THE NEW CRIMINOLOGY REVISITED

The New Criminology Revisited

Edited by

Paul Walton
Professor of Communications
Thames Valley University

and

Jock Young
Head of the Centre for Criminology
Middlesex University
Enfield

LEARNING RESOURCES
CENTRE

Havering College
of Further and Higher education

Published by PALGRAVE
Houndmills, Basingstoke, Hampshire RG21 6XS and
175 Fifth Avenue, New York, N. Y. 10010
Companies and representatives throughout the world

PALGRAVE is the new global academic imprint of
St. Martin's Press LLC Scholarly and Reference Division and
Palgrave Publishers Ltd (formerly Macmillan Press Ltd).

Outside North America
ISBN 0–333–65458–7 hardcover
ISBN 0–333–65459–5 paperback

In North America
ISBN 0–312–17415–2

This book is printed on paper suitable for recycling and
made from fully managed and sustained forest sources.

A catalogue record for this book is available from the British Library.

Library of Congress Cataloging-in-Publication Data
The new criminology revisited / edited by Paul Walton and Jock Young.
p.   cm.
Includes bibliographical references and index.
ISBN 0–312–17415–2 (cloth)
1. Criminology—Philosophy.   2. Radicalism.   3. Feminist theory.
4. Philosophy, Modern—20th century. I. Walton, Paul. II. Young, Jock.
HV6025.N49 1997
364—dc21   96–46500
                                                                          CIP

Transferred to digital printing 2002

Printed and bound in Great Britain by
Antony Rowe Ltd, Chippenham and Eastbourne

Contents

Preface

The New Criminology was first published in 1973 and has remained in print ever since. It is representative of the wave of radicalism of the time that spread through the academy into the far reaches of criminology. It reflects the dramatic changes that were occurring both in the level of crime and disorder and in the contested nature of crime and deviance as we moved out of the calm stretches of the postwar settlement into the turbulence of late modernity, which we were then entering and to which we are still attempting to adjust.

Radical criminology, which developed both in Britain and the United States at that time, has since proliferated, developed and flourished. The various currents that form its past, whether Marxist, radical feminist or anarchist, continue in fierce dispute but have in common the notion that crime and the present-day processes of criminalisation are rooted in the core structures of society, whether its class nature, its patriarchal form or its inherent authoritarianism. That is a *radical* criminology in contrast to establishment, a criminology that views crime as essentially a blemish on society that can be corrected by cosmetic means. Such an administrative criminology is technicist and piecemeal: it holds faith that the fine tuning of sentencing, police practice or the judiciary – coupled with the judicious use of target hardening, CCTV and neighbourhood watch – will do the trick. It is scarcely surprising, then, that radical criminology inhabits an academic territory of theory and dispute, of paradigm building and demolition, whereas administrative criminology holds away in a positivistic world where the accumulation of empirical facts is backed by minimalist theory.

This book represents the present-day world of radical criminology: it revisits the new criminology of the late twentieth century and tackles the central problems that the transition to the post- or late-modern era has generated. It begins with two introductions, one by each of the editors, which situate *The New Criminology* both theoretically and politically (albeit, quite naturally, with some disagreement). It then presents the reflections of some of the leading international figures in criminology on developments since 1973.

As editors we had a remarkable response to our project. Our thanks go first to all our contributors for creating such a lively collection. Special thanks must go to Ian Taylor for his staunch support of the project throughout its long gestation and to Jayne Mooney, who provided invaluable editorial advice in the later stages. Thanks also to all those colleagues who helped along the way: Andrew Cornish of the University of Wollongong, Mark Findlay of the University of Sydney, Brian Winston of the University of Wales, Cardiff, and John Lea at Middlesex University. Anya Richards and David Dawson helped word process the early manuscript, Albert Ross hung around as usual, Joseph Gabriel Mooney was a blessing and Catriona Woolner edited the final manuscript marvellously.

PAUL WALTON   JOCK YOUNG

Notes on the Contributors

John Braithwaite is Professor of Law in the Research School of Social Sciences at the Australian National University, Canberra. Internationally he is Australia's best-known criminologist. His many publications and books include *Inequality, Crime and Public Policy, Crime Shame and Reintegration,* and *Not So Just Deserts: A Republican Theory of Criminal Justice.*

Pat Carlen is Professor of Sociology at the University of Bath and was until recently Head of the Centre for Criminology at Keele University. She is the author of several key books including *Magistrates Justice, Women's Imprisonment, Women, Crime and Poverty,* and *Alternatives to Women's Imprisonment.* Her most recent book *Jigsaw: A Political Criminology of Youth Homelessness* is based on her pioneering research in this area.

Kerry Carrington is Senior Lecturer, School of Humanities, University of Western Sydney (Hawkesbury), Richmond, NSW, Australia. She teaches gender studies and feminist criminology. She is the author of *Offending Girls: Sex, Youth and Justice,* co-editor of *Cultures of Crimes and Violence, Travesty: Miscarriages of Justice,* and *Justice: Prisons, Politics and Punishment.*

Stan Cohen is Professor at the London School of Economics and the Hebrew University, Jerusalem. One of the most distinguished criminologists of his generation, his work has spanned studies of youthful disorder to crimes of the state. He is best known for *Folk Devils and Moral Panics* and *Visions of Social Control.* His recent research has been on violations of human rights and the denial of responsibility. This has resulted in the report published by the Center for Human Rights, University of Jerusalem: *Denial and Acknowledgement: The Impact of Information about Human Rights Violations.*

Elliott Currie is the foremost American critic of criminal justice policy and the author of the influential *Confronting Crime.* His recent research has focused on drugs, youth and delinquency and he is the author of the fiercely critical *Is America Really Winning the War On Crime?*.

Russell Hogg is Senior Lecturer, Law School, Macquarie University, Sydney, NSW, Australia. He teaches criminal law and criminology. He is the author of *Rethinking Law and Order* and co-editor of *Travesty: Miscarriages of Justice, Understanding Crime and Criminal Justice* and *Death in the Hands of the State.*

John Lea is Professor of Criminology at Middlesex University. He is co-editor of the recent Engels volume *The Condition of Britain*, has translated Tamar Pitch's *Limits of Responsibility*, is the co-author with Jock Young of *What is To Be Done About Law and Order?* and has just published *Crime and Post-Modernity.*

Ian Loader lectures in criminology at the University of Keele and has written numerous articles on crime and policing. He is at present working on an ESRC project on anxiety about crime and urban unease.

Jayne Mooney is Head of Criminology at Middlesex University. She has published articles on violence in public and private space, and her book *Women, Violence and Society* is to be published by Macmillan. Her research has focused on criminal victimisation and she conducted the first large-scale prevalence study of domestic violence in Britain.

John Muncie is Senior Lecturer in Criminology and Social Policy at The Open University. His publications include *The Trouble with Kids Today: Youth and Crime in Post-War Britain, Imprisonment: European Perspectives* (with R. Sparks), and *The Problem of Crime* (with E. McLaughlin).

Ian Taylor is Professor of Sociology at the University of Salford. He has published many sociological and criminological texts, including *The New Criminology* and *Critical Criminology*, with Paul Walton and Jock Young. His prescient *Law and Order: Arguments for Socialism* was published in 1981 and he edited the collection *The Social Effects of Free Market Policies*. His most recent book, *A Tale of Two Cities* written with Karen Evans and Penny Fraser, explores the two-post industrial cities Manchester and Sheffield. His current research is on gun control.

Paul Walton is Professor of Communications at Thames Valley University and was previously the Distinguished Senior Research Fellow at the Centre for Journalism, in the School of English, Communications and Philosophy, University of Wales, Cardiff. He has worked at universities across the world in North America, Australia and elsewhere. His publications and books are numerous, including *Bad News and More Bad News* with the Glasgow University Media Group; and *The New Criminology* and *Critical Criminology* with Ian Taylor and Jock Young.

Jock Young is Professor of Sociology at Middlesex University and Head of the Centre for Criminology. He is a co-author of *The New Criminology*, and author of several books including *The Drugtakers, Losing the Fight against Crime* and *The Islington Crime Survey*. He edited with Stan Cohen *The Manufacture of News* and was co-editor of *Rethinking Criminology* and *Issues in Realist Criminology* with Roger Matthews. He is at present preparing a book entitled *From Inclusive to Exclusive Society*.

1 Big Science: Dystopia and Utopia – Establishment and New Criminology Revisited

Paul Walton

Hey Pal! How do I get to town from here? And he said: Well just take a right where they're going to build that new shopping mall, go straight past where they're going to put in the freeway, take a left at what's going to be the new sports center, and keep going until you hit the place where they're thinking of building that drive-in bank. You can't miss it. And I said: This must be the place. . . . Golden Cities. Golden towns (Laurie Anderson, *Big Science*, Warner Brothers, 1982).

In an amicable but a politically critical debate, Umberto Eco recently dealt a double blow to those whose approach to the interpretation of text is either absolutist or totally relativistic. It is therefore useful to consider what the interpretation and meaning of text counts for in the social sciences. Given that many of us now accept the semiotic position that texts are polyvalent or capable of a variety of decodings – from the radical and resistant through to the ritualistic and dominant – a central issue of what limits exist to textual readings still remains.

This important academic and political debate allows us to examine whether the author's intentions have some privileged position in establishing any limits, and therefore whether some readings can be ruled out as overinterpretation. This is not a small philosophical matter, for most of what passes for social science is in fact a rereading and/or synthesis of other author's texts. Eco argues, in a series of lectures and debates entitled *Interpretation and Overinterpretation* (1992),

1

that part of the problem is that the human sciences, especially in its empiricist mode, is utilising a very limited model of Greek and Latin rationalism.

In fact, as he suggests, the Greek world was continually attracted to and fascinated by the notion of infinity. Greek civilisation delivers us much of the basis for our assumptions concerning the relationship between language and reality, which are so critically undermined by semiotics. Peculiarly enough, along with the concepts of identity and non-contradiction, both of which are essential to understanding postmodern theory, the Greeks had another fascination, namely the concept of continuous metamorphosis. It is this concept of change, so beautifully utilised by Hericlitus, 'You can't step into the same river twice', which is used along with Hegal and Rousseau by Karl Marx to create a philosophical materialism in which the object of change is the development and improvement of the human species.

Most of the debate over *The New Criminology*, with the exception of Muncie's piece in this volume, forgets that this improvement of the human condition is the sole and precise aim of the project. If *The New Criminology* is to be assessed, if authors' intentions are to count for anything, then it is against this yardstick that textual interpretation is to be made. Wonderfully enough, the Greek notion of metamorphosis is symbolised by Hermes. Hermes is an ambiguous figure for he is both father of all the arts and the god of robbers or criminals.

The aim of *The New Criminology* was to deconstruct previous theories and reveal their self-seeking or selfless character in an attempt to construct the elements of a social theory of deviance. Those who forget this objective, or seek one-sided corrections, are simply aiding establishment criminology and forgetting Hermes. Before the National Deviancy Conference, and the works that followed, British criminology was big science, with Home Office funding and dominated by one fat-cat university, Cambridge. Some things have changed since, but *The New Criminology* remains the only serious theory text with this aim.

The dominant mode of theorising in criminology remains wedded to an establishment view that the object of criminology as a science is correctionalism. Establishment criminology seeks to correct human behaviour in a manner that will reduce crime. The fact is that since the inception and development of criminology and the hundredfold multiplication of academics and social workers who have become involved in it, crime has simply increased. This fact of increasing crime rates is somehow ignored by most establishment criminologists, who are still busy receiving state grants and state funding by filling in forms that often have, as a leading question, 'How will this proposal help reduce crime?' So correctionalism on the one hand, and our so-called 'utopianism' on the other – dystopia or utopia?

Foucault taught us to look for and map out the dominant and intersecting ideologies in official use. For these carry sanctions and provide the arteries for a discourse that is both enabling and disabling. The most attractive and most emulated model of the human sciences is medicine. Well-paid, professional, state and privately funded, it has a laudable goal. It attempts to improve the human condition, eliminate pain and increase longevity. It is utopian, ultimately it seeks to abolish death. What it definitely does not generally do is to attempt to adapt and change the human body in a surgical attempt to correct society. Indeed where some of its practitioners try to do so, for example through cosmetic surgery or biogenetic engineering, medicine is revealed as politically divided and it suffers from the fiercest of ethical debates. Yet most of criminology still remains untroubled by its Frankenstein-like desire to alter human behaviour to fit society. For the correctionalists, whether it be the empiricists at Cambridge or the not so new social democrats at the London School of Economics who still embrace a version of labelling theory, it is the individual that is required to change, not society.

This 'possessive individualism' is crumbling under its own weight of numbers. Despite building more and more prisons, despite incarcerating or seeking to control (by electronic or social engineering) human activity, the centre does not hold, mere anarchy holds sway. For at the heart of society there remains the 'genetic' code of private property. It is inconceivable that a criminology wedded to the 'cure' rather than the causes of crime can in any way help permanently to resolve the crime problem. This would be the medical

equivalent of accepting that an expanding tobacco industry
and growing cancers are inevitable.

There are of course other objections to *The New Criminology*. These are what one may call omissions by virtue of
the tune. Its much vaunted male chauvinism is indeed to
be corrected, as is its Eurocentrism. However at the time of
writing (over twenty years ago), it provided a necessary paradigm of what the elements of a social theory of deviance
would look like. As Thomas Khun has observed, to be accepted as a paradigm a theory must seem better than the
other theories in existence, but it need not necessarily explain all the facts with which it is concerned. On the other
hand, neither must it explain less than previous theories.
Moreover, for a text to be coherent it has to be consistent
in its propositions.

The New Criminology meets all these criteria in its attempt
to construct a social theory of deviance. None of the critiques,
correct and useful as some of them are, have seriously
challenged its paradigmatic nature. There are however other
areas of omission – the growing importance of the media,
new technology and the rise of cultural theory are not
addressed directly in the text (see Walton, 1992; 1993), and
there is an absence of critical debate around the notion
that in general most establishment theorising treats most of
humanity as cultural dopes, or as cultural dopes manipu-
lated by moral panics (see *Cultural Dopes & Moral Panics*,
Walton, Paul; D'Alton, Stephen and Young, Jock – forthcoming). Yet all these substantive and important social omissions of *The New Criminology* aside, the deconstructwist nature
of the project itself remains intact.

To recognise the utopianism of *The New Criminology* is to
recognise its critical semiotic strategy. It seeks to produce a
community of readers who are wedded to social change. It
is this radical textual strategy that entitles *The New Criminology*
to be taken as an intellectually serious rather than merely a
respectable, professional contribution to human knowledge.

From a small marginal discipline in faculties of law and
social science, criminology has emerged as an important and
politically crucial discipline in societies that, despite massive and multiplying social control expenditure, find themselves increasingly burdened with the growing and seemingly
intractable problems of crime and deviance.

This twenty-three year-old history can be briefly described as follows: whilst the 1970s were a period of expressive cultural utopian optimism and debate, matched with expanding economies, the 1990s have seen the emergence of cultural pessimism and economic decline, along with the collapse of Marxist and many other master narrative accounts of society. For these reasons it is timely to evaluate the nature of *The New Criminology* and to assess its lasting or passing impact on the contemporary scene. One of the central achievements of *The New Criminology* was noted in a foreword by the late American Professor of Sociology, Alvin Gouldner who insisted that:

> If any single book can succeed in making 'Criminology' intellectually serious, as distinct from professionally respectable, then this study, remarkable for its combination of the analytical with the historical, will do it. It is perhaps the first truly comprehensive critique that we have ever had of totality, of past and contemporary, of European and American studies of 'crime' and 'deviance'. It is as meticulous in its treatment of the obscure, unknown theorist as it is of the most fashionable, probing both with catholic consciousness (Gouldner, 1973, p. ix).

Gouldner fundamentally argued that the reorientating power of the work lay in its ability to demonstrate that all studies of crime and deviance, however entrenched in technical or methodological differences, were also inevitably grounded in larger and more general social theories, even if these general theories were unspoken or unacknowledged in the research. What Gouldner saw in the work and what many others, both supporters and detractors, have missed is that it did this by changing the *nature of discourse* regarding crime. As he suggests, it redirects

> the total structure of discourse concerning 'crime' and 'deviance'; it does this precisely by breaking this silence, by speaking what is normally unspoken by technicians, by launching a deliberate discourse concerning the general, social theory usually only tacit in specialised work in crime and deviance; by exhibiting explicitly the linkages between technical detail and the most basic philosophical positions (ibid., p. ix).

In the subsequent debate over the impact and importance of *The New Criminology*, it is probable that all too much attention was paid to the nature of its tentative general theory of crime, and all too little to its demonstration of the fact that all discourses on crime, deviance and social problems are trading tacitly or explicitly upon their own general positions. The work was all too often written off or judged as merely Marxist, utopian or idealistic. Paul Rock, in a foreword to one of the many volumes on realist criminology, offers up the view that:

> The politics of radical criminology ignored the criminal justice policies and programs of pre-revolutionary society either as ephemeral or as wilfully calling for the impossible with the result that the fabric of the State might be stretched beyond endurance. . . . 'Bourgeois' criminology was itself dismissed as almost wholly administrative, positivist, empiricist, and ideologically compromised (Rock, 1992, p. ix).

Rock is here essentially reducing an otherwise complex argument and ongoing philosophical debate to a simple question of right and left with clear historical breaks. Rock wishes to suggest that most of the debates of the 1970s and early 1980s were merely 'facile ideological oppositions', which were somehow primarily concerned with 'what Marx and Engels really meant to say about crime and control-argument which had long since fallen prey to the law of diminishing returns' (ibid., p. xi).

This pragmatic or market view that radical or new criminology simply fell into a sterile impotent heap in the face of emerging criticism from feminism on the one hand and realist criminology on the other, is all too rugged an account of a shifting set of cultural positions that had little to do with this kind of caricature. John Muncie's views of the impact and limitations of *The New Criminology* seem nearer to actuality: thus he argues in this volume that:

> The publication of *The New Criminology* in 1973 remains a watershed in theoretical criminology. Not only is it widely assumed to have launched an oppositional, radical and

critical paradigm onto the criminological landscape, but also opened up questions regarding the role that criminologists could be expected to play in the broader realm of political activism. In its own words a criminology not committed to 'the abolition of inequalities of wealth and power' was bound to be ultimately reducible to the interests of the economically and politically powerful in society. *The New Criminology* in essence was a fierce attack on traditional positivist and correctionalist criminology, arguing that this tradition acted as little more than an academic justification for existing discriminatory practices in the penal and criminal justice systems. Rather than refocusing on the illusive search for the cause of crime, this new endeavour sought to illustrate how crime was politically and economically constructed through the capacity and ability of state institutions within the political economy of advanced capitalism, to define and confer criminality on others.

Moreover, as Muncie and others have pointed out, the work was not a Marxist tract at all, rather it was rejected by most Marxists because it held on to crime as a central social category; its object of study was the power of society to criminalise. Its originality lay as much in its ability to synthesise differing American and European theoretical traditions as in the hesitant, larger theoretical scheme offered in its conclusions.

This is not to deny that there were key omissions or failings in the work. Foremost amongst these was the nonappearance of any serious discussion of the role of gender relations and any account of women and crime. The emergence of feminist critiques of the male bastion of criminology initially took the form of taking the discipline to task for its faillure to study women's involvement in crime and criminal justice. Yet as Kerry Carrington observes in this volume,

feminist discourses have rightly and repeatedly expressed concerns about victims of crime – rape, domestic violence and sexual assault – and about the wholesale neglect of these issues within the discipline of criminology. Feminist discourses have also been strident in their critique of the treatment of female offenders by the criminal and juvenile justice systems.

Carrington further observes that:

> It is important to note that there is no one feminist position on any of these issues. The development of these positions has followed similar developments in feminist theory more generally. The initial critiques of criminology emerged out of the radical, women-centred, second-wave feminist discourses of the 1960s and 1970s. From the mid 1980s to the present, feminist discourses have developed out of a more diverse range of genealogical positions. Some of these have been explicitly committed to the enterprise of deconstructing phallocentricism, others to de-essentialising women's criminality with a view to engaging in the politics of social justice; and others with a view to centralising women as a unified subject of a masculinised social order.

She goes on to discuss whether the critique of essentialism has had a major impact on feminist models of analysis in criminology. Her position supports Pat Carlen's argument that there is no essential criminal woman. Carlen indicates the following limits to feminism as an explanation of the female offender:

> No single theory (feminist or otherwise) can adequately explain three major features of women's law breaking and that women's crimes are in the main the crimes of the powerless; the women in prison are disproportionately from ethnic minority groups, and that a majority of women in prison have been in poverty for a greater part of their lives (Carlen, 1992, p. 53).

What these arguments from Muncie, Carrington and Carlen reveal is a much more complex and diverse range of positions and discourses that have emerged from the past, and can be seen as part of the discourse initiated by *The New Criminology* in particular and critical criminology in general.

The so-called utopian or ideological position of the new criminologists in their commitment to a society without major inequalities continues to reveal that establishment criminology, by aligning itself to a supposed scientific neutrality, simply becomes a correctional criminology which: 'Must inevitably collapse into a political or moral prescriptiveness, usually of an individualistic kind and nearly always couched in terms of a conservative common sense. A practical philosophy of individual survival within existing competitive, unequal social arrangements.' The abiding insight retained by most of the positions that have emerged since *The New Criminology* was stated most clearly near the end of that text, namely that 'any criminology which was not normatively committed to the abolition of the inequalities of wealth and power was inevitably bound to fall into correctionalism (1973, p. 281). That is criminology that merely seeks to correct individual behavior instead of social structures.

Aside from feminism and realism, to which we shall return later, the most powerful post-1970s critique to appear was that of poststructuralism or postmodernism, especially in the shape of Foucault's criticism of absolute positions, namely the proposition that power lies everywhere in a never ending network of microstructures, in short that all structure and culture is both enabling and disabling and that the dominant paradigms of crime and punishment shift with the differing power of professions and beliefs.

One of the other important cognitive realisations that emerged in the post-1970s debate was that politics, social policy and theory may be related but are often best dealt with as separate issues. Stan Cohen, in this volume, answers the need to get back to a criminology that may unite these issues in the following manner:

> The critique of knowledge/power in criminology and similar subjects – our metadebates, our histories or genealogies, our persistent scepticism – takes place at a different level from our policy choices.
>
> On a 'realist' level – 'the thing' itself (crime, victims, control) – we do research, construct theories and suggest policies about what is to be done. On a sceptical level, we ask why some subjects are studied rather than others and

how they are studied – and then comment on this choice in the name of some explicit political idealogy, some vision of how the world should be, or (if so inclined) a pure philosophical scepticism. It is easy enough to 'see' the difference between these different levels.

The second . . . level of critique can tell us neither what to do nor what is good; it can only give us ground rules for what Foucault calls 'making facile gestures difficult'. Thus if there are no easy solutions to the cliched problem of 'integration between theory and practice', the task is even harder for metatheory and practice. I am uneasy about the triumphalist narrative of realism – with its impatient dismissal of sceptical questions as a romantic hangover from the past, a distinction from the demands of 'confronting crime'.

What Stan Cohen, with his usual insight, is suggesting here is that the urge to be 'relevant' on the one hand, or to be 'detached' on the other, is a necessary balancing act that can not be easily reduced to some overall, general, false integration or elision.

The argument that *The New Criminology*'s success was simply built on left-wing ideology is easily refuted. Certainly the critical movement studied the young, the marginalised and the deviant. It certainly sought to counter the bourgeois myths that the criminal and the deviant are essentially irrational, self-destructive individuals who are incoherent and parasitic. However in facilitating the documentation of the social and economic contradictions that produce sub- and countercultures, we have found pockets of resistance in some rituals and bonds of community in others, which provided solid signifiers of rational and important transformations. Having broken from the established positivistic and pluralist paradigms of earlier periods, and having refused to become zookeepers of deviance, we may have erred on the side of optimism.

What we have not done, however, is fall back on the easy assumption that criminals and deviants are merely cultural dopes. As Meagen Morris has noted in another context, all too often social theorising fails to distinguish between banal and fatal theory: 'In the former, the subject believes itself to be always more malign than the object, while in the latter the object is always assumed to be more malign, more cynical, more brilliant that the subject' (Morris, 1988, p. 190). Semiotically speaking, here lies the problem with criminology: much of its analytical work does not treat its objects with humility or decorum. It tends endlessly to reduce its rhetoric and its discourse to supposed discoveries, a series of new facts, surveys or findings that somehow are meant to fundamentally alter our view of the criminal or the criminological enterprise.

Indeed this is precisely Paul Rock's (1992) inference in his overview of the importance of realist criminology. He argues that the outcome of feminist critiques was a reluctant concession by radicals that some part of their critical enterprise required reexamination. He enthusiastically quotes Jones, MacLean and Young's statement that there exists a 'general tendency in radical thought to idealise their historical subject and to play down intra-group conflict, blemishes and social disorganisation. But the power of the feminist case resulted in a sort of cognitive schizophrenia' (Jones *et al.*, 1986, pp. 2–3).

Rock goes on to embrace both the feminist and realist criticism of critical or new criminology as if the facts simply speak for themselves. In his view, Jock Young and his realist colleagues deserve applause for publicly recanting on the new or critical position. It is true of course that, after conducting the local crime surveys from below, John Lea and Jock Young argued that the left were foolish if they simply believed all crimes were a product of the powerful: 'There was a belief that property offences are directed solely against the bourgeoisie and that violence against the person is carried out by amateur Robin Hoods in the course of their righteous attempts to redistribute wealth. All of this is alas untrue' (Lea and Young, 1984, p. 262).

What Rock conveniently forget is that realist criminology, feminist criminology and postmodernist criminology are all committed to creating a more just and equitable society. As Jock Young puts it:

> a crucial element in the discussion of the relationship between agencies and the public is accountability. Discussion

in this area has been overwhelmingly dominated by the topic of police accountability. Of course this must be extended to all agencies, with performance indicators based on public demand being devised for the array of crime-control institutions. As we have seen the public are as critical of local authority provision as they are of police performance (Young, 1992, p. 68).

Young's impulses and motives are to treat the victims and potential victims of crime as an important and crucial voice that urgently requires a democratic hearing in the development of crime solutions.

Thus another issue emerges here: whether we are evaluating the contribution of the new criminology, realist criminology, feminist criminology or the emerging postmodern criminology, the actual history and politics of contemporary society have to be evaluated and considered. The political rhetoric of the free marketeers which overlays the larger crucial justice system and inserts itself into the decision-making of sentences and officials and emphasises the punitive, restrictive role of penal agencies and pours scorn upon those who appear soft on crime. Despite the contribution of critical criminology the public discourse and agenda concerning crime is set by right wing political ideology and exacerbated and reinforced by the tabloid media.

Whilst we have apparently travelled far from the heady, master-narrative days of the general theorising of *The New Criminology* and now find ourselves amongst the uneasy new dialogues and discourses of realism, feminism and postmodernism, the journey has been fruitful. It may well turn out to be like the concept of crime itself, the most important contribution of *The New Criminology* was the neutralisation of the dominance of correctional or establishment criminology and the provision of a more believable account or discourse. This rejection and development of preexisting paradigms turns out to be a task that each generation has to confront if it wishes to reconstruct rather than merely deconstruct.

References

Carlen, P. (1992) 'Criminal Women and Criminal Justice: The limits to, and potential of feminist and left realist perspectives', in R. Matthews and J. Young (eds), *Issues in Realist Criminology* (London: Sage).

Eco, U. (1992) *Interpretation and Overinterpretation* (Cambridge: Cambridge University Press).

Gouldner, A. (1973) 'Foreword' to *The New Criminology*, in I. Taylor, P. Walton and J. Young (eds) (London: RKP).

Jones, T., B. MacLean and J. Young (1986) *The Islington Crime Survey* (Aldershot: Gower).

Lea, J. and J. Young (1984) *What is to be Done about Law and Order?* (Harmondsworth: Penguin).

Lowman, J. and B. MacLean (1992) *Realist Criminology* (Toronto: University of Toronto Press).

Rock, P. (1992) 'The Criminology That Came In Out of the Cold' in J. Lowman and B. MacLean (eds).

Walton, P. (1992) 'It's Not a Sin: The Significance of Cultural Studies' in B. Musgrave (ed.), *Signifiers: Selected Papers from the 2nd Cultural Studies Association of Australia* (Western Queensland: University of Western Queensland).

Walton, P. (1993) 'Media and Murder: Some Problems of Culture, Representation and Difference' in D. Bennett (ed.), *Cultural Studies: Pluralism & Theory* (Melbourne: University of Melbourne Press).

Walton, P. (1993) 'Youth, Subcultures, Deviance and the Media', in R. White (ed.), *Youth Subcultures, History and the Australian* (Hobart, Australia: Mercury Watch).

Walton, P. (1994) 'Out of Control: Electronic and Digital Media on the Information Super Highway', *Current Issues in Criminal Justice*, vol. 6, no. 1 (Sydney: Faculty of Law, University of Sydney).

Walton, P., S. D'Alton and J. Young, *Cultural Dopes and Moral Panics* (London: Macmillan, forthcoming).

Young, J. (1992) 'The Case for Left Realism', in Lowman and MacLean, op. cit.

2 Breaking Windows: Situating the New Criminology

Jock Young

At the end of the day, the book should be judged not so much as an academic discourse but as a political brick that was hurled through the windows of various establishments that had it coming to them (Sumner, *The Sociology of Deviance: An Obituary*, 1994, p. 284).

The retreat from theory is over, and the politicization of crime and criminology is imminent. Close reading of the classical social theorists reveals a basic agreement; the abolition of crime *is* possible under certain social arrangements . . .

It should be clear that a criminology which is not normatively committed to the abolition of inequalities of wealth and power, and in particular inequalities in property and life chances [is] irreducibly bound up with the identification of deviance with pathology . . . for crime to be abolished these social arrangements themselves must be subject to fundamental social change . . .

The task is not merely to 'penetrate' these problems, not merely to question the stereotypes, not merely to act as carriers of 'alternative phenomenological realities'. The task is to create a society in which the facts of human diversity, whether personal, organic or social, are not subject to the power to criminalize (Ian Taylor, Paul Walton, Jock Young, *The New Criminology*, 1973, pp. 281–2).

Eric Hobsbawm, in *The Age of Extremes* (1994), pinpoints the extraordinary changes that have occurred in the last third of the twentieth century. The golden age of postwar Europe and North America was a world of full employment

14

and steadily rising affluence, it witnessed the gradual incorporation of the working class into at least the trappings of full citizenship, the entry of women more fully into public life and the labour market, and the attempt in the United States to create political equality for African Americans. It was an era of inclusion, affluence and conformity. But as Hobsbawm wryly delineates, the Golden Age was followed by the cultural revolution of the late 1960s and 1970s, with the rise of individualism, of diversity, of a vast, large-scale deconstruction of accepted values. A world of seeming certainty was replaced by one of pluralism, debate, controversy and ambiguity. And whereas social commentators of the early 1960s had bemoaned the conformity of the age, the subsequent years experienced widespread disorder, rebellion and rising crime, despite the continuing increase in average incomes and the most committed attempts to socially engineer a satisfied and orderly society. It was a world where commentators of all political persuasions spoke of 'the compass' failing, where the cornerstones of society – the family, work, the nation and even affluence itself – became questioned and unobvious.

The world of criminology was touched by these upheavals, as was each subdiscipline of the social sciences, but perhaps more so – occupying as they do the crossroads of order and disorder – were law and morality. Indeed in many ways the sudden outburst of intellectual output occurring in the period 1968–75 can be seen not so much as a series of academic 'breakthroughs' occurring within the interior world of academic debate, as strident signals of the change into late modernity occurring in the world surrounding the academy. For it is at times of change that fundamental revisions of academic orthodoxy occur. Thus it is no accident that three books written at the same time but from differing political perspectives – David Matza's *Becoming Deviant* (1969), James Q. Wilson's *Thinking About Crime* (1975) and *The New Criminology* (Taylor *et al.*, 1973) – are not only revisionist, in the sense of looking back in a unique and reappraising fashion, but also share the same themes. Thus all are concerned with diversity, all are vehemently critical of positivism and all cast doubt on the metanarrative of progress, whether through social engineering or the criminal justice system.

But let us look at the specific intellectual context of *The New Criminology*; this was, as the acknowledgements indicate: 'fundamentally the product of discussions and developments in and around the National Deviancy Conference' (Taylor *et al.*, 1973, p. xv). The National Deviancy Conference (NDC) was, in the words of one author, the site of an 'explosion' of work, the 'fall out' of which was to change the terrain of criminology and the sociology of deviance for many years to come. One gauge of this explosion would be that in the first five-year period from the inception of the NDC in 1968 to 1973 there were 63 speakers from Britain, who between them produced just under 100 books on crime, deviance and social control.[1] The impact, moreover, was scarcely limited to crime and deviance, for example early work in gender studies were presented (including Mary McIntosh and Ken Plummer) and the first flourishes of what was to become cultural studies (including Dick Hebdige, Mike Featherstone, Stuart Hall and Paul Willis). The basis of such work and the widespread interest it generated (there were *ten* national conferences in the four years 1969 to 1972) were undoubtedly the first airing of what were to become known as 'postmodern' themes. As Stan Cohen (this volume) put it, 'After the middle of the 1960s – well before Foucault made these subjects intellectually respectable and a long way from the Left Bank – our little corner of the human sciences was seized by a deconstructionist impulse'. Indeed the arrival of *Discipline and Punish* in English translation in 1977 was scarcely a revelation, the themes and concepts of Foucault were already well rehearsed, the door was wide open to deconstructionism.

For the NDC was deconstructionist to a person, anti-essentialist in its stance, it evoked a myriad voices and viewpoints right to the edge of relativism, it dwelt on the social construction of gender, sexual proclivity, crime, suicide, drugs and mental state. It inverted hierarchies, it read total cultures from the demimonde of mods, rockers, teddy boys, hippies, skinheads – it traced the bricolage of the old culture by which the new 'spectacular' youth cultures constituted themselves, it focused on their media representatives and the fashion in which media stereotypes shaped and at times became reality. And beneath all this was an underlay of critique of both strands of state intervention: positivism and classicism. For the twin metanarratives of progress – social engineering and the rule of law – were consistently subject to criticism. Positivism was perhaps the main enemy: its ontology was seen to take human creativity out of deviant action, its sociology erected a consensual edifice from which deviants were bereft of culture and meaning, its methodology elevated experts to the role of fake scientists discovering the 'laws' of social action and its policy, whether in mental hospitals, social work agencies or drug clinics, was self-fulfilling and mystifying. But the rule of law also came under close scrutiny. The NDC was concerned about how the criminal justice system was selective and ineffective. That is, how crime occurred endemically yet the justice system focused on the working class and youth. Crimes of the powerful were ignored, middle-class deviancy tolerated. Prison were brutalising, scapegoating and ultimately counterproductive: two of the most blistering indictments of the prison system – *Psychological Survival* (Cohen and Taylor, 1976) and *Prisoners in Revolt* (Fitzgerald, 1977) – sprang out of this. But such irrationality in terms of social reaction to crime was not limited to the institutions of the state, but also to those of civil society. For the mass media were seen to select out deviant groups, creating folk devils and engendering moral panic (see Cohen, 1972; Young, 1971).

Two influences from North American criminology were paramount: that of labelling theory and that of subculture theory. The first was most evident; the work of Becker, Lemert and Kitsuse was, after all, the precursor of 'postmodern' developments in criminology. The second was more obscure; it was a considerable presence throughout, particularly in the work on youth subcultures, but its voice was muted (see Cohen, 1980; Downes and Rock, 1988), presumably because of its association with structural functionalism, the *bête noire* of radical sociology at that time.

From the neo-Chicagoans was gleaned a sense of diversity, of human creativity thwarted by the labelling process, of selectivity and of the self-fulfilling prophecy as the essential 'master status' of the label became accepted both by deviant and public alike. From Merton, Cloward and Ohlin, and Albert Cohen came a sense of total society, how the

contradiction between fundamental values and the structure
of society, generated crime and disorder. For deviance was
not only endemic in the neo-Chicagoan sense of diversity, it
was also ultimately related to the central values and structures of the social order, and the subcultures were attempts
to resolve such contradictions. From both these traditions
came a twofold sense of irony: the irony that the core values
and material basis of society generates crime and the way
that social attempts to tackle these problems exacerbates
the very problems it sets out to solve. That irrationality dwells
both at the core of the social order and in its attempts to
maintain equilibrium.

These twin strands of North American criminology were
transposed and woven together in British deviancy theory.
'Transposed' in that they were shifted to a society that was
more aware of relationships of class and transfixed, at that
time, with the emergence of ebullient and dynamic youth
cultures. Thus class and youth became the major social areas
around which the work pivoted (gender was to come a little
later and race/ethnicity had to wait until the 1980s). 'Woven'
in the sense that both strands, which in American criminology
were separate and antagonistic, were brought together. In a
way this was only logical because both were complementary.
The great contribution of labelling theory was its unpacking
of the dyadic nature of crime and deviance. Deviancy is not
a quality inherent in an act, it is a quality bestowed upon
an act. To have deviance one needs action and reaction,
behaviour and evaluation, rule making and rule breaking.
Yet having said this, labelling theorists, like the social constructionists who followed them, tended to bracket off action from reaction and concentrate on the latter and its
impact. They were interested in social construction; human
agency was never lost but became ephemeral and somehow existential. Subcultural theory, on the other hand, was
interested in the actual generation of behaviour; its weak-
ness was the creation of rules, the other half of the equation. Yet even though it was able to chart the determinants
of actors, the actions themselves were wooden. In *Delinquent
Boys* (Cohen, 1955) they rather petulantly inverted middle-
class morality like spoilt automata reversing their programmes;
in *Delinquency and Opportunity* (Cloward and Ohlin, 1960)

they went through a series of preprogrammed options like bearings in a pinball machine. The task of British theorisation was to try to bring these three concepts together: to deal with action and reaction, to postulate human actors who were neither capriciously free-willed nor stolidly determined, to place actors both in a microsetting and in the context of the wider society.

Finally, both theories had distinct limitations with regard to the macrolevel of analysis. Labelling theory, in particular, was concerned very fruitfully with the immediate interaction between the actor and the labelling process, but it had little theory of total society outside the clash of disparate interest groups and moral entrepreneurs. Subcultural theory was excellent in terms of its sense of contradiction between structure and culture on a macrolevel, but it had little sense of the dynamics of society as a whole (see Taylor, 1971, p. 148).

It was this task of synthesis that confronted the radical criminologists who grouped around the NDC, and it was these tasks that shaped the structure and discourse of *The New Criminology*. But before we turn to the questions such debates engendered, let us look briefly at one area of work in which the NDC was greatly involved, for it is these exploratory tasks that were the laboratory within which the framework of *The New Criminology* was developed. I have talked about transposing American theorisation onto the current British preoccupations with class and youth. It was in fact the *combination* of class and youth that was a major focus of the NDC. Thus we have papers on football hooliganism and working-class youth (Taylor, 1968), on student, middle-class drug taking (Young, 1968), on hippies (Hall, 1970), Phil Cohen's path-breaking paper on working-class youth cultures in 1970, Paul Walton on political protest and the student movement in 1971 and Paul Willis on motor bike subcultures in 1972, followed over the years by papers on youth culture by John Clarke, Mike Brake, Geoff Pearson, Geoff Mungham, Dick Hebdige and Paul Corrigan.

What is clear from these various essays is that there is a very overt attempt to go beyond the wooden, determined actors of American theorisation, to place them in a specific class position rather than invoke the notion of a universal

youth culture (see Clarke *et al.*, 1975) to place such cultures in particular local settings with a consciousness of space
and change over time, and to stress the creativity of youth
culture. For subcultures were seen as human creations, attempting to solve specific problems that were constantly
rewritten in each nook and cranny of society rather than
centrally orchestrated scripts mechanically enacted by actors deterministically allocated to their position in the social structure. There is a lineage certainly between Albert
Cohen and Paul Willis and between Cloward and Ohlin and
Phil Cohen, but there is also a wealth of difference.

   In this work there is a clear influence of English socialist historians such as Edward Thompson, Eric Hobsbawm,
Christopher Hill and Sheila Rowbotham (see Downes and
Rock, 1988; Cohen, 1980). That is, among other things, of
'writing from below', of history written from 'the material
experiences of the common people rather than from above
in the committee chambers of high office' (Pearson, 1978,
p. 119), of revealing a world that, in the title of Sheila
Rowbotham's book, was 'hidden from history' (1973). This
rewriting of social history stressed localism and specificity,
'the heterogeneity or complexity of working class culture
fragmented not only by geographical unevenness and paro-
chialism, but also by social and sexual divisions of labour
and by a whole series of divisions into spheres of existence
(including work and leisure)' (Johnson, 1979, p. 62).

   The socialist historians of this period undoubtedly had
an extraordinary influence on this second wave of subcultural theory, presented at the NDC and developed particularly around the work of the Centre for Contemporary
Cultural Studies at the University of Birmingham under the
directorship of Stuart Hall. Here we have subcultures of
imagination and creativity rather than of flatness and determinism, resistance rather than negativism and retreatism,
of a world of leisure as well as school and work, of meaning
rather than malfunction. And just as socialist and feminist
historians read from the activities and aspirations of lowly
people the dynamics and ethos of the total society, subculture becomes a text to be read and popular culture is as
relevant, perhaps more so in understanding the total society, than high culture. Thus Phil Cohen's (1972) 'mods'

and 'skinheads' tell us about urban dislocation, working-class deskilling and the destruction of community; John Clarke and his colleagues' analysis of changing youth cultural forms relates to the wider processes of embourgeoisement, mass culture and affluence (1975), Paul Willis' lads' intransigence and bloody mindedness becomes transformed to Pyrrhic resistance to wage labour and subordination (1977).

But it is not only deviant action that is given meaning in such a holistic fashion, it is the reaction against deviance. Here the other strand of North American theorisation – labelling theory – is reworked and transformed. For here, in an exactly parallel fashion, labelling theory is recast into moral panic theory. For if subcultural theory interprets the seeming irrationality of delinquency in a rational fashion, moral panic theory offers the possibility of interpreting the seemingly ill-thought-out, gut reactions of authority and the wider public to deviance in a similar manner. That is, just as on a superficial level delinquent vandalism is negativistic and unproductive yet at the same time meaningful and understandable in a wider social context, so moral panic about crime, although disproportionate, wrongly conceptu-alised and even counterproductive, becomes understandable and 'reasonable' in the light of conflicts existing in the total society.

Of course to say this does not mean that subcultural behaviour is tenable (see Matza, 1969) – it is frequently not – nor that moral panics are correct in their foundation – they are not by definition. Rather it is to stress that deviant action and the reaction against it is not mindless, non-rational behaviour, rather it is meaningful behaviour that involves mistakes in rationality (cf. Goode and Ben-Yehuda, 1994). Thus the two early formulators of moral panic – Stan Cohen (1972) and Jock Young (1971) – clearly indicate the deep-seated nature of the panic. For Cohen:

> The Mods and rockers symbolised something far more important than what they actually did. They reached the delicate and ambivalent nerves through which post-war social change in Britain was experienced. No one wanted depressions or austerity but messages about '*never having it so good*' were ambivalent in that some people were having

it too good and too quickly. . . . Resentment and jealousy
were easily directed against the young, if only because of
their increased spending power and sexual freedom. When
this was combined with a too-open flouting of the work
and leisure ethic, with violence and vandalism . . . something more than the image of a peaceful Bank Holiday at
the sea was being shattered (Cohen, 1972, p. 192).

And for Young the moral panic about a harmless drug, can-
nabis, and purposively harmless people, hippies, represented
the reaction by the hardworking citizen against groups that
disdained work and the ethos of productivity. If Cohen's
scenario in the mid 1960s represented a wider society coming
to terms with the movement out of postwar austerity and
the new affluence of the young, Young's scene of the late
1960s represented the reaction of an affluent society used
to hard work and incessant consumption to a possible world
beyond scarcity where the rigours of work were no longer
necessary and the pleasures of consumption no longer obvious. Thus, just as subcultures had to be read as a text, so
moral panics must be read likewise. Furthermore, and this
is important, each of these authors attempted to explain
both youth cultures *and* moral panics, and sought to do so
within the *same* wider context. Thus Cohen ends the first
edition of *Folk Devils and Moral Panics* with a discussion of
how mods and rockers developed in the newly found affluence of the 1960s. Later on, because the book inevitably
focused more on moral panic than folk devils, the introduction of the second edition (1980) reversed the book's
sequence and concentrated on action before reaction. And
Young, in *The Drugtakers* (1971), sought to explain the development of bohemian youth cultures as well as the moral
panic against drug use. The two strands of American
theorisation – subcultural theory and labelling theory – were
thus brought together and developed. Lastly, both authors
are concerned not only with action and reaction but with
the impact of social reaction on the deviant actors. Thus
Stan Cohen talks of how the punitive reaction of society
increases and polarises the deviance of the youths and thus
serves to confirm the original stereotypes, and Young talks
of 'the translation of fantasy into reality'. There is clearly

here what Sumner rather critically calls 'the interaction and deep interconnection between signifier (the discourse of punitive reaction) and signified (juvenile delinquency)' (Sumner, 1994, p. 263).

The study of crime and deviance is of necessity dyadic, consisting of action and reaction, but the two parts of the dyad are, in the final analysis, inseparable: they give rise to one another and profoundly affect each other. It is therefore not possible to bracket off one from the other, yet this was the unwitting situation in American theorisation at that time. Indeed contemporary social constructionism explicitly focuses only on the signifier, and contemporary American interpretation of moral panic theory manages to lose, once again, the deviant phenomenon in its rendering of moral panic theory (for example Goode and Ben-Yehuda, 1995). I will return to this at the end of the chapter.

THE NEW CRIMINOLOGY: THE EXPLANATORY AGENDA

It is out of this background that *The New Criminology* emerged. Thus the core agenda of the book elucidates the substantive and formal requirements of a fully social theory of deviance. Let us examine the framework that formed the basis of the concluding chapter.

Formal Requirements of Theory (Scope)

An adequate theory must cover fully the evolution of the deviant act:

1. Wider origins: the underlying causes of the deviant act.
2. Immediate origins: what is the immediate origin of the deviant act? For example problems faced by the individual or the group.
3. Actual act: how does the behaviour relate to the causes? For example problem solving, relationship between culture of origins and emergent culture, rationality, individual, collective solution and so on.
4. Immediate origin of social reaction.

5. Wider origin of social reaction.
6. Outcome of social reaction on deviant's further action.
7. Persistence and change of actions in terms of 1 to 6).

Substantive Requirements of Theory (Substance)

1. Human beings as both determined and determining.
2. A pluralistic diverse society.
3. A class society based on inequalities of wealth and power.
4. A sequential, processual model that is historical and open-ended.
5. A dialectic between structure and consciousness, that is, it would relate typical sets of motives (consciousness and ideologies) to situated actions (given historical contexts).
6. Holistic view of society and of the individual: the fully social conception of human action.
7. Theory: must be isomorphic (that is, symmetrical) – giving same explanations of social reaction and action, for the theorist and his object of study.
8. Empirical base: must both utilise and endeavour to explain all types of deviancy.
9. It must involve a criminology that is aware of history and the sociohistorical position of the theorists; which will treat crime not as a technicality, a surface problem needing correction, but deal with society as a totality.

There we have it, and there is very little in it that one would find fault with today. An emphasis on the symmetry of analysis of action – and reaction – is at the core of both approaches, as is the notion of locating such a process in the wider social structure. Time and process are seen as an essential part of the analysis and the implicit theoretical agenda involves a merger of subcultural and labelling theory (see Young, 1974).

The programme calls for a criminology that is isomorphic, reflexive and transcends the narrow boundaries of practical, 'jobbing' criminology (see Loader, this volume). Thus:

We have argued here for a political economy of criminal action, and of the reaction it excites, and for a politically-informed social psychology of these ongoing social dynamics. We have, in other words, laid claim to have constructed the formal elements of a theory that would be adequate to move criminology out of its own imprisonment in artificially segregated specifics. We have attempted to bring the parts together again in order to form the whole (Taylor *et al.*, 1973, p. 279).

Furthermore:

A criminology which is to be adequate to an understanding of these developments, and which will be able to bring politics back into the discussion of what were previously technical issues, will need to deal with the society as a totality. This 'new' criminology will in fact be an *old* criminology, in that it will face the same problems that were faced by the classical social theorists (ibid., p. 278).

And:

The insulation of criminology from sociology in general – symbolized institutionally in America in Robert Merton's insistence on placing the study of crime in the Department of Social Administration at Columbia – is rapidly being broken down. The 'social reaction theorists' in drawing attention to the activities of the rule-creators and enforcers . . . have redirected criminological attention to the grand questions of social structure and the overweening social arrangements within which the criminal process is played out. We are confronted once again with the central question of man's relationship to structures of power, domination and authority – and the ability of men to confront these structures in acts of crime, deviance and dissent – we are back in the realm of social theory itself (ibid., p. 268).

Thus the basis of the 'transgressive' criminology that 'abandons criminology to sociology' demanded by Maureen Cain (1990) and Carol Smart (1990) in the 1990s was part and parcel of the everyday culture of those associated with the NDC in the late 1960s and early 1970s. They would have quickly warmed to Richard Ericson and Kevin Carriere's

invocation that 'the only viable academic sensibility is to
encourage people to let their minds wander to travel intellectually across the boundaries and frontiers and perhaps
never to return to them' (Ericson and Carriere, 1994, p. 108).
This being said, it is obvious that the philosophical and
sociological debates that such an opening out would entail
would differ today. The debate with postmodernity, although
implicit in much of the early radical writing, is obviously
centre stage (see the chapters by Lea and Young in this
volume), just as the need for engagement with feminist
literature (witness the use of masculine pronouns in the last
quote from *The New Criminology*) has become essential, particularly given the incisive work of scholars such as Carol
Patemen and Anne Phillips (see Kerry Carrington, this
volume), and the pioneering research of second-wave feminists in the areas of rape, domestic violence and sexual
harassment (see Mooney, 1994).

Lastly, such a programme needs to be supplemented – as
was suggested in the later volume, *Critical Criminology* – by a
study of the victim–offender relationship, in contrast with
conventional criminology, where 'The deviant is seen as propelled by his essential propensities into the contemporary
world – his victim being the first accidental social atom into
which he collides' (Taylor *et al.*, 1975, p. 66).

THE WIDENING OF THE EMPIRICAL BASE

An integral part of this programme was a widening of the
empirical base: the solitary focus of much criminology on
class needed to be supplemented by the empirical base of
gender, ethnicity and age without either reducing one to
another or losing one dimension or another altogether, as
frequently occurs. Thus early on in *The New Criminology* it
was noted that:

> The predicament which arises [for positivism] is that crime
> is found to be well nigh ubiquitous. It is found to occur
> in all sections of society – amongst the rich and the poor,
> the young and the old – amongst men and women – and
> always in greater amounts and in different proportions

than was previously assumed. Criminological theory, however, has largely worked on the assumption that crime is an overwhelmingly youthful, masculine, working class activity (Taylor *et al.*, 1973, p. 15).

This crucial premise of *The New Criminology* stresses that crime is not a marginal, exceptional phenomenon but something that is widespread in society. It cannot, therefore, be explained by positivist accounts that ascribe such behaviour to marginal and exceptional conditions. For such theories do not attempt to explain crime, rather they seek to explain it away. But if crime is endemic, criminalisation is not. And here the critique of *The New Criminology* focuses not only on positivism but on classicism. For a central theme of the book is the problem of selectivity, that is, the fact that many are called but few are chosen. Hence the radical impact of labelling theory was rephrased in the context of class. With this in mind the book systematically examines the varieties of criminological theory in terms of their ability to deal with the facts of class. This is the basis of its revisionism.

The class distribution of crime was of course obvious; it has been commonplace in every criminology text written. The introduction of class into the analysis was in many ways the obverse of this, it was the recognition that crime occurred *throughout* the class structure but that criminalisation was *selectively* focused upon the lower working class. It was less about the class distribution of crime and more about it being a function of class relations. Instead of crime being, so to speak, the result of 'lack of class', its cause was seen as a result of relationships of class and its criminalisation, a relationship that displayed and perpetuated relationships of class.

It has frequently been pointed out that *The New Criminology* is silent on the gender distribution of crime and the implications of such a disproportionality on theories of crime in general (for example Sumner, 1994). This criticism is certainly valid, although perhaps slightly unfair given that the impact of second-wave feminism was to occur after *The New Criminology* was published. The most influential early text, Susan Brownmiller's *Against Our Will*, was for example published in 1975. Such criticisms are of course easy with hindsight, but display as much insight as pointing out that Carol Smart's *Women, Crime and Criminology* (1976) is silent on the subject of class, and indeed both texts are totally blind on race and ethnicity. The task of creating a criminology that incorporates gender, class, ethnicity and age is still in the making. Recent work, as Marcia Rice nicely points out, 'is extraordinarily partial in its focus'. For example 'black criminology . . . has focused on black men and feminist criminology . . . [is] largely concerned with white women' (Rice, 1990, p. 58). Indeed it was only recently that James Messerschmidt, in *Masculinities and Crime* (1993), came near to bringing all four structural dimensions into play within a common theory.

POLICING THE CRISIS: THE APOTHEOSIS OF RADICAL CRIMINOLOGY

Attempts to carry out such a programme are few and far between. The structure is prefigured in *The Drugtakers* (Young, 1971) and is utilised in Mike Brake's influential work on youth culture (1980), but as Downes and Rock (1988, p. 24) indicate, by far the most complete expression of such an approach is the seminal text *Policing the Crisis* (Hall *et al.*, 1978). This is not so much through any attempt explicitly to reproduce such a programme, although *The New Criminology* is clearly an influence, but rather – as I have argued – because such a comprehensive attempt to describe the wider and immediate origins of the deviant action and the reaction to it was part and parcel of the approach that developed around the NDC in these years. The book is extraordinary in that it unites concepts from deviancy theory (amplification, moral panic, control culture, signification) with those from Marcism (for example hegemony, relative autonomy, civil society, wage form). It moves in a gigantic U-curve, starting from the actual act – a mugging in Handsworth – then moving on to the immediate reaction of 'the face-to-face control' of the 'police as amplifiers', to the social production of news by the mass media, to the orchestration of moral panics, the mobilisation of public anxiety and the management of hegemony in a situation of economic crisis, and ending with the immediate causes of mugging, which lie in the 'super-exploitation' of the black labour force, the rise of a culture of hustling and a rejection of degrading work, all of this within the context of the same economic crisis that produced the social reaction. Thus both sides of the equation are covered: there is no attempt to bracket off street crime from moral panic nor to allocate it to a world of dubious aetiological validity. There is therefore no denial of the reality of street crime, no pretence that such crime does not arise out of the economic predicament of the black youth, no denial of causality:

> The position of black labour, subordinated by the processes of capital, is deteriorating and will deteriorate more rapidly, according to its own specific logic. Crime is one perfectly predictable and quite comprehensible consequence of this process – as certain a consequence of how the structures work ... as the fact that night follows day (Hall *et al.*, 1978, p. 390).

The crime itself is therefore not bracketed off from the social reaction as if it were some independent entity. Indeed the relationship between moral panic and the *real* crime problem is a key to the use of moral panic in order to maintain hegemony. Witness:

> *Certain kinds of crime* are a real, objective problem for working people trying to lead a normal and respectable life. If street crime rises, it will be primarily in *their* streets. They have a real stake in defending what little property and security they have managed to store up against the threat of poverty and unemployment. Crime threatens the limited range of cultural goods which make life worth living at all with a measure of self-respect. The demand that crime must be controlled – that people be free to walk about unmolested, that since the property of the wealthy and powerful is constantly and sophisticatedly protected there is no reason in the 'just society' why the property of the poor should be exposed to theft and vandalism – is not from this point of view an irrational one. This 'traditionalist' attitude to crime has its real, objective basis

in the material situation and cultural position of the subordinate classes (ibid., p. 149).

The concepts of 'state' and 'hegemony' appear, at first sight, to belong to different conceptual territory from that of the 'moral panic'. And part of our intention is certainly to situate the 'moral panic' as one of the forms of appearance of a more deep-seated historical crisis, and thereby to give it greater historical and theoretical specificity. . . . One of the effects of retaining the notion of 'moral panic' is the penetration it provides into the otherwise extremely obscure means by which the working classes are drawn into processes which are occurring in large measure 'behind their backs' and led to experience and respond to contradictory developments in ways which make the operation of state power legitimate, credible and consensual. To put it crudely, 'moral panic' appears to us to be one of the principal forms of ideological consciousness by means of which a 'silent majority' is won over to the support of increasingly coercive measures on the part of the state, and lends its legitimacy to a 'more than usual' exercise of control (ibid., p. 221).

The moral panic's roots are in real problems occurring in society; its rational kernel is the means by which such consensual leverage can be exerted within the population. What is irrational about the moral panic is not that it is a metaphor of social anxiety without roots but that it is *incommensurate*: that is it is *disproportional* (the anxiety is way out of proportion to the extent and changes in the size of the problem) and *miscontextualised* (mugging is seen as solely a problem of black youth, rather than a problem of poor, working-class, young people who live in inner cities) (see Lea and Young, 1984).

THE SIGNIFIER NOT THE SONG: SOME ERRORS OF SOCIAL CONSTRUCTIONISM

Colin Sumner, in his recent exegesis of the period, presents an interpretation that contrasts sharply with the above. For him, 'Conceptually the NDC had no shared view, and made few theoretical advances beyond the position reached within American sociology.' (Sumner, 1994, p. 262). The work of Stan Cohen, for example, was 'not particularly conceptually innovative' (ibid., p. 265).

For Sumner the innovation of the American deviancy theorists was that they had stumbled on the 'fact' that signifiers of deviance and those signified were only contingently related. That is, although deviance is widespread, those selected to be labelled deviants, the content of the label itself and the reaction to control them are arbitrary and inappropriate. Delinquency, for example, occurs throughout the class structure, yet it is lower-working-class youth (particularly blacks) who are selected out to be deviant, who are labelled as pathological and who are reacted to in overpunitive and counterproductive ways. All of this is true and of great significance and theoretical influence. But the conclusion drawn from this by theorists in this tradition (social constructionists, abolitionists and moral censure theorists) is that because of the contingent nature of the signifiers, the groups labelled delinquents, criminals, prostitutes and so on have no ontological reality (see Hulsman, 1986). They are merely an arbitrary sample drawn from the population at the whim of the powerful. It therefore, makes no sense to generalise about them or to devise aetiologies; rather what makes sense is to analyse and discover the causes of the labels, the moral censures themselves. After all, in this analysis the phenomenon, the social problem, has little anthological validity: it is a creature created by caprice.

It is this position that Sumner readily embraces. Indeed he notes with some satisfaction that Howard Becker 'even once used the term social censure' (ibid., p. 233), 'prefiguring' the basis of Sumner's own theory, which radically separates out the study of the label from those labelled (see Sumner, 1990). His moral censure theory is, of course, an English variety of social constructionism (see Kitsuse and Spector, 1973; Pfohl, 1977) and shares with it the same strategy: to attempt to explain the social reaction against crime, deviance or any other social problem by purposively bracketing off the phenomenon itself.

Such an approach attempts the impossible. It attempts to

explain the social reaction against deviance separately from deviance itself, indeed it denies that an explanation of the actual phenomenon makes sense. This is the problem of partiality – of denying the holistic nature of phenomena (see Young, 1994). Needless to say it is impossible to explain, say, prostitution and the public reaction to it, burglary and the attempts at its control, domestic violence and the level of social disapproval, *independently* of one another. It is one thing to suggest that the social reaction, the signifier, is inappropriate, disproportionate and counterproductive with regard to the deviant event, the signifier. It is completely another to suggest that there is no discrete problem out there, that there is no relationship between the signified event and the signification, and that the effect on the deviant actors or group is not predicated on the actual nature of the deviance.

It is impossible to understand social reaction without understanding the action that is being reacted against, it is impossible to study signifiers without knowledge of the signified. To say that the powerful more often than not get the wrong end of the stick is not to suggest that the stick is somehow conjured out of thin air or is merely a projection of their fantasies, fears and interests. This was precisely the criticism of labelling theory made in *The New Criminology* (see pp. 139–71). Furthermore, to suggest that working-class delinquents are differentially and unfairly picked upon by the criminal justice system is not to suggest that their subculture is not an entity in its own right, reflecting their deprivations and sense of injustice. Similarly, just because many women engage in prostitution does not mean that there is not something particular about street prostitution, with its own aetiology, predicaments and structure. Thus, just because crime and prostitution are legal categories that cover a multitude of subcultures and activities does not mean that the section of the population deemed to be delinquents or prostitutes by the criminal justice system is arbitrary in its nature, however arbitrary the injustice that is brought to bear upon it.

To take the heterogeneous bunch of behaviours lumped together within a legal category as the unifying base of criminology is of course a nonsense (see Carlen, 1992; Young,

1992). No causal theory could be based, say, on *all* prostitution, *all* theft, *all* drug use and so on. It is necessary to talk about discrete crimes in specific social situations. The programme of *The New Criminology* talks of specific choices involving deviant solutions in differentially experienced situations (Taylor *et al.*, 1973, p. 271). Furthermore the definition of what is criminal depends on the interaction of social reaction and behaviour, it can *never* be a constant, a given, as is positivism.

Thus not only is crime a variable that cannot be independently ascertained by either lawyer or positivist social scientist, but also the causes of crime cannot conceivably be of a blanket nature; that is, all crime cannot be caused by poverty, unemployment or market individualism, and so on. Conversely to say that all crime is not caused by poverty is not to eliminate poverty as a cause of some crime. This is a mistake stretching back to the work of Edwin Sutherland (1942); indeed it might be called Sutherland's Fallacy. Furthermore to seek a unitary explanation of crime leads to bland abstractions of breathtaking lack of utility, for example that all crime is caused by human frailty or by being male or by differential association with the wicked.

To argue, therefore, that the law, the signifier of legality, creates heterogeneous categories of behaviour under its wing is not to deny the possibility of aetiological theory, nor is it to suggest that the focus of analysis should solely be on law itself. The danger here is that, by the focusing on legal prohibitions, moral censure, moral panic, the social constructions of the powerful and so on, the phenomenon itself becomes lost from sight. The signifier becomes of greater significance than the signified, representations of deviance occlude the deviants themselves, criminology collapses into cultural studies. This can be graphically seen in Sumner's somewhat postmodern depictions of the present. For he notes that such a process of disconnection has growing validity. Its roots lie in the speed of change, the transformations wrought by modernity. Thus he writes of Stan Cohen's classic study of 'mods and rockers':

As capital expands, speeds up ever faster, dissolves new technologies in favour of hyper-technology and converts

us all into images with or without value in a rapidly de-
materializing materialism, it may be that the Mod was at
one and the same time the last stand of a coherent representation of the devil and the first form of an insub-
stantial flicker on a perpetual screen of daily denunciations
in a world where the screen is more significant than the
signifier signified.

To Cohen's credit, his analysis enabled such thoughts,
and indeed, I would say, through his particular focus on
the mass media, provoked them. Something in the text
suggests an inchoate forerunner of postmodernism, even
though Cohen himself presented a coherent connection
between signifier and signified . . .

What was to follow in the 1970s in Europe began to
disconnect signifier and signified, but Cohen, like Laing,
had already begun to suggest that the relation between
signifier and signified was 'fundamentally inappropriate'.
Insanity seemed sane and sanity seemed lunatic. Deviance
was being seen as at least as normal as normality and the
latter looked very deviant indeed. The signifiers were
becoming unhooked. They were being rendered as paro-
dies of themselves. Reality was mocked up, and mockups
became reality. Deviance became politics, politics became
deviant. Connections between images of deviance and actual
social practices became less coherent, less clear, less per-
suasive. The media spectacle was taking over at the expense of any dialectic with reality (Sumner, 1994, pp.
265–7).

Cohen's role thus becomes that of an 'inchoate' precursor
of postmodernism and the very act of bringing together
signifier and signified, which is characteristic of the British
work of the period, is seen to be regression rather than
progress. There is, of course, much to be said of the notion
that the relationship between deviant and reality in the late
modern period is distanced, distorted and mediated by the
development of the mass media. This, as Sumner recognises,
is a major focus of both the work of Stan Cohen and myself
at the time. But it is one thing to suggest that a process of
distancing and misperception is occurring within the public sphere and another to suggest that the representation is

'cut loose from its moorings' (or indeed that representation has become reality) (see Young, 1981).

Such a radical separation of the deviant from its representation (whether in the mass media or in the discourse of the criminal justice system) makes the mistake of moving from the notion of 'inappropriate' to unrelated, and of believing that there is no dialectic between signified and signifier. The importance of the work centring around the NDC was that it attempted to integrate the two sides of the dyad – action and reaction, signified and signifier – by bring together the two major strands of American theory: that focusing on subculture and that focusing on labelling. *The New Criminology*, in particular, was explicitly critical of the attempt to eliminate the interplay between the levels:

> In sum, the social reaction revolt against the structuralism of the Mertonian anomie theorists, and the subcultural critics is, for us, an overreaction. In the study of deviancy as in the study of society at large, what is required is a sociology that combines structure, process and culture in a continuous dialectic (Taylor *et al.*, 1973, p. 171).

It sought to achieve this by teasing out the radical implications of the two strands: subcultural theory, with its stress on the endemic nature of crime resulting from the injustice of opportunities within the system; and labelling theory, with its focus on the unjust application of the criminal justice system. It coaxed out the inherent radicalness of Merton and Becker from the cosy wraparound of 1960s America, and it sought to do so in an overarching analysis that involved a sociology and ontology informed by Marxism. Thus it is a sociology that starts from the 'overall social context of inequalities of power, wealth and authority', which are a product of class relations within industrial societies, and it is a sociology that is critical of the very premise of analytical individualism: 'the view of man as an atomistic individual, cut off within families or other specific subcultural situations, insulated from the pressures of existence under the prevailing social conditions' (ibid., p. 270). Indeed the major critical thrust of the book is the rejection of analytical individualism, whether in its idealist mode, that of neoclassicism, or in its vulgar materialism form, individual positivism. Untrammelled freedom of will or total determinism – both the metaphysic of the law court or of the behavioural 'scientist' – are rejected. Neither free spirit nor reified thing reflects the human condition. Furthermore, of necessity individuals exist in a social setting, ontologically they are both products and producers of society. Thus human action is both determined and determining and crime itself is 'an expression of man's situation of constraint within alienating social arrangements – and as in part an attempt (however futile and counterproductive) to overcome them' (ibid., p. 274).

REBELS WITHOUT CAUSES

If we examine the formal requirements of theory it is obvious that it is concerned both with the causes of the deviant act and the social reaction to it. That is a double aetiology of action and reaction to be explained isomorphically, using the same concepts of human nature and social order. And both must be related to the wider social structure. Thus 'a relevant theory of deviancy must treat the causal variables – motivation and reaction – as determinate and as part of a total structure of social relationships' (ibid., p. 170).

Indeed the critique of labelling theory is based on the fact that it omits an explanation of the wider and immediate origins of the deviant act and concentrates solely on the reaction against it (ibid., p. 165). *The New Criminology* explicitly expands on the notion of relative deprivation as the cause of crime and the breakdown of the meritocratic myth as a prime cause of crime (ibid., p. 137). It is therefore pointedly against those theorists who, following the tradition of labelling theory, abandon the search for the causal mechanisms that give rise to crime (cf. Muncie, this volume). That is, in particular, those influenced by social constructionism who not only – as we have seen – bracket off the deviant act from the reaction against it and focus solely on the latter, but suggest that the explanation of crime and deviancy has no ontological validity

For *The New Criminology* to advocate the causal explanation of crime is scarcely surprising, given that it is a text immersed in a theoretical tradition influenced by Marx and Engels and which develops radical interpretations of Mertonian theory. Yet of course the book is scathingly critical of certain types of causal theory. The first two chapters are devoted to demolishing positivist notions of causality that evoke absolute determinacy, that is, theories that deny human volition and meaning: those which, in the vernacular of the time, deny the *authenticity* of the deviant act. Yet human beings 'make their own history, but they do not make it just as they please; they do not make it under circumstances chosen by themselves, but under circumstances directly encountered, given and transmitted from the past' (Marx, *The Eighteenth Brumaire of Louis Bonaparte*). Thus to explain the circumstances that lead to crime does not deny human interpretation and voluntarism.

It has become commonplace, however, for some radicals to deny the possibility of ascertaining these causal sequences (see Smart, 1990). Often this is simply based on the confusion arising from misidentifying a critique of positivism as necessitating a denial of causality. But more often it is an integral part of the constructionist platform, namely that the discourses carried by the criminal justice system and the mass media play *the* crucial role in the crime problem. That is, causality is shifted from crime – as in positivism – to the process of criminalisation rather than to the interaction of both, as outlined in the programme of *The New Criminology*. But to deny that in certain circumstances (for example unemployment, poverty, marginalisation) *some* (although far from all) individuals are attracted to certain crimes (for example burglary, street robbery, theft) is not only ludicrous but renders ineffective any radical critique of society. It would render inapplicable and inconsequential the subtle and insidious lines that Elliott Currie and Ian Taylor (both in this volume) trace from market society to crime wave. But more than this it would suggest that the main source of the problem of crime in society lies within the criminal justice system, not in civil society itself. This has serious political consequences. It suggests that the most pressing task should be to do something about the criminal justice system rather than the society that produces crime in the first place. It mirrors the right-wings obsession with prisons and police: it grants by default that it is the administration of society not society itself that is the problem.

Thus it both restricts our immediate strategies and gives us tawdry utopias. However true it is that we should argue for immediate changes in the control of the police and the reduction of the prison population, we should not lose sight of the even more pressing need to make social and economic changes in the situation of those most liable to offend and those most vulnerable as victims (see Currie, 1996). To put too great an emphasis on police reform, as for example occurs in some of the most early realist work (for example Lea and Young, 1984; Kinsey *et al.*, 1986), is a failing not so much in terms of necessity (these reforms are overdue) but emphasis (they are only a small part of the solution).

The solution, for example, to the extraordinarily high black-on-black crime rate in the United States is not making the judiciary representative of ethnic minorities nor ensuring that those on death row get a fair trial. These are both perfectly laudable, progressive demands – no one to the left of Attila the Hun would disagree with them – but they will not solve the problem. The mortality rate of young black men would still remain similar to that in Bangladesh: the killing fields of Harlem, South Chicago and Watts would continue their macho business unabated even if the ethnic composition of the police perfectly reflected the community and if every trial were as fair as a liberal's conscience. Similarly there can be no doubt that the struggle to ensure that rape trials do not further victimise the victim is of great importance and the sympathetic dealing of victims by the police is a crucial demand of justice, but the most meticulously sensitive and decent criminal justice system will only make a small impact on the actual rate of rape suffered by the population. Only a change in the attitudes of men and gender relations – matters of civil society not the administration of justice – will achieve this goal.

But these are matters of immediate reforms: what is argued frequently, particularly by abolitionists, is that what is needed is an ideal, some utopian position that will allow us to orientate our long-term aims. For abolitionists this is most frequently the abolition of imprisonment but it often stretches as far as the criminal justice system as a whole (see Mathiesen,

1990; Hulsman, 1986). And in the place of the criminal justice system, alternatives to prison of various sorts are suggested.

There is no doubt that some utopian vision is needed, some critical point by which to judge progress and gain purchase in our critique of existing social arrangements (see Ian Loader, this volume). Not to do so creates a radical politics that is technicist, bitty and short term. There is also little doubt that reduction of the prison population and the building of alternatives are important areas of struggle. But whereas to focus, for example, on the abolition of prison might seem a utopian ideal, in fact it offers no firm position from which to critique the inequitable social order. We do not want alternative visions of social control but alternative visions of a just society, where both the present criminal justice system and alternatives to prison would be rendered unnecessary. Alternatives to prison may be a solution to the prison problem but they certainly are not a solution to the crime problem. For even if we were to grant that acting after rather than before the offence is committed is the best way of containing crime, and that alternatives to prison can effectively rehabilitate offenders, we would still be facing a major error with regard to crime. For the assumption, often explicitly made by the abolitionists (see Mathiesen, 1990), is that only a small number of offenders commit a large amount of crime, and furthermore at some point they inevitably come up before the criminal justice system. But there is little evidence for this: domestic violence, rape, sexual assault (and in the United States even homicide) are all serious examples of widespread crime with a multitude of offenders. Furthermore, to take less serious offences such as burglary and street robbery, it is often the case that there are few offenders at any one time, but the personnel change every month. And of course there is little evidence that the vast majority of offenders ever come up before the criminal justice system

CONCLUSION

I have argued that the significance of *The New Criminology* was that it was a representative of the discourse on crime, deviancy and culture that arose in the late 1960s and early 1970s around the activities of the NDC. Of course there was a wide current of debate but this was not as incoherent as is often suggested (for example Wiles, 1976; Sumner, 1994). With hindsight the common themes and interests become clearer, as does the relevance for the present day. The early 1970s represented a turning point in which the former certainties of the postwar settlement became the subject of debate, controversy and ambiguity. In place of absolute values we had pluralism, instead of collective solidarity, a culture of individualism; the notion of progress itself was questioned and social identities once bought off the shelf for life were constantly changing and the subject of struggle and creativity. All these themes were touched upon in the discourse of a fledgling radical criminology and continue to be so today.

In a way the programme of *The New Criminology* – the need to explain human behaviour in terms of micro context and the wider social world, to explain human agency and structure, to trace the interaction between those with powerful definitions of situations and those without and to be cognizant of the major structural elements of age, class, gender and ethnicity – is perhaps obvious to anyone not working in criminology. But a tendency towards partiality, towards emphasising one part of the social process rather than another, for instance to constructions downwards rather than upwards, towards gender rather than class and so on are common problems in any discipline that seeks to explain or discuss human behaviour. In cultural studies, for example, Paul Willis in his incisive *Common Culture* (1990) criticises the tendency to downplay the production of identity from below. He criticises, amongst other things, the orthodox Gramscian perspective, which seeks to explain popular culture too readily as a site of struggle where 'power blocks' maintain hegemony over the 'popular classes'. Thus he writes: 'What makes identity "from below" and "horizontally" is crucially missing from most accounts of hegemony. Social agents may not be seen as passive bearers but they still have not become more than brightly coloured cardboard cut-outs pasted around the hegemony board game' (ibid., p. 157).

And Angie McRobbie deplores the division of labour that has occurred between sociology, which studies youth culture, and cultural studies, which deals with texts and meanings, calling for a convergence into an 'interactive cultural sociology'. Thus she writes:

> What is needed then, in relation to the study of youth . . . is a research mode which prioritises multiple levels of experience, including the ongoing relations which connect everyday life with cultural forms. This would be a way of breaking down the division which has emerged between the study of cultural texts and the study of social behaviour and experience (McRobbie 1994, pp. 184–5; see also Ferrell and Sanders, 1995).

The work centring around the NDC was concerned with such problems, but there was more than this to it. For the emergence of such ideas and sensitivities occurred precisely at the point at which a late modern world was developing. Since the late 1960s onwards society has been driven more and more by a culture of individualism, characterised by diversity and a deconstruction of accepted values. Human action, in each and every nook and cranny of the social world is, indeed, more creative. Role making has risen to the top of the agenda rather than role taking, and the need to develop an analysis that deals with how people actively create subcultures in response to the diverse predicaments that face them has become paramount. And this is true of course across the gamut of human behaviour, some of which includes crime as a master status; some where crime and delinquency are peripheral and of relative unimportance; some where crime and criminology are of no relevance whatsoever. Similarly, in terms of the response of those in control or who are threatened by a world of pluralism and misbehaviour, the problem of maintaining hegemony has become daily more precarious, and therefore our need to explain social reaction the more obvious. It was no accident, for example, that 'moral panic' was conceived as a concept in the early 1970s. It was then that the postwar monolith of modernism, with its absolutist certainties, was failing. Moral panic, like violence, occurs not when hegemony is successful but when authority is losing its grip. And indeed, as Angie McRobbie and Sarah Thornton (1995) have shown, there was an increase in the production of such panic partly in response to vociferous developments within the proliferating mass media and partly because of the increasing difficulty of drawing a sharp demarcation between 'normal' and 'distinct' and to make distinctions that were not hotly contested.

It is for these reasons that I would contest Colin Sumner's notion that the ideas circulating around the NDC were inchoate and that *The New Criminology* had little to say on the level of academic discourse – although I thoroughly agree that the book was, as he puts it: 'unkempt'!

But he has, perhaps not surprisingly, a different interpretation of events. Rightly, seeing the labelling theory of Howard Becker as the precursor of his constructionist theory of social censure, he rather optimistically views the 'positive' part of Stan Cohen's work as a prelude to his own and Stuart Hall and his colleagues' *Policing the Crisis* as 'very much a text which openly illustrates all the marks of transition . . . from a sociology of deviance to a sociology of social censures' (Hall *et al.*, 1978, p. 295).

My own interpretation, as we have seen, is somewhat different; the agenda set up by the NDC was certainly unkempt and the debates ran us ragged, but it was remarkably prescient and it has only been recently, particularly in cultural studies, that parallel agendas have been addressed. In criminology there has been less development partly because of the constructionist turn in radical criminology and sociology of deviance in the 1980s and 1990s, which, whatever its contribution, muted discussion of such matters as aetiology, the micro context of crime and the ethnography of deviance, and partly because of the rapid and unexpected expansion of conventional criminology, which has remained stolidly within its usual habitat of empiricism and technicism.

Colin Sumner notes that *The New Criminology* should be judged more as a 'political brick' to be thrown through the establishment's window than as a piece of academic discourse. I like the idea of the brick; it was necessary then, when positivist notions ruled the roost and empiricism was unchallenged. But how much has changed? If anything the rise of criminology of the new and far right is a step back from the lukewarm, multifactor positivism of the 1950s. What are we to make of James Q. Wilson and Richard Herrnstein (1994), who adorn their text with those ghastly line drawings of William Sheldon's somatotypes? (The ones we used to show to our students, together with Lombrosian heads, to amuse them at the beginning of criminology classes.) Or, more seriously, of Philippe Rushton (1995), who in a book strongly endorsed by Hans Eysenck insists on the racial basis of violent crime, brain size, intelligence and sexual aggression, based on the supposedly greater environmental challenges that faced the white races as they confronted the cold north, compared with the blacks, who remained cosseted in Africa? And there he is, busy comparing the cranial sizes of 6325 military personnel by sex, rank and race and the penile sizes of whites, blacks and mongoloids, based surreally on self-report measurements!

Meanwhile Michael Gottfredson and Travis Hirschi (1990) have evolved a form of market positivism that, with stunning illiteracy, claims to be rooted in the work of both Thomas Hobbes and Emile Durkheim (the latter a critic of the former and both with theories totally agin that of control theory). And of course Charles Murray has managed to take 'blaming the victim' to its final conclusion by blaming the crime rate on single mothers (with precious little evidence, see Mooney in this volume) whilst *The Bell Curve*, the best-selling social science text of the decade (Herrnstein and Murray, 1994), comes up with the startling conclusion that crime is caused by the world becoming more complex so that people of low intelligence are finding it increasingly difficult to tell right from wrong. Meanwhile self-proclaimed radicals parade in the most torturous language 'the dangerous [sic] work' and 'constant flagellation' that the task of deconstruction holds for them – well we all know how difficult at times it can be to work in a socio-legal studies department.

Perhaps it is time, once again, to break a few windows: there are many more than before – some so occluded that they serve merely to conceal, some so distorted that our images of crime and justice are as unreal as the latest television crime series, some that reflect like a mirror, telling us 'reflexively' more about the writer than the real world outside.

Note

1. The NDC lasted from 1968 to 1979. Altogether there are five volumes of collected papers from the conferences, although many, perhaps the majority, of the papers were published elsewhere: S. Cohen (ed.) *Images of Deviance* (Harmondsworth: Penguin, 1971) (1968–70, York); I. Taylor and L. Taylors (eds) *Politics and Deviance* (Harmondsworth: Penguin, 1972) (1970–72, York); R. Bailey and J. Young (eds) *Contemporary Social Problems in Britain* (Farnborough: Saxon House, 1973) (1971–73, York); National Deviancy Conference (ed.) *Permissiveness and Control* (London: Macmillan, 1980) (Easter 1977, Sheffield); B. Fine, R. Kinsey, J. Lea, S. Picciotto and J. Young (eds) *Capitalism and the Rule of Law* (London: Hutchinson, 1979) (January 1979, London).

References

Brake, M. (1980) *The Sociology of Youth Culture and Youth Subcultures* (London: Routledge).

Brownmiller, S. (1975) *Against Our Will* (Harmondsworth: Penguin).

Cain, M. (1990) 'Towards Transgressions: New Directions in Feminist Criminology', *International Journal of the Sociology of Law*, vol. 18, no. 1, pp. 1–8.

Carlen, P. (1992) 'Criminal Women and Criminal Justice: The Limits to, and Potential of, Feminist and left Realist Perspectives', in R. Matthews and J. Young (eds), *Issues in Realist Criminology* (London: Sage).

Clarke, J. (1975) 'The Skinheads and the Magical Recovery of Community', in S. Hall and T. Jefferson (eds), *Resistance Through Rituals* (London: Hutchinson).

Clarke, J., S. Hall, T. Jefferson, B. Roberts (1975) 'Subcultures, Cultures and Class', in *Resistance Through Rituals* (eds), S. Hall and T. Jefferson (London: Hutchinson).

Cloward, R. and L. Ohlin (1960) *Delinquency and Opportunity* (New York: The Free Press).

Cohen, A.K. (1955) *Delinquent Boys* (New York: The Free Press).

Cohen, P. (1970) 'Youth Subcultures in Britain', NDC 6th Symposium (October).

Cohen, S. (1972) *Folk Devils and Moral Panics*, 1st edn (London: Paladin).

Cohen, S. (1980) *Folk Devils and Moral Panics* 2nd edn (Oxford: Martin Robertson).

Cohen, S. and L. Taylor (1976) *Psychological Survival* (Harmondsworth: Penguin).

Currie, E. (1996) *Is America Really Winning the War on Crime and Should Britain Follow its Example?* (London: NACRO).

Downes, D. and P. Rock (1988) *Understanding Deviance* (Oxford: Clarendon Press).

Ericson R. and K. Carriere (1994) 'The Fragmentation of Criminology' in D. Nelken (ed.), *The Futures of Criminology* (London: Sage).

Ferrell, J. and C. Sanders (eds) (1995) *Cultural Criminology* (Boston: Northeastern University Press).

Fitzgerald, M. (1977) *Prisoners in Revolt* (Harmondsworth: Penguin).

Foucault, M. (1977) *Discipline and Punish* (London: Allen Lane).
Goode, E. and N. Ben-Yehuda (1994) *Moral Panics* (Oxford: Blackwell).
Gottfredson, M. and T. Hirschi (1990) *A General Theory of Crime* (Stanford: Stanford University Press).
Hall, S. (1970) 'The Hippies: An American Moment', NDC 5th Symposium (April).
Hall, S., C. Chritcher, T. Jefferson, J. Clarke, B. Roberts (1978) *Policing the Crisis* (London: Macmillan).
Herrnstein, R. and C. Murray (1994) *The Bell Curve* (New York: The Free Press).
Hobsbawm, E. (1994) *The Age of Extremes* (London: Michael Joseph).
Hulsman, L. (1986) 'Critical Criminology and the Causes of Crime', *Contemporary Crises*, vol. 10 no. 1, pp. 63–80.
Johnson, R. (1979) 'Culture and the Historians', in J. Clarke, C. Critcher, and J. Johnson (eds), *Working Class Culture* (London: Hutchinson).
Kinsey, R., J. Lea, and J. Young (1986) *Losing the Fight Against Crime* (Oxford: Blackwell).
Kitsuse, J. and M. Spector (1973) 'Towards a Sociology of Social Problems' *Social Problems*, vol. 20, pp. 407–19.
LaCapra, D. (1972) *Emile Durkheim: Sociologist and Philosopher* (New York: Cornell University Press).
Lea, J and J. Young (1984) *What is to be Done About Law and Order?* (Harmondsworth: Penguin).
Mathiesen, T. (1990) *Prison on Trial* (London: Sage).
Matza, D. (1969) *Becoming Deviant* (Englewood Cliffs, NJ: Prentice-Hall).
McRobbie, A. (1994) *Post Modernism and Popular Culture* (London: Routledge).
McRobbie, A. and S. Thornton (1995) 'Rethinking "Moral Panic" for Multi-mediated Social Worlds', *British Journal of Sociology*, vol. 46, no. 4, pp. 559–74.
Messerschmidt, J. (1993) *Masculinities and Crime* (Lanham, MD: Rowman and Littlehead).
Mooney, J. (1994) *The Prevalence and Social Distribution of Domestic Violence: An analysis of Theory and Method*, PhD thesis, Middlesex University.
Pateman, C. (1988) *The Sexual Contract* (Cambridge: Polity Press).
Pearson, G. (1978) 'Goths and Vandals – Crime in History', *Contemporary Crises*, vol. 2, no. 2, pp. 119–40.
Pfohl, S. (1977) 'The Discovery of Child Abuse', *Social Problems*, vol. 24, pp. 310–24.
Phillips, A. (ed.) (1987) *Feminism and Equality* (Oxford: Basil Blackwell).
Rice, M. (1990) 'Challenging Orthodoxies in Feminist Theory: A Black Feminist Critique', in L. Gelsthorpe and A. Morris (eds), *Feminist Perspectives in Criminology* (Milton Keynes: Open University Press).
Rowbotham, S. (1973) *Hidden from History* (London: Penguin).
Rushton, P. (1995) *Race, Evolution and Behavior* (New Jersey: Transaction).
Smart, C. (1976) *Women, Crime and Criminology* (London: RKP).
Smart, C. (1990) 'Feminist Approaches to Criminology', in A. Morris and L. Gelsthorpe (eds), *Feminist Perspectives in Criminology* (Milton Keynes: Open University Press).

Sumner, C. (ed.) (1990) *Censure, Politics and Criminal Justice* (Milton Keynes: Open University Press).

Sumner, C. (1994) *The Sociology of Deviance: An Obituary* (Milton Keynes: Open University Press).

Taylor, Ian (1968) 'Football Mad: A Speculative Sociology of Football Hooliganism', NDC 1st Symposium (November).

Taylor, I., P. Walton, and J. Young (1973) *The New Criminology* (London: RKP).

Taylor, I., P. Walton, and J. Young (1975) *Critical Criminology* (London: RKP).

Taylor, L. (1971) *Deviance and Society* (London: Michael Joseph).

Walton, P. (1971) 'The Case of the Weathermen', NDC 8th Symposium (July).

Wiles P. (1976) *The Sociology of Crime and Delinquency in Britain* (London: Martin Robertson).

Willis, P. (1972) 'A Motorbike Subculture', NDC 8th Symposium (January).

Willis, P. (1977) *Learning to Labour* (Farnborough: Saxon House).

Willis, P. (1990) *Common Culture* (Milton Keynes: Open University Press).

Wilson, J.Q. (1975) *Thinking About Crime*, 1st edn (New York: Vintage Books).

Wilson, J.Q. and Herrnstein, R. (1985) *Criminal Human Nature* (New York: Simon R. and Schuster).

Young, J. (1968) 'The Role of the Police as Amplifiers of Deviance, Negotiators of Reality and Translators of Phantasy', NDC 1st Symposium (November).

Young, J. (1971) *The Drugtakers* (London: Paladin).

Young, J. (1974) 'New Directions in Subcultural Theory', in J. Rex (ed.), *Approaches to Sociology* (London: RKP).

Young, J. (1981) 'Beyond Consensual Paradigm Theory' in S. Cohen and J. Young (eds), *The Manufactured News* (London: Constable).

Young, J. (1992) 'Ten Points of Realism' in J. Young and R. Matthews (eds), *Rethinking Criminology* (London: Sage).

Young, J. (1994) 'Incessant Chatter: Recent Paradigms in Criminology', in M. Maguire, R. Morgan and R. Reiner (eds), *The Oxford Handbook of Criminology* (Oxford: Clarendon Press).

3 Reducing the Crime Problem: A Not So Dismal Criminology

John Braithwaite

The New Criminology appeared when I was a PhD student at the University of Queensland. It was the most important criminology book of the decade. More generally, the 1970s was the British decade in criminology, just as the 1960s had been in music. American criminology, which had dominated our thinking in the colonies during the 1960s, seemed theoretically uninspired in comparison. But by the 1980s the Cliff Richards of British criminology were back. Places such as Canada, Scandinavia and even Australia became more interesting intellectual communities for criminologists. Some of those involved in the great British criminology books of the 1970s – Maureen Cain, Stan Cohen, Frank Pearce, Ian Taylor, Paul Walton – actually left the country. Among the others who left were Kit Carson and Barry Hindess, who, while they did not write central criminological books during the 1970s, in different ways significantly influenced the British intellectual leadership of the field.

So it seemed to me an excessively British view of the world for Paul Walton to say, in inviting us to contribute chapters to this book, that the 1970s were a 'period of almost utopian optimism and debate' while the 1990s are characterised by pessimism, economic decline and a loss of faith in Marxism and other master narratives. If you are from one of Asia's newly industrialising economies you were a citizen of a Third World country in the 1970s; in the 1990s your country is set to pass Britain's per capita GDP. If you are from China, you might associate the loss of faith in Marxism with the fact that China has already surpassed Britain's aggregate GDP.

While the way *The New Criminology* wove together action and social reaction, materialist and subcultural explanation

47

will endure, the drive for a Marxist criminology will not. Paul Hirst (1975) was right to say that crime is not a Marxist category of analysis. But that was a problem with Marxism, not with criminology, as contemporary left-using realists have recognised. Martin Krygier (1990) has argued that contempt for the rule of law and for associated institutions such as an independent judiciary were central to the oppressiveness of communist regimes. Moreover this contempt for the rule of law, which included rejection of the idea that the communist state could commit crime, was more than a contingent outcome of the particular kinds of Marxists who gained control of these regimes; it was a contempt that was deeply embedded in Marxist theory.

Postmodernism in the 1990s risks an equally dangerous contempt for the rule of law. But if we were neither Marxists nor postmodernists in the 1970s and the 1990s, but epistemologically plural social democrats, there would be no need to be pessimistic, at least about the possibility of more decent criminal justice and more decent crime control. It is true that social democrats think that struggles for greater equality are central to crime control (Braithwaite, 1979, 1991; Currie, 1985; Young, 1992) and that in this regard we seem to be losing ground in the old capitalist economies, if not in the newly industrialising ones (World Bank, 1993). This is because social democrats have not learnt how to struggle for greater equality in the context of impediments that are global rather than national. Unfortunately a social science that, overreacting against the grand narratives of the 1970s, requires us to focus only on the most local of contextual analyses will never lift our gaze to the possibilities of international institutions of economic coordination that might relieve unemployment, reduce the competitive bidding down of tax rates and prevent the environmental crimes of capitalism. The long march through the international economic institutions is not easy. How to theorise optimistically about securing progress and forestalling regress within that struggle is not the topic of this chapter.

Instead I will simply revisit the possibility of an optimistic future from criminology that I recently developed in the John Barry Memorial Lecture.[1] I will advance the possibility of a normative criminology that offers guidance on the types of crime we should struggle to reduce and how. Likewise, an explanatory criminology is possible, one that suggests which practical strategies may work in reducing these types of crime. These possibilities have eluded us, however, because of an excessive emphasis on state policies within prevailing theoretical traditions. A theoretical revolution in criminology is needed to cause us to look in the right places for practical struggles that might bear fruit. Republican criminology is advanced as a theoretical alternative. Republicanism causes us to see that our most serious crime problems are actually problems with which we may be making some progress. A theoretical reorientation might help us identify the reasons for our contemporary successes in crime control so that we might apply ourselves to reinforcing them.

Criminologists are pessimists and cynics. There are good reasons for this. Our science has largely failed to deliver criminal justice policies that will prevent crime. The grand nineteenth-century utilitarian doctrines – deterrence, incapacitation, rehabilitation – are manifest failures. The return to classicism in criminology – the just deserts movement – has been worse than a failure. It has been a disastrous step backwards.

How can we extricate ourselves from our contemporary nihilism. In this chapter I will argue for a theoretical revolution that forces us to look at the crime problem in a decisively changed way. It replaces the pessimistic view that nothing works in reducing crime with an optimistic vision. The theory enables us to see that (1) the most serious crime problems in contemporary societies are precisely the crime problems we are in the best position to reduce, and (2) the changes needed to effect these reductions have gathered significant momentum in Australia since the mid 1970s.

To find the foundations for the theory that will ultimately lead to this conclusion, we need to go beyond the failed nineteenth-century theories of liberalism, Marxism and utilitarianism to the political theory that was dominant for several centuries up to the eighteenth century. That political theory is republicanism. This does not meant that I advocate the recreation of Montesquieu's or Machiavelli's or Jefferson's republic in twenty-first-century Western cities. The intellectual challenge before us is to construct models of contemporary urban republics, practical strategies for injecting republican elements into liberal urban life. So what are the lights on the republican hill[2] that we might reformulate in a contemporarily relevant way?

Cass Sunstein (1988) advances four commitments as basic to republicanism: (1) deliberation in governance, which shapes as well as balances interests (as opposed to simply doing deals between prepolitical interests), (2) political equality, (3) universality, or debate to reconcile competing views, as a regulative ideal, and (4) citizenship, community participation in public life. It will perhaps already be obvious to you how these republican values underwrite the importance of community policing as a practical strategy.

I will be as brief as I can on the philosophy of republicanism as a foundation for criminal justice policy. These foundations are discussed at length in my book with Philip Pettit, *Not Just Deserts: A Republican Theory of Criminal Justice* (Braithwaite and Pettit, 1990). This is a consequentialist theory that posits the maximisation of dominion as the yardstick against which to measure the adequacy of policy. What is this dominion that we wish to maximise?

Dominion is a republican concept of liberty. Whereas the liberal concept of freedom is the freedom of an isolated, atomistic individual, the republican concept of liberty is the freedom of a social world. Liberal freedom is objective and individualistic. Freedom for the liberal means the objective fact of individuals being left alone by others. For the republican, however, freedom is defined socially and relationally. You only enjoy republican freedom – dominion – when you live in a social world that provides you with an intersubjective set of assurances of liberty. You must subjectively believe that you enjoy these assurances, and so must others believe. Being a social, relational concept of liberty, by definition it also has a comparative dimension. To enjoy liberty fully, you must have equality of liberty prospects with other persons. If this is difficult to grasp, think of dominion as a concept of freedom that, by definition, incorporates the notions of that old republican slogan 'Liberté, Égalité, Fraternité'. Then you have the basic idea.[3]

This concept of dominion as a target for the criminal justice system has two attractive political features for progressive criminologists. First, it motivates a minimalism in state criminal justice interventions. This is the principle of parsimony: if in doubt, do less by way of criminal justice intervention.

Second, at the same time dominion requires a highly interventionist state policy to secure equality of liberty prospects. This is the relational element built into the definition. When women or Aborigines enjoy lesser liberty prospects, affirmative action, redistributive tax and economic policies are commended by the theory. So we have a theory that can require minimalism in criminal justice policy alongside interventionism in economic policy.

The principle of parsimony does important theoretical work. Pettit and I show that it motivates a theoretically driven incrementalism in criminal justice policy – actually a decrementalism. Republicans, we argue, are required to struggle politically alongside the budget-cutting economic rationalists for a progressive reduction in criminal justice intervention. The right level of punishment is not determined by the just deserts of offenders. The right level of punishment, according to the theory, is at least as low as we can take it without clear evidence emerging that crime has increased as a result of cuts to the system.

The point of all this is to show that theories are valuable when they help us to see a problem differently and to see changed and effective ways of responding to it. I will now go on to argue that republican criminology does replace a pessimism that nothing works in reducing crime with the optimistic interpretation outlined at the beginning of the chapter. To remind you, republican theory enables us to see, firstly, that the most serious crime problems in contemporary societies are precisely the crime problems we are in the best position to reduce. Secondly, the changes needed to effect these reductions have gathered momentum since the mid 1970s.

These changes are not so much in criminal justice policies, but growth in the support for an effectiveness of social movements with criminal justice agendas. Republican criminological praxis involves active support for social movements such as the women's movement, the environmental movement, the consumer movement and the social movement against drink driving. It also involves support for restorative justice and community policing, genuine community policing, for the kind of communitarian reform direction being taken with the so-called family group conferences for young offenders in New Zealand and Wagga Wagga (Maxwell and Morris, 1993; Braithwaite and Mugford, 1994).

To get to these conclusions, we need to step back for the moment from the normative theory in the book with Philip Pettit to the explanatory theory in my other recent book, *Crime, Shame and Reintegration* (Braithwaite, 1989). The two books are intended to be complementary – the one a normative theory, the other an explanatory theory.

The key explanatory idea in *Crime, Shame and Reintegration* is that reintegrative shaming is the key to crime control. This is not just about shaming a specific deterrent. It is not just about shaming that causes an internalisation of the wrongfulness of crime, so that we are punished by our own pangs of conscience. Most of us did not commit a murder last week, not because of any rational calculation of the costs and benefits of solving our problems by bumping off the person causing them. Rather we refrained from murder because murder was right off our deliberative agenda. The cultural processes of shaming murderers to which we were exposed in earlier periods of our lives rendered murder unthinkable as a means of solving our problems. The key to understanding crime control is in coming to grips with how this unthinkableness is constituted.

The notion that shaming controls crime is an old one. But so is the seemingly contradictory idea that stigmatisation makes crime problems worse. The only originality of *Crime, Shame and Reintegration* is in advancing a theoretical resolution of this contradiction. Reintegrative shaming is posited as a shaming mechanism that prevents crime, stigmatisation as a mechanism that increases the risks of crime by the shamed actor. The partitioning of shaming mechanisms into two types with these opposite effects is proposed as a missing link in criminological theory. It enables us to integrate previously irreconcilable theories – control, subcultural, labelling, opportunity and learning theories.

Reintegrative shaming is disapproval extended while a relationship of respect is sustained with the offender. Stigmatisation is disrespectful, humiliating shaming, where degradation ceremonies are never terminated by gestures of reacceptance. The offender is branded an evil person and cast out in a permanent, open-ended way. Reintegrative shaming, in contrast might shame an evil deed, but the offender is cast as a respected person rather than an evil one. Even the shaming of the deed is finite in duration, terminated by ceremonies of forgiveness–apology–repentance.

Emphasising reintegrative shaming as a strategy of crime control is not as oppressive as emphasising stigmatisation and certainly not as oppressive as imprisonment or other forms of punishment. But it can be oppressive. Here is where one must have a moral theory, a normative theory, to guide the application of the explanatory theory. In a more detailed paper (Braithwaite, 1994) I argue the republican position that shaming should only be used when its use is likely to increase dominion. The test is whether a particular form of shaming will make our society more or less free. Indeed I argue that, conceived in a republican way, shaming can not only avoid being an unconscionable threat to freedom, but the capacity to shame is essential to constituting freedom.

Consider the rights that, according to our book, republicans are required to take seriously as constraints on the pursuit of good consequences. Rights only have meaning as claims that rich individuals and corporations can occasionally assert in courts of law *unless* community disapproval can be mobilised against those who trample on the rights of others. Liberals and republicans can agree that gay men and lesbians have a right to be different outside the constraints of the criminal law. Yet because liberals are squeamish about mobilising community disapproval against those who trample on the rights of others, liberalism lacks a practical political programme for protecting gays from harassment by the police or other citizens. The liberal idea of a practical political programme is that gays should be able to take police to court when they harass them. While the republican supports this, it must viewed as a rather empty gesture. For the republican, rights to diversity only acquire genuine power when socialising institutions and community campaigns against disrespect of rights result in citizens internalising a concern to be rights-respecting. Liberal rights can be sterile legalist gestures; republican rights are active cultural accomplishments. Strong gay and lesbian rights movements are the medium for securing these accomplishments.

But how do social movements mobilise shame to bring crime under control? The first point to reiterate is that it is not *primarily* through confronting particular criminals with shame that acts as a specific deterrent, though this is not unimportant. It is deeper cultural changes that are more important. What is critical is shaming as a cultural process that constitutes self-sanctioning consciences, that constitutes the unthinkability of a crime such as homicide for most people most of the time.

Now I want to make some general points about where our greatest crime problems lie in Australia and why social movements are especially well placed to have an impact on these crimes. I want to assert without detailed justification that three types of crime are responsible for the greatest harm to persons in Australian society. These are domestic violence (Scutt, 1983; Hopkins and McGregor, 1991), occupational health and safety and other corporate crimes of violence such as those in the pharmaceutical industry (Braithwaite and Grabosky, 1985, pp. 1–41), and drink driving (Homel, 1988). Again, I will not pause to argue this, but it is easy to show that the property offenders that cause the overwhelming majority of criminal losses are white-collar criminals (Grabosky and Sutton, 1989; Wilson and Braithwaite, 1978; Braithwaite, 1979).

There is a common structural reason why these particular offences are Australia's greatest crime problems: they have all enjoyed historical immunity from public disapproval, and they have enjoyed this immunity because of the structural realities of power. The worst of Australia's white-collar criminals have not only been unusually respectable men, they have also been hailed as our greatest entrepreneurial heroes. Violent men have enjoyed historical immunity even from the disapproval of the police when they engaged in acts of domestic assault (Scutt, 1983, chapter 9; Hatty and Sutton, 1986; Wearing, 1990). This has been because of a considerable sharing of common values between the offenders and the police about the prerogative of engaging in violence in the personal kingdom of one's home.

Australian patriarchy takes the culturally specific form of a male 'mateship' culture in which gender-segregated drinking is important (Sergeant, 1973). Pub and club drinking followed by driving is something that most Australian males have done many times, something they have regarded as important to sustaining patterns of mateship and something they have found difficult to regard as shameful. As a consequence, informal disapproval of drink driving by mates and formal disapproval by the courts has been historically muted.

These then are the bases for my claim that the particular crime problems that do most harm in Australia have become our worst crime problems precisely because of the muted or ambivalent disapproval they elicit, where limited disapproval is aroused because of patterns of power.

This is also true of white-collar crime and is true generally: when a form of crime becomes more shameful, the community discovers more instances of that form of crime. So if bank robbery is shameful and insider trading is not, the community will have the impression that bank robbery is the more common and more serious of these two problems. This when we know the fact of the matter to be that 'the best way to rob a bank is to own it' (quoted in Pontell and Calavita, 1991).

In another paper (Braithwaite, 1994) it is argued that since the mid 1970s all these forms of crime have been targeted by social movements concerned to engender community disapproval of them. The consumer movement, the environmental movement, the trade union movement and even criminologists have all played significant roles in constituting the shamefulness of white-collar crime. Road safety and health professionals have been the key players, with grassroots community groups playing a lesser role, in a new social movement against drink driving that has rendered this offence shameful for the first time in our culture. With domestic violence the women's movement – refuge workers, feminist criminologists and police officers and other femocrats working within the state – has had an effect. Media current affairs programmes now carry a regular fare of stories exposing the evils of domestic violence. Police education curricula, responding to the critiques of feminist criminologists (Hatty and Sutton, 1986; Scutt, 1982), have begun to push the line that domestic violence is a crime and a priority concern for Australian police services (McDonald *et al.*, 1990; see also Stubbs and Wallace, 1986). While private condoning of domestic violence continues, the public voices that are heard today are increasingly the voices of condemnation. And this is progress.

All the social movements I have described became strong only from the mid 1970s onwards. What an irony this is for criminology when the mid 1970s was precisely the historical moment for the disillusionment of the 'nothing works' era to set in. Perhaps nothing does work particularly well if our vision is limited to statist responses to the crime problem. Republican criminology opens our eyes to the limited relevance of statist criminology – the sort that the state gives money to – to practical ongoing struggles to reduce the crime rate.

If I am right, it is precisely with respect to the crime problems that are the most severe that social movements have been making the greatest progress during the past 15 years. I do not suggest that the progress has been decisive or overwhelming – patriarchy is not about to breathe its last gasp, the environment continues to collapse and drink driving remains one of our most terrible problems. Moreover I would argue that actors within all three social movements have made a critical error in failing to grasp the difference between the negative effects of stigmatisation compared with the positive effects of reintegrative shaming of offenders. I refer to feminists who stigmatise men, to white-collar crime scholars who stigmatise pharmaceutical executives as structurally and irretrievably evil drug pushers.

But if some progress is being made in the places that count most, statist criminology is tied to statist statistical methodologies that leave it blind to such changes. The methodologies of statist criminology churn out data that are artefacts of the very patterns of power at the heart of my argument. Crimes of domestic violence were not taken very seriously by patriarchal police forces prior to the social movement against domestic violence that regained momentum in the mid 1970s. Similarly, government victim surveys provide a doubtful baseline because the interviews have been conducted in the very households that are the sites of domestic violence, presumably in many cases within sight or sound of the very persons who have committed the violent acts. In fact statist methodologies show that the problems is getting worse because an accomplishment of the social movement against domestic violence has been to provide support to women who wish to lodge complaints against violent men (Hopkins and McGregor, 1991).

One objection to directing shame against specific forms of crime is that this a utopian enterprise since shaming is not an effective mechanism of social control in modern, urbanised, heterogeneous societies. Elsewhere I have argued that there is no unidirectional historical trend either towards or away from the effectiveness of shame-based social control (Braithwaite, 1993). Like Elias (1978, 1982) and Goffman (1956), I contend that there are some features of interdependency in modern urban societies that actually increase our vulnerability to shame, and others that reduce it.

It is more important to address the specific forms of crime that are the locus of my argument here. I have already said that criminological research gives us no way of knowing whether there is more or less domestic violence today compared with the past. What we can say with some confidence, however, is that domestic violence has become more shameful compared with say Trevelyan's (1985, p. 196) description of the shamelessness of male violence in fifteenth-century England: 'Wife-beating was a recognised right of man, and was practised without shame by high as well as low. Similarly, the daughter who refused to marry the gentleman of her parents' choice was liable to be locked up, beaten, and flung about the room, without any shock being inflicted upon public opinion'. This fact is not only recorded in the history books, but in the courts as well, where, within limits, domestic violence by the head of the household continued to be a matter of right rather than shame until late in the nineteenth century.

Similarly, I view the evidence as very strong that in recent history there has been a rise in the shamefulness of environmental crimes (McAllister, 1991) and certain other types of corporate crime (Grabosky *et al.*, 1987).

In this chapter I have overplayed the contrast between preventing crime by state enforcement and preventing crime through mobilising social movements. This contrast has been

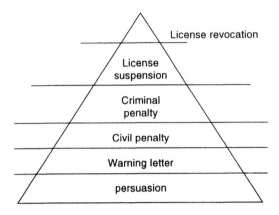

Figure 3.1 Example of an enforcement pyramid. The proportion of space at each layer represents the proportion of enforcement activity at that level.

set up in an attempt to highlight the limitations of statist criminology. But in fact my view is that both state and social movement crime control efforts are maximally effective when there is a strategic synergy between the two.

The model I like to use to communicate the required synergy is of the enforcement pyramid. Figure 3.1 is an example of a business regulatory enforcement pyramid. The idea is that the capacity of the state to escalate up the enforcement pyramid to tougher and tougher sanctions motivates the firm to cooperate with dialogic regulation at the base of the pyramid. By dialogic regulation I mean decision making where the firm sits down with an environmental regulatory agency and with greens to negotiate the solution to a pollution problem.

In Figure 3.2 we translate the same basic model to the arena of domestic violence. Kathy Daly and I (Braithwaite and Daly, 1994) have advanced the theoretical position that violence within families is least likely when those families themselves succeed in persuading their members to internalise an abhorrence of violence, to take pride in respecting the rights of women, pride in caring for others. But sometimes families will fail to accomplish this. Then they must look for outside support. In the first instance a battered woman

Figure 3.2 Example of a domestic violence enforcement pyramid

might seek help from a refuge. With a refuge worker she might then seek help from the civil law (an order restraining the man from entering his own house) and ultimately criminal enforcement by imprisonment of the man. Just as with the business regulatory pyramid, the capacity of the victim of domestic violence to pointout the inevitability of escalation to more and more dire outside intervention can be empowering for the victim.

The hope with these models is not that state enforcement will be so potent and so regularly used that it will deter rational offenders. The deterrence literature shows that to be an unrealistic hope. No, the hope is that we can provide state enforcement with a sufficient level of credibility to empower informal processes of social control, to make dialogic regulation of our most serious crime problems something that powerful actors would be well advised to attend to.

The republican envisages that a long historical process of community and state involvement in shaming acts of domestic violence will result in most citizens internalising the shamefulness of violence. Consequently most social control will work at the base of the enforcement pyramid by self-sanctioning with pangs of conscience. If this fails, the history of community shaming of violence will persuade the perpetrator that following an act of violence others will

disapprove of him. Note that no one has directly to confront the offender with shame at this level; an offender who
understands the culture will know that those who find out
about his violence will be gossiping disapprovingly. As I was
at pains to argue in *Crime, Shame and Reintegration*, on most
of the occasions when gossip hits its target, it will do so
without being heard by the target; it will be effective in the
imagination of a culturally knowledgeable subject. If the
offender is incapable of imagining the disapproval others
feel about his violence, then someone must confront him
with that disapproval. If family members are too intimidated
to do it, then a domestic violence worker must do it. If
disapproval, dialogue and counselling do not work, ultimately
incapacitative criminal law must be invoked. The republican therefore does not call simply for informalism rather
than formalism; she calls for a formalism that empowers
informalism. The effect of successful implementation of an
enforcement pyramid is, however, that most social control
is communitarian control rather than state control, and most
of the day-to-day successes are achieved by dialogic regulation, with state regulation stepping in to mop up the failures. This is also the story of Homel's (1988) work on the
reduction of drink driving in Australia – the formalism of
random breath testing empowered the informalism of dialogic regulation within drinking groups.

The real power of reintegrative shaming is at the level of
prevention – conscience building. With the very worst cases
of deep-seated violence, reintegrative shaming is quite likely
to fail, but then so is everything else. When things come to
this pass we must do our best with clumsy protective measures for victims. But the heart of a political programme
that I suspect is shared by feminism and republicanism is
to struggle for cultural and economic changes that prevent
violence long before it becomes unpreventable.

If criminology is to escape the nihilism that can turn it
into an ever more dismal science, we do need to think more
creatively about how to achieve synergy between state and
communitarian social control in a democracy. To unleash
and guide that problem-solving creativity, a radical rethinking of criminological theory might help.

Republicanism seems to me just one example of how to

see a somewhat different light on a different hill. I have sketched some similarities with how optimistic feminisms can and do motivate active citizenship to pursue feminist lights on the hill. These by no means exhaust the light worth pursuing through progressive social movements and green, social-democratic political parties.

Notes

1. This chapter is a slightly revised and expanded version of the John Barry Memorial Lecture, which was first published in *The Australian and New Zealand Journal of Criminology*, vol. 25 (1992), pp 1–10.
2. This is a reference to former Australian Labour Prime Minister Ben Chifley's characterisation of the labour movement struggle as the pursuit of the 'light on the hill'.
3. For philosophers who are shocked by such a casual definitional *gestalt*, here is a formal definition: 'A person enjoys full dominion, we say, if and only if: (a) she enjoys no less a prospect of liberty than is available to other citizens; (b) it is common knowledge among citizens that this condition obtains, so that she and nearly everyone else knows that she enjoys the prospect mentioned, she and nearly everyone else knows that the others generally know this too, and so on; (c) she enjoys no less a prospect of liberty than the best that is compatible with the same prospect for all citizens' (Braithwaite and Pettit, 1990, pp. 64–5).

References

Braithwaite, John (1979) *Inequality, Crime and Public Policy* (London: Routledge and Kegan Paul).
Braithwaite, John (1989) *Crime, Shame and Reintegration* (Melbourne: Cambridge University Press).
Braithwaite, John (1991) 'Poverty, Power, White-Collar Crime and the Paradoxes of Criminological Theory', *Australian and New Zealand Journal of Criminology*, vol. 24, pp. 40–58.
Braithwaite, John (1993) 'Shame and Modernity', *British Journal of Criminology*, vol. 33, pp. 1–18
Braithwaite, John (1994) 'Inequality and Republican Criminology', in J. Hagan and R. Peterson (eds), *Inequality and Crime*, (Palo Alto, CA: Stanford University Press).
Braithwaite, John and Peter Grabosky (1985) *Occupational Health and Safety Enforcement in Australia* (Canberra: Australia Institute of Criminology).
Braithwaite, John and Daly Kathy (1994) 'Masculinities, Violence and Communication Control' in T. Newburn and B. Stunko (eds) *Just Boys Doing Business* (London: Routledge).

Braithwaite, John and Stephen Mugford (1994) 'Conditions of Success-
ful Reintegration Ceremonies; Dealing with Juvenile Offenders', *Brit-
ish Journal of Criminology*, 34, (2), pp. 139–71.
Braithwaite, John and Philip Pettit (1990) *Not Just Deserts: A Republican
Theory of Criminal Justice* (Oxford: Oxford University Press).
Currie, Elliott (1985) *Confronting Crime* (New York: Pantheon Books).
Elias, Norbert (1978) *The Civilizing Process: The History of Manners*, trans.
Edmund Jephcott (Oxford: Basil Blackwell).
Elias, Norbert (1982) *State Formation and Civilisation: The Civilising Pro-
cess* (Oxford: Basil Blackwell).
Goffman, Erving (1956) 'Embarrassment and Social Organisation', *American
Journal of Sociology*, vol. 62, pp. 264–71.
Grabosky, Peter, John Braithwaite and Paul R. Wilson (1987) 'The Myth
of Community Tolerance Toward White-Collar Crime', *Australian and
New Zealand Journal of Criminology*, vol. 20, pp. 33–44.
Grabosky, Peter and Adam Sutton (eds) (1989) *Stains on a White Collar*
(Sydney: Federation Press).
Hatty, Suzanne and Jeanna Sutton (1986) 'Policing Violence Against
Women', in Suzanne E. Hatty (ed.), *National Conference on Domestic Viol-
ence*, vol. 2 (Canberra: Australian Institute of Criminology Seminar
Proceeding No. 12).
Hirst, Paul Q. (1975) 'Marx and Engels on Law, Crime and Morality', in
I. Taylor, P. Walton and J. Young (eds), *Critical Criminology* (London:
Routledge & Kegan Paul).
Homel, Ross (1988) *Policing and Punishing the Drinking Driver: A Study of
General and Specific Deterrence* (New York: Springer-Verlag).
Hopkins, Andrew and Heather McGregor (1991) *Working for Change: The
Movement Against Domestic Violence* (Sydney: Allen & Unwin).
Krygier, Martin (1990) 'Marxism and the Rule of Law: Reflections after
the Collapse of Communism', *Law and Social Inquiry*, vol. 15, pp. 633–63.
Maxwell, Gabrielle M. and Allison Morris (1993) *Family, Victims and Cul-
ture: Youth Justice in New Zealand* (Wellington: Social Policy Agency).
McAllister, Ian (1991) *Community Attitudes to the Environment, Forests and
Forest Management in Australia* (Canberra: Resources Assessment
Commission).
McDonald, B., J. Elliot, T. Logan, N. Norris, C. Norris, J. Shostak and S.
Kusher (1990) *The New South Wales Police Recruit Education Programme:
An Independent Evaluation* (Sydney: NSW Police Department).
Pontell, Henry and Kitty Calavita (1991) *Bilking Bankers and Bad Debts:
White-collar Crime and the Savings and Loan Crisis*, paper presented at
the Edwin Sutherland Conference on White-Collar Crime (Bloomington:
Indiana University).
Scutt, Jocelynne (1982) 'Domestic Violence: The Police Response', in C.
O'Donnell and J. Craney (eds), *Family Violence in Australia* (Melbourne:
Longman Cheshire).
Scutt, Jocelynne (1983) *Even in the Best of Homes* (Melbourne: Penguin).
Sergeant, Margaret (1973) *Alcoholism as a Social Problem* (Brisbane: Uni-
versity of Queensland Press).

Stubbs, Julie and D. Wallace (1986) *Domestic Violence: Impact of Legal Reform in NSW* (Sydney: New South Wales Bureau of Crime Statistics and Research).

Sunstein, Cass (1988) 'Beyond the Republican Revival', *Yale Law Journal*, vol. 97, pp. 1539–90.

Taylor, Ian, Paul Walton and Jock Young (1973) *The New Criminology: For a Social Theory of Deviance* (Sydney: Routledge and Kegan Paul).

Trevelyan, G.M. (1985) *A Shortened History of England* (Harmondsworth: Penguin).

Wearing, Rosemary (1990) *A Longitudinal Analysis of the 1987 Crimes (Family Violence) Act in Victoria* (Canberra: Report to Criminology Research Council).

Wilson, Paul R. and John Braithwaite (eds) (1978) *Two Faces of Deviance: Crimes of the Powerless and Powerful* (Brisbane: University of Queensland Press).

World Bank (1993) *The East Asian Miracle: Economic Growth and Public Policy* (Washington, DC: World Bank).

Young, Jock (1992) 'Ten Points of Realism', in J. Young and R. Matthews (eds), *Rethinking Criminology: The Realist Debate* (London: Sage).

4 Criminology Ltd: The Search for a Paradigm
Pat Carlen

INTRODUCTION

Glance at the criminology shelves of any academic library . . . and there they are! 'New', 'critical', 'Marxist', 'feminist', 'radical', 'realist' or 'postmodernist' criminologies, each signalling a distance from other discourses on crime by endorsing their own with a distinctive brand name. This article discusses the 'class', 'racism', 'gender' and 'object of criminology' debates that have been central to criminologies since the publication of *The New Criminology* (Taylor *et al.*, 1973), and argues that, in their theoretical or political self-consciousness, many of the brand-name criminologies have been constrained by a globalism, a realism, a populism or a political correctness (of the times) that have been theoretically and/or politically limiting. By way of conclusion, it is argued that the search for a comprehensive, realist and politically correct paradigm should be abandoned in favour of a return to the much more complex, open-ended and utopian perspectives proposed by Taylor, Walton and Young (TWY) in 1973.

CLASS AND CRIME DEBATES

Publication of *The New Criminology* (*The New Crim*) gave immediate new impetus to the perennial class and crime debates provoked early in the century by Willem Bonger (1967, first published 1916), continued by Rusche and Kirchheimer in 1939 and revived in the late 1960s and early 1970s by conflict theorists Quinney (1969, 1974, 1977, 1990) and Turk (1969). Since 1973, four main trajectories have been travelled by class and crime analysts in search of a paradigm. Here they are categorised as *Marxist, socialist, realist* and *abolitionist.*

TWY themselves (1975), as well as their earliest critics (for example Hirst, 1975), were quick to point out that it was difficult to reconcile the utopianism and sociologism of *The New Criminology* with any coherent Marxism. Yet, following publication of *The New Criminology*, the search for a Marxist theory of crime was on – and immediately stymied by Marx's failure to provide either a theory of criminal law or an explicit theory of the state. To help remedy these omissions, Cain and Hunt (1979) edited a comprehensive compilation of Marx's writings on law, while TWY joined with the Conference of Socialist Economists' Law and State Group to publish *Capitalism and the Rule of Law* (Fine *et al.*, 1979). At the same time there was a refocusing of the criminological gaze towards the writings of Marxist theorists and historians such as Pashukanis (1978) and Thompson (1975). Along this trajectory, the search for a Marxist theory of *crime* was rapidly transformed into a diversity of intellectual labours directed primarily at construction of a critical theory of *law*.

Taylor and Young continued to work at a politics of crime. Taylor's endeavours resulted in his *Law and Order: Arguments for Socialism* (1981). Contemporaries also evincing a concern about crime, class and socialism included Hall *et al.* (1978), Carlen (1976, 1979), Hirst (1979), Box (1983, 1987), as well as all the abolitionists (see below). Young, however, although equally committed to socialism, was already absorbed by the very specific issue of the relationship between theoretical criminology and the politics of crime control. Increasing frustration at the left's failure to influence law and order policies provided the spur for his development of the paradigm known as left realism.

In the mid 1970s, left-wing fears that radical critique might be neutralised by incorporation into state apparatuses had resulted in the new criminologists (later to be auto-critiqued as 'left idealists' by Young, 1986) temporarily eschewing policy debate. In the mid 1980s it was the realisation that this stance had been in part responsible for the highjacking of law and order issues by the radical right that provoked the left realists' first injunction – to take crime and its effects seriously. As far as class and crime politics are concerned, Young and his associates (Lea and Young, 1984; Kinsey *et al.*, 1986; Young, 1987, 1992; Lea, 1987; Matthews, 1987; Young and Matthews,

1992) have tirelessly confronted the challenge of right-wing criminologists such as Wilson (1975) and 'underclass' theorists such as Murray (1984, 1990). These 'right-wing realists' have argued against materialist and liberal theories of crime on the ground that the (supposed) amelioration of social conditions by welfarist policies has not reduced official crime rates – and may even have increased them. Nonetheless the populism and globalism inherent in the left realists' synthesising and increasingly elaborated theoretical edifice seem to involve a prejudgment of crime issues that could lead to theoretical and political dead-ends. Uncritical use of victim surveys is one example of an empiricist and populist tendency towards theoretical closure (Jones *et al.*, 1986; Elias, 1993). Appeals to global and moralistic notions of individual responsibility and free will is another. Such appeals certainly tap a vote-winning populism, but they also put at risk all opportunity to show how individualised problems of criminal justice are also issues of social justice in general (see Young, 1986, p. 29; Carlen, 1988, 1992, pp. 58–61).

The fourth radical trajectory tenaciously held to by theorists of class and crime has been that of abolitionism. Inherent in much radical critique since the birth of the prison, abolitionism is a complex theoretico-political programme. Its justification is to be found in the contention that popular and operative definitions of crime in class societies have all but ignored the institutionalised illegalities of the powerful. Instead they have focused on the crimes of the disadvantaged, who as a consequence have disproportionately suffered imprisonment. The strategy of abolitionists is to support short-term penal reforms *only* if they both contribute to an erosion of prison systems and do not increase inequality. The resurgence of the abolitionist thrust in the 1970s was inspired by the works of Mathiesen (1974) and Dodge (1979), as well as by some radical reforms in the Dutch penal system (Hulsman, 1981, 1982). Since then it has primarily been in the works of abolitionists that a few elements of a utopian criminology have continued to be found (for example Bianchi and Swaaningen, 1986; Scraton *et al.*, 1991; Carlen, 1990, 1993a, 1993b; Sim, 1993; see also P. Young, 1992).

RACISM AND CRIME DEBATES

For *fin de siècle* readers the two most startling silences in *The New Criminology* relate to race/racism and gender. Black people and women are mentioned only to illustrate aspects of the experiences of a global 'Man'. Lea and Young (1984) subsequently raised the issue of black people and street crime in their *What Is To Be Done About Law and Order*, but only after the *Scarman Report* (1982) on the Brixton riots had discussed the issue of institutionalised racism within the police. The 'black subculture' theory implicit in *What Is To Be Done* provoked Paul Gilroy (1982, 1987) to accuse both its authors and the authors of *Policing the Crisis* (Hall *et al.*, 1978) of perpetuating a popular and mistaken view that black culture and political traditions are crimogenic. What we *do* know, however, is that for over a decade official statistics and detailed studies have indicated that disproportionate numbers of black people in Britain and North America are perennially charged with crimes and imprisoned, and that this anomaly cannot be wholly accounted for by black defendants either having longer criminal records or being convicted of more serious crimes. The most recent work on race and criminal justice in Britain focuses on citizenship (Cook and Hudson, 1993) and thereby continues in the tradition of Hall *et al.* (1978) and Gilroy (1982, 1987) of raising questions of race, racism and crime within broader questions of state and class. Regrettably, and notwithstanding the more sophisticated theories of Hall and Gilroy, some other criminologists have invoked a crude realism implying that all theories should have a one-to-one relationship with the empirical referent (see for instance Chiquada, 1989; Rice, 1990), that is, that all theories of crime should 'add-in' a component on racism. As I argue below, insofar as the 'adding in' fallacy inhibits the questioning of common-sense knowledge it is theoretically limiting. However injunctions about the 'political correctness' of 'adding in' have been much more frequent in writings on gender and justice than in those on race, racism and crime.

GENDER AND CRIME DEBATES

During the past two decades there has been a greater focus
on gender and crime than there was prior to the 1970s. In
the earlier work the emphasis was on feminisms and stereotypes of femininity. More recently there has been a shift
towards investigations of masculisms and masculinities.

Since the 1970s three major contributions have been made
to the understanding of women's lawbreaking and the social response to it. First, it has been established that women's
crimes are committed in different circumstances from men's,
that women's crimes are the crimes of the powerless (Messerschmidt, 1986; Carlen, 1988; Worrall, 1990; Carrington, 1993).
Secondly, it has been shown that the response to women's
lawbreaking is constituted within typifications of femininity
and womanhood that further add to women's oppression
(Carlen, 1983; Haln-Rafter, 1985; Edwards, 1984; Eaton, 1986).
Thirdly, writers from a variety of standpoints have asked
whether the development of a feminist criminology is a
possible theoretical project (Cousins, 1980; Brown, 1986; Cain,
1990; Smart, 1990; Carlen, 1992), whether the focus on women
is a 'proper' concern of feminism (Allen, 1988; Smart, 1990),
and whether a feminist jurisprudence is desirable and/or
possible (see Boyle *et al.*, 1985, for Canada; Dahl, 1987, for
Norway; MacKinnon, 1987, and Fineman and Thomadsen,
1991, for the United States; Redcar, 1990, and Grbich, 1991,
for Australia; and Smart, 1989, for England). Good historical work on women and crime has been produced by Beattie
(1980), Walkovitz (1980) and Zedner (1991) – to name but
three writers in a growing field. British criminologists currently addressing issues of masculisms and masculinities include Hanmer *et al.* (1989), Scraton (1990), Sumner (1990),
and Carlen (1994b).

The major concerns of feminists about criminology have
been the absence of women from crime texts, the theoretical propriety (or not) of developing feminist theories of
women's lawbreaking, the degree of correspondence between
a theory and its empirical referent, and the political risks
attendant upon campaigns for justice for women. Discussion of these issues has not only enriched women and crime
debates. Insofar as they have called into question the object

of criminology, they have also been central to criminology's most important concerns.

'OBJECT OF CRIMINOLOGY' DEBATES

In speaking of 'The Object of Criminology' in 1985, Stan Cohen said that his interest lay in 'the dual sense in which criminology has to accept a certain object (officially-designated crime) as its subject matter, but at the same time the criminologist as an active subject is busy constituting what this object is or should be' (Cohen, 1988, p. 235). Exactly the same as my interest here. For the most limiting effect of theories in search of a master narrative on crime is the implication that they always–already know what criminology's object is – for all times and all places. Examples are to be found in the theoreticist, realist–essentialist and politicist tendencies inherent in some of the most recent debates about 'criminology's object'.

A tendency towards *theoreticism* can be found in critiques that claim all criminological theory is tainted by its empirical referent (officially designated crime). In its antipolicy and antiproblem orientation the theoreticist tendency is most marked in the work of feminist anticriminologists such as Brown (1986) and Smart (1990). It seems to stem from two major fears: first, that to focus on an empirical referent such as crime, which has pre-given ideological and institutional meaning, entails an essentialist trap from which there is no escape; second, that radical ideas or strategies used in the service of the state are necessarily subverted by administrators whose aims are far from those of the women's movement. Fear of the power of the empirical referent to subvert innovation in theory and politics has also resulted in the theoreticists promulgating a strange contradiction: combining a plea that explanations of crime should transgress the limits of empiricist criminology (that is, *all* criminology from a theoreticist viewpoint) with an insistence that their own particular brands of theory should not be contaminated in the process (see, for instance, Hirst, 1975, on criminology and Marxism; and Brown, 1986, and Smart, 1990, on criminology and feminism).

The *realist–essentialist* tendencies (which limit critiques implicitly invoking some always–already known master paradigm for explaining crime phenomena) insist on tinkering with theories to make them reflect the 'truth' of a specified empirical referent. Two main strategies are 'adding-in' (for example 'black people', or 'men', or 'women', or 'black women' – see for instance Rice, 1990), and the essentialising of *some* desired characteristic of a phenomenon (for example insisting that women prisoners are *not* victims but survivors – see Shaw, 1992).

Finally, the *politicist* tendency may refuse to raise questions not seen to be politically correct (for example 'Do black people break the law more frequently than white?' or 'Are women in court treated more leniently than men?'); conflate politics with theory by developing theories to fit populist notions of crime (see, for left realists, Jones *et al.*, 1986, pp 3–4; and for feminists, on allowing women 'to speak for themselves' (Smart 1990), or insisting on a global privileging of certain concepts (as in the gender centrism of some feminist theorists, for example Cain, 1989, 1990; Smart, 1989).

AGAINST CRIMINOLOGY LTD: FOR AN EVER-NEW CRIMINOLOGY

The argument so far has been that the search for a master narrative on the meanings of 'crime' is limiting, and usually involves theoreticist, realist–essentialist or politicist tendencies that lead to analytic cul-de-sacs. Many of these tendencies are rooted in fears about the ideological effectivity of the empirical referent as already defined by official statistics, and I have discussed elsewhere the deadening effects that such apprehensions can have on theory production (Carlen, 1990, 1992, 1993b, 1994a). I will therefore end this chapter by arguing that *one* way of keeping criminologies alive and ever-new may be by repeatedly playing them through the self-denying theoretical practices of poststructuralisms at the same time as infusing them with a utopianism that, like poststructuralisms, always and already assumes that things could be otherwise.

Poststructuralisms are many, though they all share a 'dissatisfaction with the subject as a "programmed individual"' (Grbich, 1991, p. 63). The poststructuralism that I am advocating both recognises and denies structuralism. In relation to criminology, the effectivity of the structures of social process and consciousness, sociologically grouped (and often conflated) under the signs of 'crime', 'criminal' and 'criminal justice', are recognised. But they are then denied any necessary unitary being in theories, subjectivities or practices. Such a poststructuralism is structuralist insofar as it attributes a nominalist reality (see Fuss, 1989) to the concepts of 'crime', 'criminal' and 'criminal justice'. It is poststructuralist when it adopts the methodological protocol of Bachelard (1940) that systems of thought must say 'no' to their own conventions and conditions of existence. It is structuralist insofar as it takes comfort from Saussurian linguistics, which demonstrate that individual words themselves have no essential meaning but only acquire meaning via syntagma, which through differentiation assign the value of a specific sign (Saussure, 1974). It then becomes poststructuralist by raising the spectre of otherness (Lacan, 1979) or the desire for (and knowledge of) meanings that lie beyond the text (or context). These latter also make possible (via 'differance' – Derrida, 1976) the construction and simultaneous deconstruction of the text (context, theoretical object) itself. In other words, the poststructuralist perspective on crime for which I am arguing is one that will allow recognition of the value (that is, effectivity) of already known structures of crime production at the same time as denying that they always and already have perennial applicability to any specific society, social formation or individuated subjectivity. The theoretical imperative would be to fashion objects of knowledge which would not presuppose correspondence with either already-known empirical referents or politically correct stances. Such an imperative would inhibit ideological injunctions or inclinations either to 'add-in' or automatically to privilege specific concepts (for example class, gender, race). This is not to deny that theorists *must* privilege certain concepts when fashioning a theoretical system. But it is to reiterate the argument that the ordering of concepts should be justifiable on the ground of theoretical production rather than political pragmatism. Nor is it contended that theories will not be influenced by politics. It is merely asserted (yet again!) that a theory cannot be read off from a politics – and vice versa.

And finally, of course, it is recognised that while criminological debate flourishes, new brand-name criminologies are bound to be produced – if only to denote otherness and difference. So be it. But let us not celebrate the master narratives suggested by the brand names. Let us instead aim for the complexity, the open-endedness and the utopianism implicit in so much of *The New Criminology*. Then, by striving for the loss of identity, authorship and ideology inherent in 'poststructural' knowledge production, successive criminologies may successfully lose their brand names... in the production of something brand new.

References

Allen, J. (1988) 'The "Masculinity" of Criminality and Criminology: Interrogating Some Impasses', in M. Findlay and R. Hogg (eds), *Understanding Crime and Criminal Justice* (Sydney: The Law Book Co.), pp. 1–23.
Bachelard, G. (1940) *The Philosophy of No*, trans. G.C. Waterson (London: Orion Press).
Beattie, J. (1980) 'The Criminality of Women in Eighteenth Century England', in D.K. Weisberg (ed.), *Women and the Law*, vol. I, (Massachusetts: Schenkinan), pp. 197–238.
Bianchi, H. and R. Swaaningen (eds) (1986) *Abolitionism* (Amsterdam: Free University Press).
Bonger, W. (1967) *Criminality and Economic Conditions*, trans H.P. Horton (New York: Agathon Press, first published 1916, Little, Brown).
Box, S. (1983) *Crime, Power and Mystification* (London: Tavistock).
Box, S. (1987) *Recession, Crime and Punishment* (London: Tavistock).
Boyle, C. *et al.*, (1985) *A Feminist Review of Criminal Law* (Canada: Minister of Supply and Services).
Brown, B. (1986) 'Women and Crime: the Dark Figures of Criminology' *Economy and Society*, vol. 3, no. 15, pp. 355–402.
Cain, M. (1989) *Growing Up Good* (London: Sage).
Cain, M. (1990) 'Towards Transgression: New Directions in Feminist Criminology', *International Journal of the Sociology of Law*, vol. 18, no. 1, pp. 1–18.
Cain, M. and A. Hunt (eds) (1979) *Marx and Engels on Law* (London: Academic Press).
Carlen, P. (1976) *Magistrates' Justice* (Oxford: Martin Robertson).

Carlen, P. (1979) 'Radical Criminology, Penal Politics and The Rule of Law', in P. Carlen and M. Collison (eds), *Radical Criminology* (Oxford: Martin Robertson), pp. 7–24.

Carlen, P. (1983) *Women's Imprisonment* (London: Routledge & Kegan Paul).

Carlen, P. (1988) *Women, Crime and Poverty* (Buckingham: Open University Press).

Carlen, P. (1990) *Alternatives to Women's Imprisonment* (Buckingham: Open University Press).

Carlen, P. (1992) 'Criminal Women and Criminal Justice: the Limits to and Potential of Feminist and Left Realist Perspectives' in R. Matthews and J. Young, (eds), *Issues in Realist Criminology* (London: Sage).

Carlen, P. (1993a) *Underclass, Crime and Imprisonment* (Bonger Institute, University of Amsterdam, 4th Bonger Lecture).

Carlen, P. (1993b) 'Gender, Class, Racism and Criminal Justice', in G. Bridges and M. Myers (eds), *Against Global and Gender-Centric Theories* (London, Routledge).

Carlen, P. (1994a) 'Why study women's imprisonment? Or anyone else's?', *British Journal of Criminology*, special issue on prisons, vol. 33/4.

Carlen, P. (1994b) 'Virginia, criminology and the anti-social control of women', in T. Blomberg and S. Cohen (eds), *Law, Punishment and Social Control: Essays in Honour of Sheldon Messinger* (Chicago: Aldine de Gruyter).

Carrington, K. (1993) *Offending Girls* (Sydney: Allen and Unwin).

Chiquada, R. (1989) 'The Criminalization and Imprisonment of Black Women', *Probation Journal*, vol. 6, No. 3, pp. 100–5.

Cohen, S. (1988) 'The object of criminology: reflections on the new criminalization', in S. Cohen, *Against Criminology* (New Jersey: Transaction Books), pp. 235–76.

Cook, D. and B. Hudson (1993) *Racism and Criminology* (London: Sage).

Cousins, M. (1980) 'Men's Rea: A note on Sexual Difference, Criminology and the Law', in P. Carlen and M. Collison, *Radical Issues in Criminology* (Oxford: Martin Robertson).

Dahl, T.S. (1987) *Women's Law: An Introduction to Feminist Jurisprudence* (Oslo: Norwegian University Press).

Derrida, J. (1976) *Of Grammatology* (London: Johns Hopkins Press).

Dodge, C. (1979) *A World Without Prisons* (Lexington, Mass: Heath).

Eaton, M. (1986) *Justice for Women* (Buckingham: Open University Press).

Edwards, S. (1984) *Women on Trial* (Manchester: Manchester University Press).

Ehrenreich, B. and D. English (1979) *For Her Own Good* (London: Pluto Press).

Elias, R. (1993) *Victims Still* (Newbury Park: Sage).

Fine, B., R. Kinsey, J. Lea, S. Picciotto and J. Young (1979) *Capitalism and The Rule of Law* (London: Hutchinson).

Fineman, M. and N. Thomadsen (eds) (1991) *At the Boundaries of Law* (New York: Routledge).

Fuss, D. (1989) *Essentially Speaking: Feminism, Nature, Difference* (London: Routledge).

Gilroy, P. (1982) 'Police and Thieves', in CCCS Birmingham University *The Empire Strikes Back* (London: Routledge), pp. 143–82

Gilroy, P. (1987) *There Ain't No Black in the Union Jack* (London: Routledge).

Grbich, J. (1991) 'The Body in Legal Theory', in M.A. Fineman and N.S. Thomadsen (eds), (1991) op.cit., pp. 61–76.

Hall, S., C. Critcher, T. Jefferson, J. Clarke and B. Robert (1978) *Policing The Crisis* (London: Macmillan).

Haln-Rafter, N. (1985) *Partial Justice: State Prisons and Their Inmates 1800–1935* (Boston: North Easton University Press).

Hanmer, J., J. Radford and B. Stanko (1989) *Women, Policing and Male Violence* (London: Routledge).

Hirst, P. (1975) 'Marx and Engels on law, crime and morality', in I. Taylor, P. Walton, and J. Young (eds), *Critical Criminology* (London: Routledge & Kegan Paul), pp. 203–32.

Hirst, P. (1979) 'Law, socialism and rights', in P. Carlen and M. Collison' (eds). *Radical Criminology* (Oxford: Martin Robertson), pp. 58–108.

Hulsman, L. (1981) 'Penal Reform in the Netherlands: Part I Bringing The Criminal Justice System Under Control', *Howard Journal*, vol. 20, pp. 150–9.

Hulsman, L. (1982) 'Penal Reform in The Netherlands: Part II', *Howard Journal* vol. 21, pp. 35–47.

Jones, T., B. Maclean and J. Young (1986) *The Islington Crime Survey* (Aldershot: Gower).

Kinsey, R., J. Lea and J. Young (1986) *Losing the Fight Against Crime* (London: Blackwell).

Lacan, J. (1979) *The Four Fundamental Concepts of Psychoanalysis* (Harmondsworth: Penguin).

Lea, J. (1987) 'Left Realism: A Defence', *Contemporary Crises*, vol. II, no. 4, pp. 371–404.

Lea, J. and J. Young (1984) *What is to be Done About Law and Order?* (Harmondsworth: Penguin).

MacKinnon, C. (1987) 'Feminism, Marxism, Method and The State: Toward Feminist Jurisprudence', in S. Harding (ed.), *Feminism and Methodology* (Milton Keynes: Open University Press).

Mathiesen, T. (1974) *The Politics of Abolition* (Oxford: Martin Robertson).

Matthews, R. (1987) 'Taking Realist Criminology Seriously', *Contemporary Crises*, vol. II, pp. 371–401.

Messerschmidt, J. (1986) *Capitalism, Patriarchy and Crime: Towards a Socialist Feminist .Criminology* (Totowa, NJ: Rowan & Littlefield).

Murray, C. (1984) *Losing Ground: American Social Policy, 1950–1980* (New York: Basic Books).

Murray, C. (1990) *The Emerging British Underclass* (London: IEA).

Pashukanis, E. (1978) *Law and Marxism* (London: Ink Links).

Quinney, R. (1969) *Crime and Justice in Society* (Boston: Little, Brown).

Quinney, R. (1970) *The Social Reality of Crime* (Boston: Little, Brown).

Quinney, R. (1974) *Critique of Legal Order* (Boston: Little, Brown).

Quinney, R. (1977) *Class, State and Crime* (New York: Longman).

Redcar, R. (1990) (ed.) *Dissenting Opinions* (Sydney: Allen & Unwin).

Rice, M.A. (1990) 'Challenging Orthodoxies in Feminist Theory: A Black

Feminist Critique', in L. Gelsthorpe, and A. Morris, *Feminist Perspectives in Criminology* (Buckingham: Open University Press), pp. 57–69.

Rusche, G. and O. Kirchheimer (1939) *Punishment and Social Structure* (New York: Columbia University Press).

Saussure, F. (1974) *Course in General Linguistics* (London: Fontana).

Scarman, Lord Justice (1982) *The Scarman Report* (Harmondsworth: Penguin).

Scraton, P. (1990) 'Scientific Knowledge Or Masculine Discourses? Challenging Patriarchy in Criminology', in L. Gelsthorpe and A. Morris, *Feminist Perspectives in Criminology* (Buckingham: Open University Press).

Scraton, P., J. Sim and P. Skidmore (1991) *Prisons Under Protest* (Buckingham: Open University Press).

Shaw, M. (1992) 'Issues of Power and Control: Women in Prison and Their Defenders', *British Journal of Criminology*, vol. 32, no. 4.

Sim, J. (1993) 'The Abolitionist Approach: A British Perspective', in R. Dobash, A. Duff and S. Marshall (eds), *Penal Theory and Penal Practice* (Manchester: Manchester University Press).

Smart, C. (1989) *Feminism and The Power of Law* (London: Routledge).

Smart, C. (1990) 'Feminist Approaches to Criminology: Or Postmodern-woman Meets Atavistic Man', in L. Gelsthorpe, and A. Morris, *Feminist Perspectives in Criminology* (Buckingham: Open University Press).

Sumner, C. (1990) 'Foucault, gender and the censure of deviance', in L. Gelsthorpe and A. Morris, *Feminist Perspectives in Criminology* (Buckingham: Open University Press).

Taylor, I. (1981) *Law and Order: Arguments for Socialism* (London: Macmillan).

Taylor, I., P. Walton, and J. Young (1973) *The New Criminology* (London: Routledge and Kegan Paul).

Thompson, E. (1975) *Whigs and Hunters* (London: Allen Lane).

Turk, A. (1969) *Criminality and the Legal Order* (Chicago: Rand McNally).

Walkowitz, J. (1980) *Prostitution and Victorian Society* (Cambridge: Cambridge University Press).

Wilson, J. (1975) *Thinking About Crime* (New York: Basic Books).

Worrall, A. (1990) *Offending Women* (London: Routledge).

Young, J. (1986) 'The Future of Criminology: the Need for A Radical Realism', in R. Matthews and J. Young (eds), *Confronting Crime* (London: Sage).

Young, J. (1987) 'The Tasks of A Realist Criminology', *Contemporary Crises*, vol. II, no. 4, pp. 337–56.

Young, J. (1992) 'Ten Points of Realism', in J. Young and R. Matthews (eds), *Rethinking Criminology* (London: Sage).

Young, J. and R. Matthews (1992) 'Questioning left realism', in R. Matthews and J. Young (eds), *Issues in Realist Criminology* (London: Sage).

Young, P. (1992) 'The Importance of Utopias in Criminological Thinking', *British Journal of Criminology*, vol. 32, no. 4, pp. 423–37.

Zedner, L. (1991) *Women, Crime and Custody in Victorian England* (Oxford: Clarendon Press).

5 Postmodernism and Feminist Criminologies: Fragmenting the Criminological Subject

Kerry Carrington

The genre of postmodernism has contributed to increasing scepticism about essentialism in social theory. This chapter considers the implications of postmodernism for the development of anti-essentialism in feminist analyses of the criminological subject. My argument neither romanticises nor hysterises postmodernism, but seeks to locate the emergence of this discourse in a genealogical field in which the subject has become understood as increasingly fractured. It is also important to recognise that a variety of intellectual resources have been crucial in the genealogical development of non-universalist ways of thinking about issues such as gender, crime and criminal justice. Only more recently has postmodernism become one of these.

POSTMODERNIST GENRES

Postmodernism has become a buzzword used to describe a wide range of objects, conditions, and experiences, including a style of architecture, painting, or performance, the development of global information technologies and the diversification of forms of work, sexuality and living in contemporary societies (Hebdige, 1988, p. 182). The genre of postmodernism suggests that modernity has undergone a rapid succession of transformations with the emergence of mechanical and electronic means of reproduction. These transformations in production, consumption and signification have cut across an elitist aesthetics based on authorship and excellence. In postmodernity there is no authenticity, but renditions of former representations. This is why Baudrillard (1983, 1992) describes the postmodern as the replacement of the real by a hyperreality of simulation (simulcrae). Nothing is new. The artist, the pop star, the criminologist, the poet, the novelist do not create a song, poem, a book, or an image out of nothing – but through a constant reworking of the antecedent. The cycle of reflection, nostalgia, deconstruction and reconstruction is always incomplete. Madonna's shifting persona and seductive style, for example, bear all the hallmarks of a postmodern consumer culture where notions of authenticity, surrender to postmodern fabrication and replication (Schwichtenberg, 1993, p. 130). Nor is there any past or future – but a never-ending present shadowed by the past – as Chambers describes:

> With electronic reproduction offering the spectacle of gestures, images, styles and cultures in a perpetual collage of disintegration and reintegration, the 'new' – a concept connected linearity, to the serial prospects of 'progress', to 'modernism' – we move into a perpetual recycling of quotations, styles and fashions: an uninterrupted montage of the 'now'. (Chambers, 1986, p. 190).

The postmodern condition has been variously described as an epoch characterised by simultaneous continuity and discontinuity; the profusion of cultural diversity; the implosion of meaning, the collapse of cultural hierarchies; the dominance of the image, the text, the preference for the popular, the end of grand narratives, certainties or stable referents (Frow, 1991; Smart, 1992). Lyotard (1986) refers to this list of postmodern conditions as 'the derealisation of society'. He elaborates: 'The postmodern would be that which, in the modern, puts forward the unpresentable in presentation itself ... that which searches for new presentations, not in order to enjoy them but in order to impart a stronger sense of the unpresentable' (Lyotard, 1986, p. 81).

Postmodernism seems infinitely flexible. It has been 'stretched across different debates, different disciplinary and discursive boundaries' (Hebdige, 1988, p. 181). It allows you to associate it with any political position whatsoever (Frow,

1991, p. 7). Such vagueness and elasticity can become a licence for schematisation. Consider for example Bauman's sweeping generalisation about the emergence of a new kind of political technology wholly unreliant on legitimation because 'The twin technique of panoptical power and seduction . . . were increasingly put in charge of the reproduction of the social order' (Bauman, 1990, p. 14).

Curiously, what is said about postmodernity, as a set of conditions transcendent of some antecedent, was said about modernity. So the postmodern is not necessarily a condition, or epoch, or style *decisively* distinguishable from the past, as commonly suggested, but a discursive rupture in the conditions of possibility, which is very much genealogical. There is nothing at all *new* about this, as the genealogical excavations in Foucault's many works demonstrate (for example, *The History of Sexuality*, 1980). Perhaps another way of talking about the collapse of grand narratives, totalities and the postmodern condition is to consider it in relation to the emergence of governmental power (of specific and limited governmental technologies, tactics or rationalities through which the social body has become increasingly produced and managed); the reduction of importance of sovereign and juridical forms of power in the ongoing production of both subjectivity and the social through the multiple pathways of discourse (Foucault, 1991, pp. 87–103).

Nevertheless the currency of postmodernism as an intellectual resource, and particularly its critique of the discourses of modernism, is sufficiently important to argue about. As Huyssen puts it, 'The postmodern must be salvaged from its champions and its detractors' (Huyssen, 1990, p. 234). The postmodernist critique of modernity has been wide-ranging, taking issue with the modern sense of self and subjectivity, the progress view of history as linear and evolutionary and the modernist separation of art and popular culture (Nicholson, 1990, p. 3). The postmodernist project of deconstruction has sought to deconstruct three key aspects of modernism (sometimes called the enlightenment project) – its essentialising conception of history, politics, society and the transcendental subject, its teleological search for origins or causes, and its utopian solutions to the problems of modernism (Hebdige, 1988).[1]

The postmodernist critique of modernism has had an uneven reception in feminist discourses. A postfeminist discourse has embraced a postmodernist genre to deconstruct the notion of an essentialist category of women's culture, writing or discourse. Women's identities are conceptualised as fragmented and multiple and not unified by some fictive female essence (cf. Flax, 1987; Schwichtenberg, 1993; Nicholson, 1990; Weedon, 1987). This feminist encounter with postmodernism has been considered a liability for other feminists precisely because it challenges the notion of a unified single experience based on sex. The following attempts to link the debates about postmodernism and the fragmentation of the subject to debates in feminist discourses about essentialism and the criminological subject.

ESSENTIALISM AND FEMINIST CRIMINOLOGIES: RELEVANT TO ALL – SPECIFIC TO NONE!

Feminist discourses have rightly and repeatedly expressed concerns about victims of crime – of rape, domestic violence and sexual assault – and about the wholesale neglect of these issues within the discipline of criminology (Allen, 1988; Cain, 1986; Heidensohn, 1985; Naffine, 1987; MacKinnon, 1983; Smart, 1976). Feminist discourses have also been strident in their critique of the treatment of female offenders by the criminal and juvenile justice systems (Allen, 1990; Campbell, 1981; Carlen, 1988; Daly, 1989; Hancock and Chesney-Lind, 1985; Mukherjee and Scutt, 1981, Smart, 1989).

It is important to note that there is no one feminist position on any of these issues. The development of these positions has followed similar developments in feminist theory more generally (Grosz, 1989). The initial critiques of criminology emerged out of the radical, woman-centred, second-wave feminist discourses of the 1960s and 1970s. From the mid 1980s to the present feminist discourses have developed out of a more diverse range of genealogical positions. Some of these have been explicitly committed to the enterprise of deconstructing phallogocentricism (Smart, 1989, p. 86), others to de-essentialising women's criminality with a view to engaging in the politics of social justice (Carlen, 1992, pp. 65–7) and others with a view to essentialising women as a unified subject of a masculinised social order (Allen, 1990, pp. 86-8). After reviewing some of these shifts in feminist discourses about crime, criminal justice and the law, I want to address an issue other feminist scholars (cf. Nicholson, 1990) have felt compelled to address in relation to their own areas of research. How has the feminist interrogation of crime, the operation of the law and criminal justice gained from its encounter with postmodernism?

A feminist discourse emerged in the 1960s that inserted the analysis of gender into disciplines that had hitherto ignored or misrepresented half of humanity. Some have called this liberal feminism (Grosz, 1989). Irrespective of what you call it, this is exactly what feminist scholars did with criminology in the 1970s, and what some still do today. This feminist discourse criticised both the omission of women from the discipline as well as the misogynist representation of women within it. They thought that existing criminological theories could be remedied by simply correcting the many false images of women constructed in them (cf. Naffine, 1987, pp. 2–5). The great value of this work has been the mass of critical attention directed to the misrepresentation of women within criminological discourse and the folly of biologically reductionist accounts of female crime that assign to the female population fixed sex-related characteristics (for example the Lombrosian notion that women's criminality is innately related to their reproductive capacities or sexual organs, as deconstructed by Campbell, 1981, p. 36, Heidensohn, 1985, p. 111, and Smart, 1976, pp. 27–30).

However the invocation of social explanations of female criminality (for example that women's criminality can be explained as the product of male oppression, gender inequality, their confinement to the domestic sphere and the female role, and so on) have simply replaced one set of reductionisms with another (Cousins, 1980). The female offender has emerged in this feminist discourse as a unitary subject. She is a hapless victim of a patriarchal legal system 'which sees and treats women the way men see and treat women' (MacKinnon, 1983, p. 644). So while most of the feminist challenges to criminology in the 1970s and early

1980s developed rigorous critiques of its misogynous content, rarely were these accounts critical enough of the concept of criminality or the discipline of criminology itself. The central failing of criminology was simply its failure to adequately address the female sex (Cousins, 1980, p. 111). This point was made forcefully by feminist scholars in the 1980s (cf. Brown, 1986, p. 367; Howe, 1987, p. 5).

More recent feminist challenges to criminology have inverted the essentialist formulae. The central failing of criminology is now its inherent phallocentricism; its failure to confront its sex question with regard to men (Allen, 1989, pp. 20–21; Van Swaaningen, 1989, p. 288; Cain, 1990, p. 11). These critiques have in Cain's terms transgressed the discipline of criminology (Cain, 1990, p. 6) and fit loosely into Carlen's typification of an anticriminology position (Carlen, 1991, p. 53).

Defending and challenging the force of gender essentialism has become a major area of contention in feminist criminology,[2] as it has in feminist theory and social theory more generally. Gender essentialism projects onto all men and women capacities or attributes that are historically and culturally specific (Fraser and Nicholson, 1990, p. 28). It assumes 'that a unitary, "essential" women's experience can be isolated and described independently of race, class, sexual orientation, and other realities of experience' (Harris, 1990, p. 585). The commonalities of sex subordination are said to make it meaningful to adopt essentialist positions and to speak transhistorically and cross-culturally about women's experiences. Gender essentialism can be detected in accounts of universal female ·oppression, as well as in appeals to a female essence, because both impose a unity upon its object of inquiry – women (Fuss, 1989, p. 2). The flip side of this is the attribution of a shared masculinist interest to all men, or to certain institutions such as the state or the law, which are regarded as patriarchal, phallogocentric or masculinist in essence, effect or nature.

A major problem with essentialism for feminist criminology, as Cousins suggested over a decade ago, is that neither the category law nor the category women are homogenous entities capable of supporting a singular relation between them (Cousins, 1980). Carol Smart too has argued that the law is not a simple tool of either patriarchy or capitalism (Smart, 1986, p. 117). To assume so is to assume that the law has a unified object, no autonomy from other state instrumentalities and a singular essential relation with the female sex. The law is a tactic of government, not an instrument of the state (Foucault, 1991). An essentialist position also assumes that the affectivity of sexual difference acts upon the minutiae of specific discourses and penal practices from the vantage point of some exterior sovereign power. Sometimes discourses about sexual difference may be effective within the tactical use of the law, as it is in certain restricted respects in the processing of delinquent girls (cf. Carrington, 1993, pp. 28–35). But there is no pregiven unity to such relations (Cousins, 1980, pp. 114–15). The criminological subject, like the legal subject, has no fixed status associated with gender or sex.

Essentialist feminist analyses of female delinquency have tended not only to overstate the centrality of discourses authorised around sex, but in so doing have actually *misread* their effects. By positing the affectivity of discourses about sex in some sovereign form of patriarchal power that operates from the outside upon the field of juvenile justice they have failed to see the production of these discourses within this particular site of government.[3] Obviously the latter is what I attempted to do with readings of specific case studies of delinquent girls (see Carrington, 1993).

In defence of gender essentialism it has been argued that while women's experiences differ according to race and class position, their position in relation to the men of their own class or race has been one of subordination (Allen, 1990, p. 5). Hence the shared experiences of subordination are said to make it meaningful to adopt essentialist positions and to speak with authority about 'women as a group'. Others have argued more cynically that essentialist positions, while problematic, are inescapable (Fuss, 1989, pp. 3–6) and that feminists need to retain the idea of women as a group if for no other reason than rhetorical purposes (Fuss, 1989, p. 36). The main problem with these defences is the rather dubious assumption that women's experiences are monotonously similar, regardless of their endlessly varied cultural, spatial and historical specificity. In any case the rhetorical effect of talking about 'women as a group' can be used either way, positively or negatively (that is, women are good drivers, women are bad drivers; women are less criminal, women are more devious). Essentialism, whatever form it takes, cannot cut across the reductionism of binary opposites such as these.

Nevertheless the defences of gender essentialism have multiplied and developed in ways that have become more difficult to challenge. A feminist discourse emerged in Australia during the 1980s, strongly influenced by what was called 'French Feminisms'. It took male theory or phallocentricism as its object 'using the perspective of women's experience' to produce feminist ways of knowing (Grosz, 1989, p. 97). One particularly interesting development was the rejection of behaviourist and rationalist conceptions of the body, which regard it as neutral in the formation of consciousness (Gatens, 1983). Borrowing from psychoanalytic discourses, the feminine imaginary body and the masculine imaginary body are said to correspond to the female body and male body respectively (ibid., p. 155). Thus the body is not neutral in regard to the formation of consciousness. It is sexed. While Gaten's insists that this assertion does not imply a fixed essence to the masculine or feminine, it is difficult to see how there can be any historical variability in female or male sexed bodies if their correspondence to an imaginary body always corresponds. In a subsequent refinement of this argument Gatens argues that the neutral body of laws and public apparatuses assumed by the liberal state is in fact implicitly masculine (Gatens, 1991, p. 82). She says: 'Man is the model and it is his body which is taken for the human body; his reason which is taken for Reason; his morality which formalised into a system of ethics' (Gatens, 1991, p. 83).

These more sophisticated defences of essentialism in feminist theory have had a commensurate impact on the development of feminist criminologies. The concept of the sexed body has entered into the discursive field of feminist discourses about the law (see Smart, 1990). Feminists have begun to the take issue with 'the law' as a phallogocentric culture (ibid., p. 201), and criminal justice as having played an important historical role in the masculinisation of the modern social order (Allen, 1990). Feminists have also begun

to interrogate criminology as a form of masculinist thinking about women. Criminology is now regarded not just as
sexist discourse but a phallocentric one (Allen, 1988, 1989,
p. 20; Van Swaaningen, 1989, p. 288, Cain, 1990, p. 11)
because 'Criminological theory is written largely by men and
about men, whilst a universal validity is simply taken for
granted' (Van Swaaningen, 1989, p. 288).

It is difficult to disagree with these seemingly plausible
assertions. On the basis of recorded statistical sex differences
maleness does appear to be the strongest predictor of crime
and delinquency. The fact that boys far outnumber girls
coming before the Children's Courts is empirically well
founded and clearly supported by Australian and international collections of juvenile crime statistics (see Carrington,
1993, p.18). In 1991 six times as many men as women were
convicted of a criminal offence in the state of New South
Wales (81 715 men compared with 13 751 women) (NSW
Bureau of Crime Statistics, 1992, p. 301). Thus the criticism
that criminology has left untheorised the relationship between masculinity and crime is a forceful one.

The difficulty begins when this general *description* of recorded sex differentials becomes the *end* of the analysis and
when a feminist politics is read off from these overinterpreted
statistical sex discrepancies. The criminal then emerges in
this feminist discourse as a phallocentric phenomenon – as
nearly always male whose victim is nearly always female (cf.
Allen, 1990, p. 252). While this is true of certain crimes,
such as sexual and domestic violence, men, not women, are
the vast majority of victims of violence, including non-reported
assaults (National Committee on Violence, 1990, p. 33). In
any case the formulation of 'the problem' as a product of
phallocentricism, has led to demands for the law to be much
more vigilantly enforced on men 'as men'. A major flaw in
this argument, as Hogg and Brown suggest, 'is that it rests
on an idealised conception of the way the criminal justice
system, in particular the police, operate with respect to the
so-called "public" sphere' (Hogg and Brown, 1992, pp. 8–9).
They explain:

The argument that police should simply enforce the law
in the case of domestic assault (and other forms of vi-

olence against women) by arresting and charging offenders, as they would in any other assault, ignores the particularism and selectivity that characterise policing outside, as well as within the domestic sphere. It therefore oversimplifies the problems entailed in getting the police to behave differently, by reducing them to the problem of police sexism. However, many men as well as women are vulnerable to both violence and the tendency for such violence to be officially and popularly denied and disregarded. An example can be found in the most public of male domains, the pub (Hogg and Brown, 1992, pp. 8–9).

Three empirical studies, two statistical and one ethnographic, have suggested that the levels of unreported victimisation of intramale violence are as high as the levels of unreported domestic violence (Deverey, 1992; Hommel, Thommeny and Tomsen, 1989; Victorian Community Council Against Violence, 1990). The National Committee on Violence, established in 1987 by the prime minister in association with the Australian states, concluded that

> the vast majority of those who commit crimes of violence are males. . . . With the important exceptions of sexual assault and domestic violence, men are also more likely to become victims of violence. Males comprise approximately two-thirds of Australian homicide victims, and 75 percent of victims of serious assault recorded by police (National Committee on Violence, 1990, p. 33).

The committee also concluded that the victims of violence, like their perpetrators, come from relatively disadvantaged backgrounds, that infants up to one year old are the age group at greatest risk of homicide (the female sex is the most likely offender here), and that Aboriginal Australians have a much higher risk of victimisation, up to ten times greater in the case of homicide (ibid., p. xxiii). Rather than dismiss these empirical details as unwelcome nuisances to the continuum of male violence argument, feminist criminologies would do better to construct genealogies of intrasex, intrafamilial, and intersexual violence, and to interrogate the sites and means of their production before assuming any universal significance about the sex of the victim or the offender.

There is of course one major practical advantage with essentialism. Essentialist explanations of sex differences are convenient because that which is assumed universal, singular or deterministic hardly warrants any attention to empirical detail. All those nuisances and discrepancies, like the ones above, can be relegated to status of irrelevance or incorporated into an essentialist tautology (that is, men victimised by male violence are victims of a phallocentric culture or hegemonic masculinity. Ironically these men become exemplary as victims of male violence only more so than women!) In other words teleological feminist truths, 'that the law is the law of patriarchy' and that violence is the product of a 'hypermasculine male', can be exempt from any thorough genealogical investigation. In any case, where the theoretical construct of universal gender oppression doesn't fit the facts, it seems the facts tend to be sacrificed.

One particular example is the recurring claim that the criminal justice system is masculinist, in that it operates in the interests of one sex – men. A major problem with this argument (apart from its empirical fallibility), at least in an Australian context, is that the dramatic overrepresentation of Aboriginal girls and women (and their men) in the justice system contradicts an insistence on an essential relationship between it and sex. I am not suggesting that discourses about sexuality are not authoritative in contexts where court action is taken against Aboriginal girls or women. Sometimes Aboriginal girls are criminalised because of their sexual encounters with white boys. But discourses of racial hygiene cannot be easily separated from such instances (cf. Carrington, 1993, p. 44). Nor am I suggesting that there is an essential relationship between race and criminal justice that simply displaces an essential relationship between criminal justice and sex. What I am suggesting is that despite the immense genealogical relevance of colonialism on the contemporary administration of criminal justice in Australia, and the way this positions Aboriginal women very differently from non-Aboriginal women, this glaring relevance has been persistently absent from feminist research on female crime and delinquency in this country.

The only feminist text to explore a history of crimes 'involving Australian women', for example, concentrated exclusively on crimes involving non-Aboriginal women (cf. Allen, 1990). Yet Aboriginal women comprise nearly 50 per cent all female custodies and almost 14 per cent of all female prisoners in Australia, although they account for less than 2 per cent of the Australian female population (McDonald, 1990, p. 9; Biles, 1989, p. 10). Aboriginal girls constitute the single most overrepresented group of girls who regularly appear before the New South Wales Children's Courts (Carrington, 1993, pp. 37–8). There is hardly an Aboriginal woman in Australia untouched by the operation of criminal justice in her life, either directly or through the repeated criminalisation of her children, her kin, her men, or through her own victimisation of various crimes. Very few non-Aboriginal women are subject to anything resembling the extensive management of their lives, families and communities by the criminal justice system, with the exception of a few who live in areas connected to families identified as police targets (that is, some housing commission communities). The massive rate of criminalisation among Aboriginal women contradicts the dogmatic insistence that criminals are a phallocentric phenomenon, as well as the assertion that women are positioned as a unified group before the law.[4] It seems, however, that the specificity of Aboriginal women's experiences with the law *must* remain submerged within essentialist feminist discourses to maintain the credibility of the general claim that the criminal justice system is masculinist in that it generally operates in interests on one sex – men.

Hilary Allen (1987), in *Justice Unbalanced*, has also taken issue with attempts to explain the treatment of women in the criminal justice system by refering to some general force of sexual oppression. She argues:

Such an explanation demands as its initial premise the assertion of 'the patriarchy', as an all-embracing, all-powerful system of male dictatorship, which determines, more or less violently, all the forms and outcomes of social relations, including those of psychiatry and the law. This is certainly a convenient way to explain away all the discre-

pancies in the treatment of men and women. . . . At a substantive level, it blurs the edges of all the specific questions that might otherwise be asked about the nature and
extent and form of this discrepancy in sentencing, by unifying it with all the other social divisions of gender, wherever and however they occur. . . . This is a form of analysis
which lends a surface of intelligibility to everything in
general – behind which everything in particular seems
suddenly indistinct (Allen, 1987, p. 12).

As Hilary Allen's argument suggests, because of the assumption that the female sex is singular in its relation to a
masculinist legal system little attention has been paid to the
striking differences among those of the same sex. The vast
majority of the female population rarely come into contact
with the criminal justice agencies. Those who do have very
little in common with the vast majority of women insulated
from the effects of criminal justice, as the specific empirical
detail of feminist inquiries such as Pat Carlen's have
documented (Carlen, 1985, 1988). Maybe what is important
is not some seamless web of women's oppression, but the
production of differences in levels of criminalisation and
victimisation among them. This obviously calls for a feminist
politics of alliances rather than a false unity of sisterhood
premised on a utopian overthrow of the masculinisation of
the social order. It also demands a genuine recognition of
the diversity of women's experiences and a recognition that
there is no single problem or solution but a tapestry of commonalities by no means universal, interlaced with difference and
even conflict (Fraser and Nicholson, 1990, p. 35). These political
realisations are precisely those being promoted in postmodernist feminist discourse (cf. Flax, 1987; Nicholson, 1990).

After two decades of developments in feminist criminologies
we have an internally inconsistent feminist discursive territory that on the one hand reduces criminality and violence
to the effects of masculinity (or a male sexed body) while
on the other deconstructs or mitigates women's crimes as
understandable responses to their oppression by men. So
on the one hand Lombroso is denounced as a misogynist
monster and on the other the shadow of Lombroso is invoked to explain the innate criminality of the male sex. There
are some major exceptions of course (for example Allen,

1987; Carlen, 1988, Howe, 1991; Smart, 1989). I have three major difficulties with the current state of this discursive terrain. It rests on a false universalism that insists on a singular relationship between sex and the law. Such an insistence is then Eurocentric in its application and has produced profound silences within feminist research about the actual girls and women whose lives are affected by the operation of criminal justice. And finally such insistence has led to a simplistic feminist politics demanding the criminal justice system institute the rule of law over men. This position rests on a popular misconception that the criminal justice system actually divests most of its resources into the investigation of serious crime. How naive. The bulk of the resources of the mundane daily functioning of the criminal justice system are directed at the management of social marginality, and particularly its social visibility (see Hogg, 1991; Carrington et al., 1991; Carrington, 1993). This kind of power operates not through some juridical mechanism of sovereignty (be it patriarchal or some other totalising structure of domination), which has as its central point the application of law, but through techniques of normalisation (Foucault, 1980, pp. 89–91) and specific technologies of government (Foucault, 1991, p. 103), such as the custodial mechanisms of summary justice. Remember, Aboriginal women comprise nearly half of these female custodies. The types of feminist discourses I have been criticising have not only failed to grasp the politics of the criminal justice process and its mechanisms of power, but have actively silenced major discrepancies in the patterns of victimisation, violence and criminality in and among· the female sex. A little more attention to the specificity of the margins and less devotion to the unexamined claims about universal female oppression would make feminist criminologies at least a little more relevant to a few more women – rather than 'relevant' to all and specific to none.

POSTMODERN ENCOUNTERS OF A FEMINIST KIND?

The genre of postmodernism has promoted among many things, an anti-essentialist thinking deeply sceptical of the kind of claims to universality criticised above. Totalising

discourses construct grand narratives that depend on subjects having fixed essences. These discourses assume the
existence of a unitary or transcendental subject and are
referred to variously as essentialist, monocausal, teleological, enlightenment or universalist metanarratives.

Postmodernism suggests that it is no longer possible to
posit general or universalistic solutions or answers to problems concerning contemporary life, because 'human order
is vulnerable, contingent and devoid of reliable foundations'
(Bauman, 1992, p. xi). A corollary of this is that we can no
longer find comfort in explanations of social phenomena
based on essentialisms, grand narratives, secure foundations
or fixed subjects. The production of subjectivity, like the
production of truth, is contingent, fragmentary and multi-
farious. It is just not possible to impose a unity upon the
diversity of subjectivities, nor on the processes of their production. Thus in post-discourses the subject is fragmented,
fluid and diverse. The following implications of this for a
postmodern feminism have been suggested.

> Thus, the categories of postmodern-feminist theory would
> be inflected by temporality, with historically specific insti-
> tutional categories like the modern restricted, male-headed,
> nuclear family taking precedence over ahistorical, func-
> tionalist categories like reproduction and mothering. Where
> categories of the later sort were not eschewed altogether,
> they would be genealogised, that is, framed by a histori-
> cal narrative and rendered temporally and culturally spe-
> cific. Moreover, postmodern-feminist theory would be
> nonuniversalist. . . . Finally, postmodern-feminist theory
> would dispense with the idea of a subject of history. It would
> replace unitary notions of woman and feminine gender
> identity with plural and complexly constructed conceptions
> of social identity, treating gender as one relevant strand
> among others, attending also to class, race ethnicity, age
> and sexual orientation (Fraser and Nicholson, 1990, p. 34).

The question is how has the feminist interrogation of crime,
the operation of the law and criminal justice gained from
such an encounter with postmodernism? It could be argued
that the postmodernist critique of subjectivity has had a

considerable impact on the conceptualisation of the legal or criminal subject as fragmented and diverse. But why should postmodernism be privileged as the sole source of this critique? The argument that legal personality is fragmented, that it is attached to statuses and not fixed sexed subjects is not new. For example in 1980 Cousins wrote: 'The heterogenous collection of statuses and capacities in law, which mostly seem to bear upon the organisation of sexual differences, cannot be made commensurate with the categories "men" and "women"' (Cousins, 1980, p. 119).

There has been a whole series of critiques of the essentialism of second wave feminism from other feminist positions, not necessarily associated with the genre of postmodernism. One of the most notable epistemological critiques of essentialism in feminist criminology has come from one of its oft-quoted supporters. Maureen Cain has consistently argued that the structures of gender, race and class are not reducible to each other in feminist forms of knowledge or any other (Cain, 1986). Other notable critiques from within feminism have come from those seeking to de-essentialise the criminal, the victim and the criminal justice system. Notable texts in this critical genre include Carlen's edited collection *Criminal Women* (1985) and subsequent book *Women, Crime and Poverty* (1998), and Smart's *Feminism and the Power of Law* (1989).

Pat Carlen has consistently urged the abandonment of reductionist accounts of women and crime and tried to dispel the myth of the 'essential criminal woman' (Carlen, 1985, p. 10). She says that much of feminist criminology has pursued 'global, a-historical, monocausal and essentialist explanations' of women's offending (Carlen, 1985, p. 9) and has since embarked on an ambitious project of politically engaged deconstructionism (Carlen, 1992, pp. 59–60). She argues that 'The essential criminal woman does not exist' (Carlen, 1985, p. 10). Rather the heterogeneous effects of sex and gender combine with the differential effects of other statuses (that is, class and race) to produce a constellation around which women's offending occurs, is understood and punished (Carlen, 1985, p. 9). She has since pointed to the following limits of feminism as an explanation of female offending:

No single theory (feminist or otherwise) can adequately explain three major features of women's lawbreaking and imprisonment, that women's crimes are, in the main, the crimes of the powerless; that women in prison are disproportionately from ethnic minority groups, and that a majority of women in prison have been in poverty for the greater part of their lives (Carlen, 1992, p. 53).

Carol Smart's project of deconstructionism has also made a substantial, if somewhat ambivalent,[5] contribution to the sustained critique of a unified subject in both law and feminism. Her book *Feminism and the Power of Law* (1989) criticises the quest for a feminist jurisprudence for its essentialism and determinism. She points out how male power is constructed in this grand theory as omnipotent and how 'women are completely over-determined', as if they are constructed by men (Smart, 1989, pp. 76–7). The quest for a feminist jurisprudence, she says, elevates the law's claim to truth and may simply lead to the replacement of one truth claim with another equally as totalising. She suggests that:

> the last thing we need is a feminist jurisprudence on a grand scale which will set up general principles based on abstractions as opposed to the realities of women's (and men's) lives. It is not just that it would be a difficult task to achieve but it would run counter to the main direction of feminist thinking which is moving away from universalising strategies (ibid., p. 69).

The critique of essentialism has certainly had a major impact on feminist modes of analysis, in criminology as elsewhere. But how much of this reconstruction is the product of the self-reflexive character of discourse rather than the currency of postmodernism and its encounter with feminism is impossible to know. The status of women as a unified category has long been the subject of contestation within feminism. Black women, for example, have not needed postmodernism to tell them that women are not a unified subject of history and culture (cf. Harris, 1990).

The production of discourses are contingent and variable – self-referential and reformulating. They have no single source, ownership or authenticity, and their power effects are just as inescapable for feminist discourses as they are for any other, including postmodernism. So there is no reason to privilege the genre of postmodernism as the sole site and source of reconstruction in feminist discourse. But postmodernism has occupied an important place in the genealogy of antiessentialism. For this reason, if no other, it is likely to continue to exert a strategic, albeit limited, influence over the production of specific feminist knowledges about gender, crime and criminal justice. Well at least for those attempting a more humble analysis of 'power within the concrete and historical framework of its operation' (Foucault, 1980, p. 90).

Notes

1. Essentialism is a form of analysis in which social phenomena are understood not in terms of the specific conditions of their existence, but in terms of some presumed essence or interest (Hindess, 1977, p. 95). Thus membership of a social category (that is, women, working class) is understood to produce certain shared interests even if these are not recognised by the members themselves. Essentialism therefore imposes a unity upon its object of inquiry by assuming that members of a social group have similar interests or essences (that is, women, blacks, workers). The postmodernist critique argues that because the subject is fragmented, contingent and variable, the insistence on a fixed transcendental subject or essence is fictive and unnecessarily totalising.
2. Teleological discourses search for functionalist determinations, causes or origins of social, historical and political phenomena. Postmodernist critique instead insists on the arbitrary and mediated nature of the contemporary life and its diverse representation in text and discourse. Postmodernism abandons the search for teleological truths. See for example the debates in and between Allen (1989), Brown (1986), Cain (1986), Carlen (1985), Dahl (1986), Daly (1989), Gelsthorpe (1986), Harris (1990), Howe (1987), MacKinnon (1983), Smart (1986, 1989), Van Swaaningen (1989).
3. Utopian solutions to the problems of contemporary life posit a misplaced faith in the transcendental subject of history on the inevitable march towards enlightenment. Postmodernisms seek solutions in much more local and limited ways through invention in an on the present, rather than revolutionary transcendence from the past.
   There is no doubt that the justice authorities sometimes develop an intense and moralistic concern with the sexual behaviour of girls,

and sometimes their criminal behaviour is sexualised. However to see this concern simply as a form of social control that seeks to repress adolescent *female* sexuality only, while turning a blind eye to the sexual transgressions of boys, is to miss the crucial point that the regulation of socially injurious forms of male sexuality, such as incest, rape and carnal knowledge, also operate through technologies of government centred on the corporeality of young women. While the effect of these technologies of government may limit and order the corporeal positions legitimately available to girls, they are primarily intended to control male not female sexual deviance through the prevention of arousal. Whilst this is all dreadfully misguided, the issue is not as simple as some masculinist criminal justice system systematically and wilfully neglecting the sexual transgressions of boys, but rather an inability to reconstruct male sexuality into something capable of being civilised, and hence culpable for sexual deviance.

Essentialist feminist understandings of male sexuality that see heterosexuality as an innate expression of male power (the continuum of male violence argument) does nothing to disrupt the common understandings upon which the justice authorities make these decisions. They just flip the attribution of blame to the other side of the binary.

4. For example Judith Allen asserts 'Sexual difference made women of whatever class a unity, a group whose interests might seriously imperil the liberty of men' (Allen, 1990, p. 88).

5. The arguments in Smart's book (1989) and other recent writings (1990) tend to oscillate between a deconstructionism and an essentialism. On the one the hand feminist jurisprudence is criticised for its essentialising discourses about male power, while on the other 'the law' is continuously referred to as phallogocentric, masculine and so on. So the problem with the quest for a feminist jurisprudence is not so much its essentialism, but the crudity of that essentialism and its privileging of law in the hierarchy of knowledges. The general argument advanced by Smart that law is phallogocentric in that it is a knowledge and practice commensurate with masculinity (Smart, 1989, p. 86), reconstructs the feminist essentialism she so superbly deconstructs as nonsense.

References

Allen, H. (1987) *Justice Unbalanced: Gender, Psychiatry and Judicial Decisions* (Milton Keynes: Open University Press).

Allen, J. (1988) 'The masculinity of criminality and criminology: Interrogating some impasses', in M. Findlay and R. Hogg (eds), *Understanding Crime and Criminal Justice* (Sydney: Hogg R., Law Book Co.).

Allen, J. (1989) 'Men, Crime and Criminology: Recasting the Questions', *International Journal of the Sociology of Law*, vol. 17, pp. 19–39.

Allen, J. (1990) *Sex and Secrets: Crimes Involving Australian Women Since 1770* (Oxford: Oxford University Press).

Baudrillard, J. (1983) *Simulations* (New York: Semiotext(e)).

Baudrillard, J. (1992) 'Simulations', A. Easthorpe and K. McGownan (eds),

A Critical and Cultural Theory Reader (Sydney: Allen & Unwin).

Bauman, Z. (1992) *Imitations of Postmodernity* (London: Routledge).

Biles, D. (1989) *Aboriginal Imprisonment – A Statistical Analysis*, Research Paper no. 6 (Royal Commission into Aboriginal Deaths in Custody, Research Unit, AGPS, Canberra).

Brown, B. (1986) 'Women and crime: the dark figures of criminology' *Economy and Society*, vol. 15, no. 3, pp. 355–402.

Cain, M. (1986) 'Realism, Feminism, Methodology, and Law', *International Journal of the Sociology of Law*, vol. 14, pp. 255–67.

Cain, M. (1990) 'Towards Transgression: New Directions in Feminist Criminology', *International Journal of the Sociology of Law*, vol. 18, no. 1, pp. 1–18.

Campbell, A. (1981) *Girl Delinquents* (Oxford: Basil Blackwell).

Carlen, P. (1988) *Women, Crime and Poverty* (Milton Keynes: Open University Press).

Carlen, P. (1992) 'Criminal Women and Criminal Justice, the Limits to, and Potential of, Feminist and Left Realist Perspectives', in R. Matthews and J. Young (eds), *Issues in Realist Criminology* (London: Sage).

Carlen, P., J. Hicks, J. O'Dywer, D. Christina and C. Tchaikovsky (1985) *Criminal Women* (Cambridge: Polity Press).

Carrington, K. (1993) *Offending Girls: Sex, Youth & Justice* (Sydney: Allen & Unwin).

Carrington, K., M. Dever, R. Hogg, J. Bargen and A. Lohrey (1991) *Travesty! Miscarriages of Justice* (Sydney: Pluto Press).

Chambers, I. (1986) *Popular Culture* (London: Methuen), pp. 3–13.

Chesney-Lind, M. (1974) 'Juvenile Delinquency and the Sexualisation of Female Crime', *Psychology Today*, July, pp. 4–7.

Cousins, M. (1980) 'Men's Rea: A Note on Sexual Difference, Criminology and the Law', in P. Carlen and M. Collison (eds), *Radical Issues in Criminology* (Oxford: Martin Robertson).

Dahl, T. (1986) 'Taking Women as a Starting Point: Building Women's Law', *International Journal of the Sociology of Law*, vol. 14, pp. 239–47.

Daly, K. (1989) 'Criminal Justice Ideologies and Practices in Different Voices: Some Feminist Questions about Justice', *International Journal of the Sociology of Law*, vol. 17, pp. 1–18.

Deverey, C. (1992) *Mapping Crime in Local Government Areas* (Sydney: NSW Bureau of Crime Statistics & Research).

Flax, J. (1987) 'Postmodernism and Gender Relations in Feminist Theory', *Signs*, vol. 12, pp. 621–33.

Foucault, M. (1980) *The History of Sexuality: Volume I* (New York: Vintage Books).

Foucault, M. (1991) 'Governmentality', in *The Foucault Effect: Studies in Governmentality* (London: Harvester Wheatsheaf).

Fraser, N. and Nicholson, L.J. (1990) 'Social Criticism Without Philosophy: An Encounter between Feminism and Postmodernism', in L.J. Nicholson (ed.), *Feminism/Postmodernism* (New York: Routledge).

Frow, J. (1991) *What was Postmodernism?* (Sydney: Local Consumption Publications).

Fuss, D. (1989) *Essentially Speaking Feminism, Nature and Difference* (London: Routledge).

Gatens, M. (1983) 'The Critique of the Sex/Gender Distinction', *Beyond Marxism* (Sydney: Intervention).

Gatens, M. (1991) 'Corporeal representation in/and the body politic', *Cartiographies: poststructuralism and the mapping of bodies and spaces* (Sydney: Allen & Unwin).

Gelsthorpe, L. (1986) 'Towards a Skeptical Look at Sexism', *International Journal of the Sociology of Law*, vol. 14, pp. 125–52.

Grosz, E. (1986) 'Conclusion: What is Feminist Theory', in C. Pateman and E. Gross (eds), *Feminist Challenges* (Sydney: Allen & Unwin).

Grosz, E. (1989) 'The In(ter)vention of Feminist Knowledges', *Crossing Boundaries: Feminisms and the Critique of Knowledges* (Sydney: Allen & Unwin).

Hancock, L. and M. Chesney-Lind (1985) 'Juvenile Justice Legislation and Gender Discrimination', in J. Murray and A. Borowski (eds), *Juvenile Delinquency In Australia* (Australia: Methuen).

Harris, A.P. (1990) 'Race and Essentialism in Feminist Legal Theory', *Standford Legal Review*, vol. 42, pp. 581–616.

Hebdige, D. (1988) *Hiding in the Light* (London: Routledge).

Heidensohn, F. (1985) *Women & Crime* (London: Macmillan).

Hinders, B. (1977) *Philosophy and Methodology in the Social Sciences* (Brighton: Harvester).

Hirst, P. (1981) 'The Genesis of the Social', *Politics & Power 3* (London: Routledge & Kegan Paul).

Hogg, R. (1991) 'Policing and Penalty', *Journal for Social Justice Studies*, vol. 4, pp. 1–26.

Hogg, R. and D. Brown (1992) 'Policing Patriarchy: Unwelcomed facts on domestic violence', *Australian Left Review*, no. 144, pp. 8–9.

Hommel, R., J. Thommeny and S. Thomsen (1989) 'Causes of public violence: Situational versus other factors', paper presented at the National Conference on Violence, Canberra.

Howe, A. (1987) 'Social Injury' Revisited: Towards a Feminist Theory of Social Justice', *International Journal of the Sociology of Law*, vol. 15, pp. 423–38.

Howe, A. (1991) 'Postmodern Penal Politics', *Journal for Social Justice Studies*, vol. 4, pp. 61–72.

Huyssen, A. (1990) 'Mapping the Postmodern' in L. Nicholson (ed.), *Feminism/Postmodernism* (New York: Routledge).

Lyotard, J. (1986) *The Postmodern Condition: A Report on Knowledge* (Manchester: Manchester University Press).

MacKinnon, C.A. (1983) 'Feminism, Marxism, Method and the State: Toward a Feminist Jurisprudence', *Signs*, vol. 8, no. 4, pp. 635–58.

McDonald, D. (1990) *National Police Custody Survey August 1988*, Research Paper no. 13 (Royal Commission into Aboriginal Deaths in Custody, Research Unit, AGPS, Canberra).

Mukherjee, S. and J. Scutt (eds) (1981) *Women and Crime* (Sydney: Allen & Unwin).

Naffine, N. (1987) *Female Crime: The Construction Of Women In Criminology* (Sydney: Allen & Unwin).

NSW Bureau of Crime Statistics (1992) *Crime Statistics* (Sydney: Bureau of Crime Statistics).

National Committee on Violence (1990) *Violence: Directions for Australia* (Canberra: Australian Institute of Criminology).

Nicholson, L.J. (ed.) (1990) *Feminism/Postmodernism* (New York: Routledge).

Schwichtenberg, C. (1993) 'Madonna's Postmodern Feminism: Bringing the Margins to the Center', *The Madonna Connection* (Sydney: Allen & Unwin).

Smart, B. (1992) *Modern Conditions, Postmodern Controversies* (London: Routledge).

Smart, C. (1976) *Women, Crime & Criminology* (London: Routledge & Kegan Paul).

Smart, C. (1986) 'Feminism and Law: Some Problems of Analysis and Strategy', *International Journal of the Sociology of Law*, vol. 14, pp. 109–23.

Smart, C. (1989) *Feminism and the Power of Law* (London: Routledge).

Smart, C. (1990) 'Law's Power, the Sexed Body, and Feminist Discourse', *Journal of Law & Society*, vol. 17, no. 2, pp. 194–210.

Tyler, D. (1986) 'The Case Of Irene Tuckerman: Understanding Sexual Violence and the Protection of Women and Girls, Victoria 1890–1925', *History of Education Review*, vol. 15, no. 2, pp. 52–67.

Van Swaaningen, R. (1989) 'Feminism and Abolitionism as Critiques of Criminology', *International Journal of the Sociology of Law*, vol. 17, pp. 287–306.

Victorian Community Council Against Violence (1990) *Violence In And Around Licensed Premises* (Melbourne: Victorian Community Council Against Violence).

Weedon, C. (1987) *Feminist Practice and Poststructuralist Theory* (Oxford: Blackwell).

6 Intellectual Scepticism and Political Commitment: The Case of Radical Criminology[1]

Stan Cohen

Willem Bonger was an important, even legendary figure in Western criminology, and fifty years after his death we should all be aware of this heritage. This chapter, however, does not directly deal with the *content* of Bonger's contribution to criminology and sociology – in the Netherlands or in general. This contribution is considerable, and needs reassessment with all the seriousness that serious thinkers deserve.[2]

I have decided rather to honour Bonger's memory and the tragic way his life ended, by trying to stay with the spirit rather than the content of his work. This is a dangerous enterprise; it would be easier to talk about crime and economic conditions, crime and race, or any of Bonger's other interests. 'Spirit' is a tricky matter to judge. It is hard enough to know what our living friends, family and colleagues think; harder to assume that we know what the dead thought; even harder to speculate on what they *would* have thought if they were living in our times. I feel though, that I can safely assume that the subject I have chosen is indeed something that concerned Bonger in his long and productive life.

Like all our 'radical' cohorts in Britain in the mid 1960s I read those publications of his that had been translated into English[3]. This left little more than the simple label of 'economic determinism – 1908'. I had only a vaguest knowledge of the rest of Bonger's life and thought. Looking for more details in the biographical and academic material that Ellie Lissenberg kindly sent me, I was immediately struck by one theme revealed in Bart van Heerikhuizen's intellectual biography *W A Bonger: Socioloog en Socialist (1987).* This theme is the connection between Bonger's academic and political work.

If my reading is correct, I see a career marked by honesty, doubt and marginality. In politics, as he moved from the doctrinal Marxism of the Second International to social democracy, he found himself in conflict with his fellow party members for being too 'soft', not orthodox enough. But in the 1930s (in van Heerikhuizen's words): 'he was surprised to find that he was once more a member of the opposition'. Now the journal he edited (*De Socialistische Gids*) was *too* Marxist for his social democratic friends and was closed down. His academic life was also marked by controversy; he was never afraid to choose subjects and express thoughts that ran against the current of the time.

This, however, is not just the old story of internal intellectual honesty and internal political doubts. There was a conflict between the demands of these two worlds – a conflict perhaps endemic and irreconcilable. I quote the eloquent last paragraph of van Heerikhuizen's English summary of his thesis:

> Bonger lived in two worlds: the world of social-democratic politics and the world of social-scientific research. On both sides he was considered by many as a marginal man, a partial stranger: professor in the party, socialist at the university. At times this must have been painful for him. Yet his precarious position contributed to the detachment and wonder with which he looked at subjects that were considered by others as completely self evident. Bonger's outstanding features – his intellectual tenacity and integrity – are associated with this double loyalty: sociologist and socialist (van Heerikhuizen, 1987, p. 322).

As soon as I read these sentences I knew that I had a good justification for choosing what I wanted anyway to write about. To choose a subject that has no resonance with your own life and values has never made sense to me. And this particular expression of 'double loyalty' is brutally close to the problems I have lived with, especially for the past decade.

I will start by stating crudely the problem about the 'two worlds' of intellectual and political life. I will then introduce the case that I know best because it has occupied my academic thought for much of this time: the attempts over the last twenty five years to create a 'radical criminology'. After suggesting a few conclusions specific to this case, I shall return to the wider problem of intellectual doubt and political action.

THE PROBLEM CRUDELY STATED: DOUBT AND ACTION

The problem goes something like this: intellectual and academic life in general and the social sciences in particular, thrive best and depend upon a spirit of scepticism, doubt and uncertainty. The answers are provisional; thought is ambiguous; irony is deliberate. All this can best be achieved when one is free from the pressures of everyday demands – especially those to be 'relevant' and to fit and tailor your ideas to serve the managers of society. Uncompromising intellectual honesty does not usually please politicians and civil servants.

Political life, on the other hand – and in this context I include social policy, welfare, social work, social control and criminal justice – calls for some immediate commitments. Decisions have to be made, clear public statements made, bets placed, budgets drawn up, doubts temporarily laid aside. You have to respond to values that are binding and encourage neither scepticism nor irony: social justice, humanitarianism, doing good, equality, citizenship, public safety, the needs of victims.

All this is familiar. But the familiar is always with us.

THE CASE INTRODUCED: 'RADICAL CRIMINOLOGY'

My case is the story of the development of 'critical', 'alternative' or 'radical' theories about crime, law and social control over the last twenty five years. Various stages and many versions of this story have been chronicled before[4] – so there are no hidden plots, unknown heroes or surprise endings. My interest here lies less in the story's details than in its wider lessons.

Whether such narratives are called the history of ideas, the sociology of knowledge or (more fashionably these days) 'archeologies' or 'genealogies', they tend eventually to degenerate into self-serving defences of present intentions and claims. The narrative takes on a triumphalist note: mistakes are rectified, false paths abandoned, excesses moderated, new directions sighted, the final metaphysical goal achieved: 'correct' theory and practise. This is not going to be my reading. I will leave you with vague directions rather than achieved destinations.

The following is how the story might be told in a three-part Walt Disney serial.

Episode One: Deconstruction

After the mid 1960s – well before Foucault made these subjects intellectually respectable and a long way from the Left Bank – our little corner of the human sciences was seized by a *deconstructionist* impulse. What does this pretentious term mean?

First, there is the everyday sense of 'deconstruction' as a breaking up of something that has been built. Second, this is the metaphor that best captures the spirit of those movements that tried to undermine the dominant theories of crime and structures of social control. Third, there is the sense in which these movements either explicitly or (more often) unknowingly, parallel the formal theory of deconstructionism in literary criticism, cultural studies and feminism. Pretentious as this sounds, it is this last sense that connects the insular (and insulated) world of criminology with the wider debates of postmodernism.

The connection appeared the moment that criminologists began constructing a counter-discourse – known variously as 'alternative', 'critical', 'new', or 'radical' criminology. Similar stories can also be told about psychiatry (with its counter-discourse of anti- or critical psychiatry) and law (with its counter-discourse of critical legal studies). In all these areas, deconstruction took (and still takes) place in the everyday, metaphorical and formal senses.

The initial impulse drew on a heady intellectual mixture – soon to disintegrate under its weight and internal inconsistency – of critical theory, romantic utopianism, new-left Marxism, phenomenology, interactionism and something like deconstructionism proper. It took the form of radical scepticism about accepted disciplinary paradigms, cognitive categories and methods of enquiry (positivist criminology, the very concept of crime, the medical model of mental illness, liberal legal theory). This is the level of theory or – in Foucault's term – *knowledge*. At the same time the critique was directed at the dominant structures and ideologies for the control of crime and deviance – the physical apparatus and visible mechanism of the system (prisons, criminal justice agencies, mental hospitals). This is the level of policy or *power*.

Social movements were directed at weakening, by-passing or even abolishing conventional structures of legality, punishment, control and treatment; innovative and radical alternatives were advocated or actually set up; deviant groups themselves struggled against 'oppression' and for 'liberation' from techniques of control and categorisation; social theory and political ideologies were advanced to rationalise these movements; counter-cultures appeared in criminology, law, sociology, social work and psychiatry aimed – no less – at reconstituting their disciplines and professions.

I've described elsewhere the content of these movements (Cohen, 1985). At the level of *power*: decentralisation and decriminalisation (against state power and monopoly); deprofessionalisation, informal justice, delabelling (against bureaucratic classification and professional power); decarceration, prison abolition, community control (against segregation and isolation in the closed, total institution). Behind all this, a common vision of inclusion rather than exclusion: decentralised community control, somewhere out of the reach of the state criminal justice system.

At the level of *knowledge*, counter theories were directed against positivist criminology (and other such 'normalising sciences'). You are all acquainted with the mainstreams in the anticriminology discourse: labelling theory, critical criminology and (best known in Holland) abolitionism.

Sometimes these manoeuvres were relatively modest. At the level of *power* – traditional liberal reformism; at the level of *knowledge* – new concepts, concerns and methods. Often the message was more ambitious and utopian: the very systems of power and knowledge identified with the modern state were to be broken up and returned to the people. The 1960s gave courage to attack the Big Enemies: scientism, dehumanisation, determinism, reification, fake neutrality, the denial of politics.

So (with crucial internal differences that must be explained in any detailed telling of this tale), the counter-criminology discourse began to deconstruct the very concept of crime. Version one was sceptical labelling of labelling, social reaction, definition, relativism, normalisation, tolerance, diversity, moral panics and so on.

In Version two – original radical criminology – the sands are shaped by the political economy and the needs of capitalism. The essence behind the facade of legality and justice is a system to protect an unjust, unequal and repressive social order. The main object of criminology – conventional street crime – is ideologically constructed and exploited by the powerful to divide the working class and justify repressive law-and-order campaigns. 'Real' crime lies elsewhere, the crimes committed by the powerful themselves: corporate crime, state crime, the unnamed 'crimes' of exploitation, racism, sexism and the abuse of power.

Version three, abolitionism, took the most uncompromising and literal reading of the deconstructionist project. The object of abolition is not just(!) prisons, not just(!) punishment, but the whole apparatus of criminal justice and the very concept of crime itself. The vision is a society without punishment, where human-inflicted pain is reduced to the minimum. You are familiar with the abolitionist case for finding alternatives to the rituals of punishment organised by penal law. That is: cognitive (knowledge) alternatives (in a language of 'problem', 'conflict', and 'trouble' more congruent with ordinary people's experience) and policy (power) alternatives (in systems of mediation, conciliation, reparation and other ways to resolve conflict).

My caricature does little justice to the textures of the emerging discourse. Nor does it credit its contribution in turning criminology into a subject of intellectual richness. And it makes us sound much dumber than we really were. I draw these crude lines only to extract the three metaproblems that will become crucial in the later episodes of the story. These I will call *essentialism, idealism* and *negative scepticism.* The last is most relevant to my subject here.

1. *Essentialism.* The mystery posed by deconstructionism is this: underneath the surface (progressive penology, liberal legalism or whatever) is there an essence to be revealed – or just an infinite series of multiple meanings? In the early phase of critical criminology, this was the submerged) conflict between, on the one hand, more libertarian and subjectivist theories such as labelling, interactionism, phenomenology and ethnomethodology, and on the other, versions of sociological positivism – including Marxism – that depended on some notion of a fixed reality, a hidden master narrative behind the surface appearance.

2. *Idealism.* What is the relationship between the intellectual exercise of deconstruction – unmasking, breaking down categories, ruthless scepticism – and what is going on or what can be changed in the real world? As we will see, the main criticism of early critical criminology was that it was mere 'left idealism' – a facile intellectual inversion of the categories of positivist criminology, a word game that would not affect policy and politics.

3. *Negative scepticism.* This is our question here: does the deconstructionist, postmodernist project – 'de', 'anti', 'counter' – carry with it any moral, intellectual or political obligation to suggest actual alternatives? Or is radical scepticism (the critique) or negativity (refusal, 'abolitionism' in the ordinary sense of the word) justified in its own terms?

This is to run ahead of the story. We now have to return to anticriminology somewhere at the end of the 1970s.

Episode Two: Reconstruction

If the mid 1960s saw the dawning of the Age of Aquarius – idealism, optimism, utopianism, the sense that everything was possible – then the mid 1970s heralded a bleaker, more pessimistic time: the Age of Realism. Again, I've described in detail elsewhere the manifestations this spirit took in our area. First, in the sphere of policy, among *liberals* there was disenchantment, disengagement, a sense of lowered horizons and expectations. Good intentions lead to disastrous consequences, benevolence ends up as coercion, less harm is better than more good, everything costs too much and anyway nothing works.

Among *radicals* there was a wearier cynicism. Reforms had not been implemented at all, but if so, only for the wrong reasons or else co-opted and absorbed in such a way as to blunt their radical edge. The old structures (prisons, professions, state bureaucracies) had turned out to be not only more resilient than we supposed, but even more powerful (despite community control, rates of incarceration increased; despite decentralisation, the reach of the centralised state widened). The new alternatives were not manifestly more humane, just or effective. And worse, all sorts of previously unimagined problems and dangers had been created: the net of social control widened, coercion disguised.

There were different ways to make sense of the news. Conservatives said 'we told you so'. Liberals thought the ideas had been taken too seriously. Abolitionists continued to say that the original ideas had not been taken seriously enough. Other members of the original radical cohort began a more profound stocktaking – leading eventually to what is now called 'left realist criminology'. Again, a caricature.[5]

The original deconstructionism of the 1960s is dismissed as romantic, utopian and politically irresponsible because of its negativity. 'Left idealism' was theoretically misconceived in its simplistic attempt to reverse the discourse of criminological positivism by mere word magic. Its content too was misconceived, as follows.

Firstly, it was wrong to gloss over the significance of street crime. Instead of demystifying the crime problem as a product of media myths, moral panics, faulty categorisation or false consciousness, crime must be acknowledged as a real problem for the powerless. The weak and the marginal are the *targets* of crime. There is a rational core to their fear and insecurity. Victimisation studies have rediscovered old victims (the working class, the elderly, ethnic minorities) and discovered some 'new' ones – notably women victims of male sexualised violence. Indeed it was the feminist critique of the 'romantic' strain in original deconstructionism that presented the model with its most serious anomalies. The result, in any event, is that the damaging, brutalising and demoralising consequences of conventional crime must be confronted rather than glossed over.

Secondly, it was wrong to see the origins and functions of the criminal justice system in repressive terms or as mere reflection of class interest. This crude instrumentalism must be replaced by a more nuanced appreciation of the rule of law as a historical victory of democratic legality over arbitrary power.

Thirdly, it was wrong to abandon the traditional causal questions of positivism. This did not mean reviving psychological determinism, but it did mean restating the causal connection in which crime emerges in modern capitalist societies such as Britain and the United States, that is, poverty, deprivation, racism, social disorganisation, unemployment, loss of community and the power of gender.

Finally, above all it was wrong to try to abandon the discourse of the old criminology and to try to construct an alternative with its own problematic. Radical criminology must make itself politically relevant by operating on the same terrain that conservatives and technocrats have appropriated. 'Law and order' is not naturally a conservative issue; a socialist vision of law and order can also be constructed. But not by taking the risks of the 1960s: at worst, being marginalised as freaky, at best, as 'interesting – but not leading anywhere'. The point is to be relevant. This leads to the following:

1. A renewed appreciation of certain aspects of the old system. The criminal law model must be affirmed to deal with street crime and expanded to control the crimes of the powerful – corporate crime, environmental crime and (especially) crimes of men against women: rape, sexual harassment, pornography. The police, instead of being attacked as oppressors, must be democratised and made more accountable. Similarly, the formal judicial system is defended as a strategy to protect the weak against the powerful.
2. The soft parts of the system (welfare, social work, treat-

ment, rehabilitation), instead of being attacked as they used to be as disguised forms of social control, should now be defended in the face of the conservative onslaught on the welfare state.

3. The overall policy/political message supports reformism: the pursuit of immediately achievable political goals rather than long-term, utopian or revolutionary alternatives.

In Britain in particular, left realism has emerged as the dominant voice in the radical movement and is already creating its own theoretical discourse that contains (1) the claim to have developed a new paradigm, (2) a complex intellectual autobiography to justify realism as being *faithful* to the spirit of critical criminology rather than (as abolitionists charge) a betrayal, and (3) even an appeal to 'realist' (that is, antirelativist and antinominalist) philosophy.

This entire self-critique is interesting and important. I will comment, though, only on the elements that are relevant to my subject of intellectual doubt and political action. Here the self-critique overlaps (and indeed has been constructed in response to) the more hostile *external* criticisms of the 1960s package. I'm referring not to conservatives nor to disenchanted liberals, but to those traditional liberals who are upset that the original radical attack so undermined the ideology of progress and rationality. This – it is claimed – has lent strength to the enemy – with disastrous consequences to the progressive 'civilizing' reform project.

I could give many examples of such criticism, but I will take one from a source familiar in Holland. This is an address (at the last International Society of Criminology Conference in Hamburg in 1989) given by Dr Jan van Dijk, the director of research and information in the Dutch Ministry of Justice (van Dijk, 1989). Dr van Dijk accuses criminological criticism itself of contributing to a mood of despair and disillusionment in which the commitment is abandoned to humanise the prisons and criminal justice system. Such criticism, he notes, is 'post modernist in the derogatory sense'; it undermines the utilitarian and humanistic traditions that informs penal reform. So, for example, he claims that the liberal case against rehabilitation and for 'just deserts' leads to warehousing; that the abolitionist case that prisons are beyond redemption, inhibits the drive for prison reform; that the 'hostile scepticism' towards community alternatives (on the grounds of 'net-widening' and so on) unwittingly lends political support (as he alleges has happened in the Netherlands) for *re*-expanding the prison system.

So (in van Dijk's words) criminologists – lured by abstract notions such as 'just deserts' or 'abolitionism', and 'fellow travelling with post-modernist or radical ideas' – have deserted their traditional cause: finding a rational and humanitarian approach towards the problem of crime. Such abstract notions are 'not very helpful for those who seek to reform the criminal justice system'.

Now of course Dr van Dijk is right about that. But is this the end of the story – a joyous rapprochement between academics and Ministry of Justice officials to reform prison? As a fellow traveller I would first say, haven't we heard this message before? Perhaps a century ago – when academic criminology originally became joined to the penal reform project. Is the whole task of constructing an intellectually respectable subject now to be abandoned to bolster the platitudes of progressive penal reform?

Secondly, is this *really* the way ideas affect social policy? Or isn't this rather like saying that functionalist sociology *causes* inequality and that Freudian psychology *causes* human unhappiness? Are prisons like they are now because their managers read postmodernist theory – or rather because they are doing what they've always done (for more than a hundred years): that is, 'reforming' the penal system. And surely prisons expanded during the 1980s (in low-imprisonment counties such as Holland and high-imprisonment countries such as Britain and the United States) in response to realities (such as the drug problem) and political contingencies that have nothing to do with the critical discourse.

And thirdly, why should 'abolitionism', 'labelling' and so on be merely 'abstract notions', while 'rationality', 'humanitarianism' and the 'civilising process' are not?

We need a better theory of the complex relationship between ideas/knowledge and policy/power than Dr van Dijk even hints at.[6] But his bitter attempts to blame the messenger for the news points directly to the wider lessons we might extract from the curious story of radical criminology.

Episode Three: Instruction

We could, of course, agree with the realist case – and that of 'progressive' critics such as van Dijk – against the original radical impulse. The counter-theories were modified in the light of experience, new findings, anomalies and a recommitment to rationality. Reconstruction was thus perfectly natural and signals the maturation of radical theory rather than any dramatic mutation or reversal. In response to the 'aetiological crisis' (the failure to explain rising crime rates) and 'radical victimology', the new paradigm emerged. Left realism is, in Jock Young's terms (1988), simply 'critical criminology come of age'.

But we cannot, I believe, end the triumphalist narrative at this point. In addition to (or instead of, as some philosophers urge us) asking 'is it right?' we might ask 'why do you say something like that?' This might mean speculating on the supposed biographical (rather than logical) maturation and sense of responsibility and 'realism' alleged to come from middle age and getting tenure, or on the generational transformation from the culture of the 1960s – the joys of 'trashing', attacking the old order, the sense of alternative realities, the unbounded optimism – to the lowered horizons and defensiveness of the next decade; or the revisions through which the Western radical tradition is passing – confronted by feminism, the ecological movement, the dramatic transformations in state socialism. The legitimacy of 'conservative' concerns is acknowledged and there is more receptiveness to reformist politics (what used to be dismissed as 'working within the system').

The political context is crucial to my subject here. At first sight at least, this looks like a clear case where the tension between sociological scepticism and socialist commitment is resolved by abandoning an intellectual route that offered no immediate political relevance. In Britain at least – where the realist course has been most dramatic – this is clear enough: left realism is social democratic or Labour Party criminology, produced by socialists appalled by the long years of Thatcherite conservatism and convinced that the original 'left-idealist' paradigm offered nothing to counter this.

Besides the sociology of knowledge explanations ('why are

you talking like that?') we must also confront the realist
message in its own right. Here the debate with abolitionism
still remains instructive and by no means settled. Aside from
the bitter question (of limited interest to the outsider) about
which side is the 'true' heir to the critical legacy, many of
the abolitionist/realist differences remain important. Abolitionism is an anomaly: although sharing the original deconstructionist impulse, it can hardly be accused of negative
scepticism; far from being nihilist, most abolitionists are seen
as quaintly optimistic. Quixotically – according to their realist critics – they remain committed to 'thought experiments'
about a future society, sceptical about purely instrumental
and utilitarian justifications of the criminal law, reluctant to
support means that are incongruent with the desired end
state, insistent that there is no simple congruence between
everyday cognitive categories and the discourse of penal law,
reluctant to take crime or criminology seriously, and so on.

But the instruction for which I'm searching lies not in
the details of the debate between abolitionists and left realists. The question is not who is being more 'realistic' – but
rather what is the point of intellectual work that seems to
lead to scepticism, irony and self-doubt. After all the 'trashing' (the terms used in critical legal studies for the negative critique) is there some essence to be revealed, which
tells us how to act – or just another set of meanings, another text to be decoded and so endlessly on? Is negative
scepticism good in itself even if no well-grounded proposals
for institutional change are offered? Does its value lie precisely in its ability to distance itself from the professed aims
of progressive crime control policy (or liberal legal ideology)?
Is the refusal even to suggest 'constructive' alternatives something of which to be proud?

If the answers to all these questions are an unqualified
'yes', then no wonder liberal supporters of progress and
rationality are so unhappy. They hardly want to hear this
news about their *own* (as well as the conservative) project:
'Whatever it looks like, that's not it. And whatever it is, it's
bad'. Nor can socialists to be happy about an epistemology
that offers them only this non-connection between theory
and practise. Therefore, left realist criminology.

Now, as someone whose values come from the same socialist or communitarian liberal vision (the values I assume Bonger would share) I should be satisfied with the realist solution. And indeed I respect their political stance and their attempt to stake out a clearly radical opposition to today's grim coalition between enterprise and capitalism and neutered administrative criminology. Unlike their harsh critics from the left, I see no reason to question their continued commitment to socialist theory and practise. But why does their sociology leave me uneasy? With a sense that this is a premature closure of the debate, a denial of the tension between intellectual doubt and political action? Have not some important theoretical problems, insights been forgotten in order to respond to a particular set of political contingencies?

Before returning to criminology and to our general problem, let us look for instruction elsewhere.

Further Instruction

Moving from the immediately relevant to the apparently irrelevant, there are three areas that might illuminate our original problem of 'double loyalty': critical legal studies, feminism, and deconstruction 'proper' (in literature, philosophy, cultural criticism).

Critical Legal Studies
Critical legal studies (CLS) is something of an intellectual anomaly. Though it formally appeared at a time (the late 1970s) when the first wave of critical criminology was already under drastic self-revision, its spirit is that of the 1960s. It draws on the same mixture of new left and critical theory; it appeals to the same project of 'advancing human liberation'; it shares the commitment to attacking dominant orthodoxies (in this case, the paradigm of liberal legalism); it rewrites history to show the contingent and transitory nature of current arrangements; and it is hostile to rules, formalism and bureaucracy in the name of visionary alternatives (such as 'society without law').

But precisely because CLS appeared later on the scene, it registered more clearly the metaproblems behind the deconstructionist enterprise.[7] Also, unlike criminology, it explicitly works with texts. Thus the issue of essentialism becomes clear: if law is 'unmasked' as not a repository of noble liberal principles, then what is it? In essence, an instrumental ruling-class plot, a mask of domination? A set of multiple meanings liable to further and further deconstruction? Or (an intermediate position recommended in such moderate expositions as Gordon's), a more 'plastic medium of discourse that conditions how we experience social life?' (1988, p. 15).

Just as in radical criminology, this debate results from grafting onto the original critical project (demystifying the law as an instrument of domination) those strands in postmodernist thought that resist any idea of fixed meaning, order or essence. And hostile outsiders are correct to note that any claim to decode the discourse according to a master narrative (whether of progress, rationality or historicism) is quite incompatible with pure deconstructionism. I shall return to this question – but here I want to note the sharpness of this theoretical debate in CLS compared with its premature burial in radical criminology.

The same can be said about the question of idealism. Its version in critical legal studies is this: what is the connection between decoding legal consciousness – exposing its inconsistencies, anomalies and 'foolishness' – and any recognisable political agenda? However elegantly one unmasks the contradictions of liberal legalism or takes apart its concepts ('contract', 'property', 'consent') or breaks up its dichotomies (substance/process, public/private, voluntary/ involuntary) – so what? the critics answers to this question are – to say the least – elliptic. At least, though, they do not merely denounce 'left idealism' as self-indulgence.

This leads onto the problem of negative scepticism. In its most outrageous declarations, CLS proclaimed trashing to be good in itself, even if no well-grounded proposals for institutional change were offered. Its virtue lies precisely in its negativity. This, of course, was the same message in the original attempt by anticriminology to distance itself from 'correctional' concerns. And this is the literal meaning of abolitionism (as defended by Mathiesen, though quite contradicted by the fact that most abolitionists are very busy working out practical alternatives).

This negativity worries both realists and critics (internal and external) of CLS. These worries are justified – without them this chapter would have no subject. They are only partially confronted by the critique (and in my view this is much as we should expect). In CLS, taking legal discourse apart, seeing how it works and then reinterpreting it is supposed to give you the energy and motivation to look for alternatives. You then pose the question, as abolitionists do: what would society look like if these were implemented? From a common hostility to formalism, professions and state monopolies, emerges the communitarian vision of decentralised, informal social control.

Realists, as we have seen, are not only unhappy with 'pure' scepticism, but less sympathetic now to the content of this type of negative critique. The trashed values of liberal democracy must be reconfirmed, legal reforms supported. CLS is more ambivalent (and hence in my mind, more realistic!) than either realists (with their new-born faith in formalism) or abolitionists (with their absolute rejection of anything to do with the criminal justice apparatus). They allow that justice, legality, the rule of law and rights are shorthand symbols for desired values that hide latent utopian possibilities. And they also recognise that under certain conditions it is useful to maintain the pretence that laws have an objective fixed set of meanings that can be invoked in the struggle against arbitrary power. For those involved in this struggle – whether in Third World military dictatorship or the current upheavals in Eastern Europe – the critique must indeed look at best a distraction, at worst, counterproductive. What can the progressive struggle mean, if its goal is dismissed by the intellectual avant garde as illusory?

I agree wholly with this way of defending legal formalism; all of us know the derision that greets the pristine critique in societies like these. This, however, is a point about the political *specificity* of the critique and not the sceptical enterprise itself.

Feminism

The few words I want to say about feminism derive not so much from the large substantive overlap between feminist work and the fields of law, crime and social control (abortion, birth control, family, law, pornography, divorce, rape, sexuality, prostitution, labour law and so on). My interest is more theoretical (how feminist theory has used deconstructionism) and political (how feminist resolutions of the tension between theory and practice are more convincing than those in general critical theory).

Both in the loose sense of the 1960s 'de-' movements and the particular area of literary theory, feminist work has been 'deconstructionist' in spirit. Take the three central subjects of gender roles, sexuality and the differences between public/private or market/family. In each case, standard categories are questioned, fixed dichotomies broken down, the natural exposed as ideological, hidden forms of power revealed, self-serving legitimations unmasked. In each case the truth lies either in an essence ('patriarchy') or in a set of contingent and infinitely variable meanings. This is the issue of essentialism. And then there is the problem of idealism: the presentation of alternative, liberating possibilities, either in the realm of the practical (for example legal reform) or the imaginary (androgyny, desexualisation, the dissolution of categories).

The 'strong' version of radical feminism goes along the whole deconstructionist path. In the radical discourse on rape, for example, the legal categories of 'will', 'spheres of consent', 'relationships' and 'exemptions' all dissolve, and eventually it is difficult to tell the difference between normal heterosexual intercourse and rape. For radical feminists such as MacKinnon (1982), rape becomes merely the paradigmatic case of male power. For Olson (1983) the dichotomy between market and family is exposed as false, as impoverishing, as inhibiting the possibilities of change (1982).

The weaker – in this context, 'realist' case – argues the opposite. All ·the talk about the 'dissolution' of categories, the 'reconstruction' of social life, the creation of a new 'referential system' is irrelevant to the political agenda. Policy lies in the spheres of legal reform, protection through formal legality and so on. This, of course, is to oversimplify the debate within feminist theory. But even in this form, its resonance for the critical criminology should be obvious.

Deconstructionism

Finally – before returning to criminology – something about formal deconstructionism in literary and philosophical theory. This now fashionable way of contemplating texts and language sounds totally remote from criminology. It is not by chance, however, that critics of criminology (for example van Dijk) have spotted the connection with postmodernism. As I've argued elsewhere, the highly specific message of critical criminology must be seen not just in terms of the cultural idealism of the 1960s, nor even of general critical theory, but the long and powerful lines of Western intellectual thought that Steiner calls the 'dissent from reason'.

The original moment of critical criminology was part of the wider postmodern scepticism about the faith that with good will, scientific knowledge and rationality, human and social problems could be solved. At the heart of this attack on objectivity and reason, the language revolution was critical: the breaking of the relationship between the word and the world. No longer could we assume this connection, no longer could there be an observation that was theory-free. The truth value of any claim was either up for grabs (wholly relativist) or mere ideology (hiding a hidden essence).

In the 1960s these ideas were torn from their complex theoretical origins and translated into guides for action – guides that led (without us being aware) in quite opposite directions. When we took the essential path, the language of others was depicted as mystifying while ours was liberatory. We knew what were people's 'real needs'. With pessimism, we discovered repression everywhere; with optimism we proclaimed that we could transform reality. When we took the relativist, subjectivist path, then reality was negotiated meaning, a variable language game. The accepted language (of 'crime' or 'mental illness') was only one way of making sense of the world, the particular language game that had achieved currency for entirely contingent reasons. And throughout we confused demolition – taking the elements apart to make the structure collapse ('left idealism') – with deconstruction: showing that despite its anomalies and inconsistencies, the building goes on standing.

Twenty years ago we had never heard the word 'deconstruction'. But now we know. Deconstructionism proper is the

culmination of this challenge to the enlightened faith in
reason, progress and objective knowledge. It denies the
possibility of rational discourse. In a disciplined and rigorous form and by reading texts (hence its appeal to students
of law) it poses the same questions that appeared so incho-
ately in the 1960s: is there an objective access to reality?
Do our discourses correspond to a reality independent of
consciousness?

Precisely because pure literary deconstructionism –
Derrida's relentless break with the instituted wisdom of language – is so bizarre and irrelevant to a subject like criminology, this is why it is so instructive.[8]

The realist case becomes obviously correct: a libertarian
textual theory that equates radical politics with the free play
of an infinitely pluralised meaning, offers little more than
an impotent gesture of defiance. It becomes impossible to
defend this version of 'sceptical theory' (the term I used
twenty years ago to describe the 'great refusal' by criminologists to accept the common sense, the obvious, the surface).

We could hardly have imagined, however, the wild directions that philosophical scepticism were to take. Literary
deconstructionism is an extreme form of the sceptical tradition that 'makes manifest the fact that any radical shift of
interpretative thought must always come up against the limits of its seeming absurdity' (Norris, 1986, p. xii). The particular absurdity in life, if not literature, lies in knowing
that this line of thought cannot be followed through into
action. As Norris goes on, such philosophers have long
recognised that 'thinking may lead them inescapably into
regions of scepticism such that life could hardly carry on if
people were to act on their own conclusions' (ibid.).

Deconstructionism works at a 'giddy limit' that suspends
all we take for granted about language and experience. It is
'an activity of thought which cannot be consistently acted
on – that way madness lies – but which yet possesses an
inescapable rigour of its own (ibid., p. xiii).

Without actually appealing to this philosophical debate,
this is just the objection to critical theory that comes from
realists and liberals. As one such critic notes about the 'excessive' or 'radical' scepticism in critical legal studies that
insists on pushing any premise to its furthest level of justifi-

cation, this 'is less appropriate to practical matters such as law than it is to, say, philosophy' (Brosnan, 1986). This simple point is surely irrefutable: however rigorous the work of sceptical deconstructionism might be (in fact the *more* rigorous it is) – the critique, trashing, genealogy or whatever – no moral, political, practical or policy lines follow.

To me, however, this does not mean we should abandon these intellectual journeys. It *does* mean we should abandon the silly idea that they will tell us 'what is to be done.' As Norris remarks about literary deconstructionism: 'Its proponents have never pretended that life could be conducted in a practical way if everyone acted consistently on sceptical assumptions' (Norris, 1986, p. 128). Language continues more or less to communicate, life goes on. Norris again: 'Decontructionism neither denies nor really affects the common sense view that language exists to convey meaning. It *suspends* that view for its own specific purpose of seeing what happens when the writs of convention no longer run' (ibid., p. xiii).

This type of 'suspension' is precisely what critical theory and movements such as CLS and abolitionism (at their best) encourage. This, of course, is neither an immediately practical nor a very appealing political strategy. And, at their worst and silliest, abolitionism and CLS do indeed pretend that life could be conducted in a practical way by acting on sceptical assumptions. This is one reason why realists and other critics have lost patience with radical scepticism. They are altogether correct in saying that no amount of talk about the contingency of categories, the historical specificity of the punishment response or the vision of reconciliation will help city dwellers to protect themselves from mugging, drug abuse, rape or pollution. To travel the subways of New York, I need more help than a deconstructed map of the category of 'mugging'.

So the call for a politically relevant form of 'help' is justified. But this can be done by suspending, not junking some hard-won theoretical insights. Otherwise we forget that language is not a simple representation of social reality, that metaphors (for example the 'war against crime') compete with each other rather than being self-evident. Otherwise we forget that the public discourse of crime control reflects the interests of the powerful; that it is saturated with images that justify the social order as natural, necessary and even just. To claim that this discourse serves 'everyone's' interest in protection is to lose any critical reading of 'texts' such as official criminal statistics, public opinion polls or victim surveys.[9] And to say that people want justice and legality is to argue that of course the discourse of legality draws its legitimacy from a widely held, if inchoate, sense of the ideal. But this hardly tells us how to reach this ideal.

For this project, the point is not to choose between scepticism and realism but to show in concrete situations just where intellectual subversion might or might not lead. Take the sceptical (and wholly idealist) project of 'dissolving' categories. However soluble the categories of, say, positivist criminology or legal liberalism, they might still provide the best (or only) way of improving services, achieving social justice, compensating the victim, empowering the weak – or whatever. As one feminist commentator on projects such as 'desexualisation' notes: 'Having achieved a position from which to enter the struggle over definition, we are confronted with the avant garde's observations that sexual difference, sexual identity, sexuality itself are fictions, and that the perpetuation of these categories can only further enhance the workings of power' (Martin, 1988, p. 17). Women might not be able to speak as women: 'our oppression may easily be lost among the pluralities of new theories of ideologies and power' (ibid., p. 17).

But this is a political point; it raises questions of strategy, tactics, alliances. Deconstructionism itself does not necessarily undermine the utility of any discourse, still less the importance of any values or the desirability of any practise. This is clear when we look not at Derrida-like extravaganzas, but the position advanced by pragmatic philosophers such as Richard Rorty. The message is more moderate – but it is also firmly opposed to any sort of realism. Yes, language is contingent – all we have are different language games for making sense of what interests us. None has any privileged status. Rorty presents not an alternative epistemology, but denies the need for epistemology at all. This does mean that the choice depends on what works, not what is true.

Even if we concede that an infinite number of meanings are possible, we are still left with two old questions. First, the traditional logical question: why does one meaning system become dominant? And second, the political and value question: by exactly what pragmatic criterion does one meaning system work better than another? This last question is crucial for those of us working in 'practical' areas such as law and crime control as opposed to deconstructing literary texts: what are the implications of these theories for concrete social policy choices and political actions?

BACK TO CRIMINOLOGY

My answer to that final question is less an answer than a partial evasion. For the critique of knowledge/power in criminology and similar subjects – our metadebates, our histories or genealogies, our persistent scepticism – takes place at a different level from our policy choices.

On a 'realist' level – the 'thing' itself (crime, victims, control) – we do research, construct theories and suggest policies about what is to be done. On a 'sceptical' level we ask why some subjects are studied rather than others and how they are studied – and then comment on this choice in the name of some explicit political ideology, some vision of how the world should be, or (if so inclined) a pure philosophical scepticism.

It is easy enough to see the differences between these different levels. On one level, for example, we might describe an act of rape, explain why it happened, document the extent of the women's fear of victimisation and propose viable social policy. This is different from claiming that rape is a logical extension of male power or that a male-centred epistemology cannot comprehend the phenomenon.

How to connect these levels? Some of this task is phoney: a prison manager in Holland should not be expected to produce a Foucault-type analysis of social control any more than a Foucault analysis of knowledge-power tells us how to judge whether a theory of delinquency 'works' or whether a social worker is doing a good job. Some of the task, however, is real, because claims at one level turn out to inform what happens at another. This is no more than any self-respecting sociologist knows anyway. If we have consistently looked at rape from a male world view (a metapoint, an ultratheoretical claim) then how can we begin to construct a social policy?

The second- (or third-, or fourth-) level critique can tell us neither what to do nor what is good; it can only give us the ground rules for what Foucault calls 'making facile gestures difficult'. Thus if there are no easy solutions to the cliched problem of integration between theory and practise, the task is even harder for meta-theory and practise. I am uneasy about the triumphalist narrative of realism – with its impatient dismissal of sceptical questions as a romantic hangover from the past, a distraction from the demands of 'confronting crime'. Nor have I argued for a pure deconstructionism that leads nowhere except to the paralysis of infinite philosophical redress. Both these solutions are legacies from the confused politics of the 1960s: the urge on the one hand to be 'relevant', and on the other to detach ourselves from what others define as relevant.

There must always be a tension between these demands and it is all too easy either to respond only to one or to look for false integration. Studying criminological knowledge and power can indeed only be achieved by scepticism, by detachment, but not being the slightest bit interested in 'relevance'. This work is superior because it tries to transcend the discourse itself. On the other hand, realists (from left, right or centre) must surely be right in asserting that there is something 'out there' independent of our closed circuit of knowledge/power. This is the 'superior' reality that demands immediate reaction: fear, damage, loss of life, injury, suffering, victimisation, massive investment of money, skill and energy.[10] To dismiss these matters as ancillary to the business of metatheorising, is something like dismissing the traditional concerns of literature – imagination, creativity, moral worth, literary value – as irrelevant. What Frank Kermode calls the 'flight from literature' might indeed have its echo in the realist slogans about denying the grim facts of urban life.

We all know this – because inside every relativist, scepticist and deconstructionist there is a little realist, a closet positivist, struggling to get out. He or she, however, should not feel obliged to retreat from the insights derived from critical and deconstructionist thinking. It is an act of bad faith to bracket off this knowledge – deriving as it does from the best of the message of the 1960s, the sense of 'unravelling, rethinking, refusing to take for granted – thinking without limits' (Gitlin, 1987, p. 7).

The problem of deconstruction is that it took up only half of this message – the reflexive, sceptical, sociology of knowledge question – and pushed it to its giddy limits. This is the impulse that culminates in today's paradigm of postmodernity, in which there are no dominant schools, no sense of evolution or progress, no authoritative aesthetic discourse, only pastiche, plagiarism, collage and endless self-referentiality.[11]

The other half of the message of the 1960s was the drive to make moral and political positions explicit, a commitment to reshape our theoretical and policy agenda to meet the needs of people and the demands for social justice. It is here – and not by 'being realistic' or by 'thinking without limits' – that we find the criteria to judge whether what we are doing is 'right'. It is here that realist criminologies are working – justifiably, in my view – to create an anthropology that better fits the demands of a reconstituted socialism or social democracy.

But does this political stance demand all the new epistemological fervour of realism? Surely it is possible to be sceptical and ironical at the level of theory – yet at the level of policy and politics to be firmly committed. This is just the position that antirealist philosophers such as Rorty are trying to defend. His ideal is the 'liberal ironist'.[12] A liberal (in his version) is a person who thinks that cruelty is the worst thing we can do, that human suffering and humiliation should be diminished.[13] An ironist is a person who faces up to the contingency of his or her central beliefs and desires – someone sufficiently historicist and nominalist to have abandoned the idea that these beliefs and desires refer back to something 'real', 'essential', beyond the reach of time and chance. The opposite of irony is not just realist metaphysics ('real interests', 'true desires', the 'quest for truth', 'progress') but also the appeal to common sense:

'the watchword of those who unself-consciously describe everything important in terms of the final vocabulary to which
they and those around them are habituated') (Rorty, 1989,
p. 74).

I personally agree more with Rorty's irony than with his
political position, which looks much like a triumphalist defence of liberal capitalism. My point here though is that
liberal (or any other) irony is not mindlessly relativist, nihilist or irresponsible. It is quite possible to recognise the
contingency of your values, language and conscience, yet
remain wholly faithful to them.

DOUBT AND ACTION: AGAIN

This returns us, by a long route, to where we started: Bonger's
problem of double loyalty – to sociology (intellectual) and
to socialism (political). I have argued elsewhere (Cohen,
1987) that this is really a *triple* loyalty: first, an overriding
obligation to honest intellectual enquiry itself (however sceptical, provisional, irrelevant and unrealistic); second, a political commitment to social justice, and third (and potentially
conflicting with both), the pressing and immediate demands
for short-term humanitarian help. We have to appease these
three voracious gods.

How? Not, I have argued here, by giving into one to the
exclusion of the others. Each strongly tempts. We have seen
the appeal of 'detached' radical scepticism – but we are
fooling nobody if we think that this stance can be sustained,
not in our subjects (justice, suffering, violence, guilt, punishment) and not in our time. And as for political systems built
on essentialism and teleology, they have turned out to be
poor intellectual guides and even worse when translated into
practise. Nor can we return to the Garden of Eden of intuition, common sense, kindness and compassion. Such sentiments need to be framed by a theory and informed by a
political strategy.

But if there is more than one god to appease, this does
not mean we should be using all our precious time searching for false symmetry, for the modern alchemist's stone of
'integration'. Both the liberal, idealist theory of knowledge

and the materialist metaphysics that dismisses such knowledge as ideology, share the illusory commitment to 'getting it right', finding the correct fit between theory and practise. We don't have to surrender to the pretentious charms of postmodernist fragmentation, to be able to live without such integration. Although much of this chapter is a defence of the spirit of the 1960s, here surely is one part of that legacy too flawed to revive: our hope that somewhere, integration is possible, not only between the intellectual and political but also between this gestalt and our innermost personal lives, our true selves.

Allow me a personal example. I work now in the field of human rights violations by Israelis against Palestinians in the Occupied Territories. Despite my deep theoretical scepticism about the discourse of pure legality (the apolitical model of civil rights), I accept this as the only 'realistic' weapon to ensure moral accountability (for example of soldiers guilty of atrocities). Despite my sympathy with some abolitionist ideas, I have no doubt that such accountability requires punishment. At the same time I don't feel inhibited about writing critiques of this model (which are then criticised by any liberal colleagues for giving ammunition to the right). Despite our commitment to particular long-term political goals, I spend more time working (help, solidarity) with individual victims. Despite my conflicts with colleagues who think that the university should be 'free of politics', I feel (willingly) obliged to teach courses ('Introduction to Criminological Theory' or 'Crime and Politics') in as wholly a detached and objective way as possible.

I am simplifying these examples – but the lack of easy 'integration' is typical rather than unusual, or (at least I would like to think) a product of my own cognitive defects. These worlds are split – as Bonger's were. All we can do, is find the best guide to each one – then confront the tension that results. This is hard going. In the end the only guides are, first, our sense of social justice and, second, whatever time we have in the twenty-four-hour day.

Others, of course, have laid down more sophisticated instructions. Of the critics of our century, it is peculiarly Foucault whom I find most helpful and even inspiring. 'Peculiarly' because his postmodernist disengagement is seen by many as entirely unhelpful. This, for example, is Michael Waltzer's reading in his recent study of social criticism and political commitment in the twentieth century (Waltzer, 1989). He sees Foucault as the supreme example of the critic – someone who specialises in complaint – who cannot be a *social* critic, because of his deliberate attempt to step back, to distance himself from his own 'community', to make no virtue of 'connectedness', to refuse engagement with all reform projects. My guess is that left realist criminology would agree with Waltzer's dismissal of Foucault. Note, for example, Ian Taylor's sense of the political task, along with his 'friends in the developing tradition of realist criminology': 'sociology should not remain content with the task of critique, but it must be involved in the project of reform and social construction organised around a coherent, specific conception of the public interest'.[14]

Foucault is seen as negative, pessimistic, hostile to any such project of social reconstruction – the pure, nihilistic critic. This is not my reading. I take literally his model of the specific intellectual who does not make too many general injunctions but works in his or her own field, eternally questioning the self-evident, dissipating what is accepted and familiar. It is this reproblematisation in the role of intellectual that allows him 'to participate in the formation of a political will (in which he was his role as citizen to play)' (Foucault, 1988, p. 265).

True, Foucault does not supply us with the guiding values for knowing what is good, for knowing (as he prefers it) 'whether the resolution is worthwhile'. But we don't need him for this. We need him for a sense of wonder, the intellectual ethics that demands 'to make oneself permanently capable of detaching oneself from oneself (which is the opposite of the attitude of conversion)' (ibid., p. 262) This means that 'There are times in life when the question of knowing if one can think differently than one thinks, and perceive differently than one sees, is absolutely necessary if one is to go on looking and reflecting at all' (Foucault, 1984, p. 8).

There is an apocryphal story about a British sociology professor thirty years ago who was criticised for teaching totally untheoretical courses year after year. His reply was 'I give them the facts – and then let their Marxist intuition do the rest'. We live in more complicated times. We have been taught to be sceptical about what constitute 'facts' and even more sceptical about systems such as 'Marxism' to arbitrate our intuitions. But a postmodern version of that old certainty might still, oddly, apply: an honest deconstruction (which is not *denial*) of the facts plus an intuitive sense of the values.

To resolve the conflicting demands of honesty and relevance is facile but false. Ideally, though, these demands should be informed by similar values. The ruthless scepticism needed for good intellectual work need be only a little less ruthless for honest politics and even for the ordinary human solidarity and decency that motivates help for our fellows – whether offender or victim.

The problem of sceptical, postmodernist thought is not so much that it is politically unrealistic but that its slogans (such as 'the end of history' or the 'death of rationality') are so intellectually naive. For most of the world, the old truths of racism, naked injustice, mass starvation and brutal physical repression still apply. In these parts of the world, just to be a sociologist, to state these old truths openly and honestly, is an act of courage and consequence. In the January 1990 Newsletter of the American Sociological Association, an obituary appeared for two sociologists murdered in November 1989 in El Salvador – just for using their research skills to expose their country's social injustice. As one of their colleagues writes: 'It is not a coincidence that all the professors had their brains blasted out of their skulls. It is not a coincidence that all the tools of the social scientists – their computers and typewriters – were physically destroyed in the attack. This massacre was not only an attack on these individuals, but an attack on reason itself'.[14]

If there is an inconsistency in sometimes speaking out for reason and humanitarianism but sometimes questioning this faith, this inconsistency is a product of intellectual honesty. If the old ways of connecting facts and intuition make little sense, neither do the detachments of postmodernism.

Where would Willem Bonger have stood in the little criminological corner of this contemporary discourse? It is almost certain that Bonger would indeed have been attracted by the realist programme, precisely because this is a criminology reconstituted for a leftist social democracy. There are many references in his 1936 textbook, *An Introduction to Criminology*, to the damaging and demoralising effects of crime, its cost to the body politic, the suffering caused to the victims and offenders alike. And certainly he had little time for the notion of the criminal as a social rebel.

On the other hand Bonger stressed that throughout – who could not? – the way the definition of crime is shaped by the conflict between rulers and ruled. And I would also like to think that he shared one part at least of Foucault's scepticism – the powerful drive to see familiar things in a new way. Remember van Heerikhuizen's final words about Bonger: the detachment and wonder with which he looked at subjects that were considered by others as completely self evident' (van Heerikhuizen, 1987, p. 322).

Our task is seemingly impossible: to combine detachment with commitment. There is only one universal guide for this: not to use intellectual scepticism as an alibi for political inaction. I'll give the last word to a poet rather than a sociologist. In his famous poem *In Praise of Doubt*, Brecht harshly condemns 'the thoughtless who never doubt'. But just as harshly he condemns 'the thoughtful who never act':

> They doubt not in order to come to a decision but
> to avoid a decision . . .
> Therefore if you praise doubt
> Do not praise
> The doubt which is a form of despair.

We, the living, can know nothing of Bonger's last moments of despair. We can only decide at what point to stop praising doubt.

Notes

1. I am deeply grateful to Professor Elisabeth Lissenberg and her colleagues in the Willem Bonger Institute of Criminology, University of Amsterdam for inviting me to give this lecture (Bonger Memorial, 1990). I received many helpful comments from them and my other friends in The Netherlands. I am grateful also to members of the Amherst Seminar, with whom I had an earlier opportunity to discuss some of these ideas.

2. The most comprehensive account of Bonger's intellectual contribution is to be found in Bart van Heerikhuizen, *W.A. Bonger, Socioloog en Socialist* (doctoral thesis, University of Amsterdam, 1987, and Groningen: Wolters-Noordhoff, 1987). It is to be hoped that this will be published in England.

3. Notably, of course, the abridged English translation of *Criminality and Economic Conditions* (with Austin Turk's introduction) – the version of Bonger known through the *The New Criminology*.

4. My own version appears in *Against Criminology* (New Jersey: Transaction, 1989). For a version that vindicates the emergence of 'radical realism', see Jock Young, 'Radical Criminology in Britain: The Emergence of a competing Paradigm', *British Journal of Criminology*, vol. 28 (Spring 1988), pp. 159–83.

5. I list only the realist claims that are relevant to our theme of intellectual scepticism. For full statements, see Jock Young 'The Failure of Criminology: The Need for Radical Realism', in J. Young and R. Matthews (eds), *Confronting Crime* (London: Sage, 1986), and subsequent publications by Young and his colleagues at the Middlesex Polytechnic Centre of Criminology, England (listed in 'Realism: A Selected Bibliography', December 1988).

6. A depressingly relevant example of just how problematic this relationship is, is to be found in Dirk van Zyl Smit's fascinating study of criminology and Afrikaner nationalism in South Africa. Geoff Cronje, one of the two founders of criminology in South Africa, studied criminology in Amsterdam with Professor Bonger in 1933 and was awarded his doctoral degree by the University of Amsterdam. From Bonger he picked up – 'correctly' or not – the determinist thread of Marxism. Cronje returned to South Africa to deploy this, not to advance social justice and democracy, but to justify the inevitable emergence of Afrikaner *volk* – threatened by the British, by communism and by liberalism. From this there emerged an elaborate 'scientific' justification for racism in criminology and apartheid in society. See Dirk van Zyl Smit, 'Adapting and Adopting Criminological Ideas: Criminology and Afrikaner nationalism in South Africa', *Contemporary Crises*, vol. 13 (1989), pp. 227–51.

7. I do not provide detailed citations of the key writings (by Kennedy, Kelman, Gabel *et al.*) in the CLS canon. A good source remains the various articles in *The Stanford Law Review*, vol. 36 (1984). See also Peter Fitzpatrick and Alan Hunt (eds), *Critical Legal Studies* (Oxford: Blackwell, 1987). A very accessible summary is Robert W. Gordon, 'Law and Ideology', *Tikkun*, vol. 3 (Jan/Feb 1988), pp. 14–19, 83–6.

8. I suggest 'instruction' about our scepticism/action problem only. Literary theory is even more instructive on the essentialist problem – especially if we accept the claim that the methods for reading a text can be used to 'read' social reality. Once (in opposition to liberal humanist inquiry) the text is interrogated, broken up, unpacked, we can move in two different directions: either towards the quest for the secret subtext (of power, class or gender) or towards exposure to another set of meanings, an infinite contextualisation. On

this conflict (in its early stages!), see Frederic Jameson, *The Political Unconscious* (Ithaca: Cornell University Press, 1982).
9. Sophisticated statements of the realist position do not, of course, forget such critical readings. Thus Young explicitly lists the political advantage of radical criminology over its conservative competitors: 'It is sensitised to the fact that crime statistics are social constructs and that their reality is not something "out there" as positivism and evaluation' (Young, 1988, p. 175). Realists also acknowledge that 'fear of crime' is often a convenient semiotic shorthand, a metaphor to capture a sense of urban decay, displacement and marginality.
10. For a vivid sense of the consequences of criminal victimisation, see the standard research on crime injuries. A current report, for example, estimates that between 1979 and 1986, 2.2 million people were injured by violent crime each year in the USA, one million of whom received medical care, with an average hospital stay of nine days. See *Injuries From Crime* (Washington: Bureau of Justice Statistics, 1989). This made up 30 per cent of the hospitalisation days caused by traffic accidents. No one would deny the sickening details of such crime injuries; to say that these could be called something other than crime looks strangely besides the point. But to say that more injuries result from hidden abuses of power remains an important point. And why haven't the remaining 70 per cent of hospitalisation days produced a discipline of 'traffic accidentology' that commands the same resources as criminology?
11. For some commentators, however, sociologists have little choice but to follow the directions of postmodernity. The post 1960s deconstructionist movements, rather than being rectifications of previous blunders, 'can best be understood as a mimetic representation of the postmodern condition' (Zygmunt Bauman, 'Sociology and Postmodernity', *Sociological Review*, vol. 36, November 1988, p. 806).
12. Richard Rorty, *Contingency, Irony and Solidarity* (Cambridge University Press, 1989). For a sceptical review of Rorty's casualness about the 'truth', see Bernard Williams, 'Getting it Right', *London Review of Books*, vol. 11 (23 November 1989), pp. 1–3.
13. Philosophers do not read criminology. So there is little reason for Rorty to cite the striking similarity between this version of liberalism – placing a supreme value on preventing cruelty, humiliation and pain – and Christie's defence of abolitionism: Nils Christie, *Limits To Pain* (Oxford: Martin Robertson, 1981).
14. Ian Taylor, 'Sociology and the Condition of the English City', Inaugural Lecture, Department of Sociology, University of Salford, November 1989, p. 30. The criminological part of this wider sociological project is 'rescuing the public spaces of the modern English city from despoliation and crime'.

References

Bauman, Z. (1988) 'Sociology and Postmodernity', *Sociological Review*, vol. 36, pp. 804–30.

Brosnan, D. (1986) 'Serious But Not Critical', *Southern California Law Review*, vol. 60.

Christie, N. (1981) *Limits to Pain* (Oxford: Martin Robertson).

Cohen, S. (1985) *Visions of Social Control* (Cambridge: Polity Press).

Cohen, S. (1987) 'Appeasing Voracious Gods', *Canadian Criminology Forum*, vol. 8, pp. 132–48.

Cohen, S. (1989) *Against Criminology* (New Jersey: Transaction).

Fitzpatrick, P. and A. Hunt (eds) *Critical Legal Studies* (Oxford: Blackwell).

Footnotes (American Sociological Association) (1990) 'In Memoriam', p. 2

Foucault, M. (1984) *The Uses of Pleasure* (London: Penguin).

Foucault, M. (1988) 'The Concern for Truth', in L.D. Kritzman (ed.), *Michael Foucault: Politics, Philosophy and Culture* (London: Routledge).

Gitlin, T. (1987) *The Sixties: Years of Hope, Days of Rage* (New York: Bantam Books).

Gordon, R.W. (1988) 'Law and Ideology', *Tikkun*, vol. 3, pp. 14–19, 83–6.

Heerikhuizen, B. van (1987) *W.A. Bonger: Sociology en Socialist* (Groningen: Noordhoff).

Jameson, F. (1982) *The Political Unconsciousness* (Ithaca: Cornell University Press).

MacKinnon, C. (1982) 'Feminism, Marxism, Method and the State' (Part 1), *Signs*, vol. 7, pp. 215–41.

MacKinnon, C. (1983) 'Feminism, Marxism, Method and the State' (Part 2), *Signs*, vol. 8, pp. 635–83

Martin, B. (1988) 'Feminism, Criticism and Foucault', in I. Diamond and L. Quigley (eds), *Feminism and Foucault: Reflections on Resistance* (Boston: Northeastern University Press).

Norris, C. (1986) *Deconstructionism: Theory and Practice* (London: Methuen).

Olson, F. (1982) 'The Family and the Market: A Study of Ideology and Legal Reform', *Harvard Law Review*, vol. 96.

Rorty, R. (1989) *Contingency, Irony and Solidarity* (Cambridge: Cambridge University Press).

Taylor, I. (1989) 'Sociology and the condition of the English City', inaugural lecture, Department of Sociology, University of Salford,

van Dijk, J. (1989) 'Penal Sanctions and the Process of Civilisation', *International Annals of Criminology*, vol. 27, pp. 191–294.

van Heerikhuizen, B. (1987) *WA Bonger, Socioloog en Socialist*, PhD University of Amsterdam.

van Zyl Smit, D. (1989) 'Adapting and Adopting Criminological Ideas: Criminology and Afrikaner Nationalism in South Africa', *Contemporary Crises*, vol. 13, pp. 227–51.

Waltzer, M. (1989) *The Company of Critics* (London: Peter Halban).

Williams, B. (1989) 'Getting it Right', *London Review of Books*, vol. 11, pp. 1–3.

Young, Jock (1986) 'The Failure of Criminology: The Need for a Radical Realism', in J. Young and R. Matthews (eds), *Confronting Crime* (London: Sage).

Young, Jock (1988) 'Radical Criminology in Britain: The Emergence of a Competing Paradigm', *British Journal of Criminology*, vol. 28, pp. 159–83.

7 Crime and Market Society: Lessons from the United States[1]

Elliott Currie

Enormous changes are taking place in Europe – East and West – and, of course, not only in Europe but around the world. How we deal with those changes in the 1990s – the decisions we make about social and economic policy – will shape our global future far into the twenty-first century. So it is especially critical that we engage now in a full and global debate about the choices before us. At the heart of the debate – here in England, in Europe both East and West, in Latin America – is the issue of the role of 'market forces' – the balance of public and private, of the pursuit of common ends versus individual gain as organising principles of social life. In the United States, I am afraid, at least among our more conservative pundits and the mass media, the debate is generally regarded as largely settled, the choices already made. The enormous changes rocking Europe today are seen as one expression of the worldwide vindication of conservative social policies and economic values: of the triumph of 'free markets'. From this perspective, the only people who have reservations about the presumed victory of those policies and those values – as a former US secretary of the treasury, William Simon, said recently – are a 'handful of soreheads who don't know how to compete'. Well, that's one American view: I would like to offer another, and considerably less celebratory one. For lost in the celebration, in the United States at any rate, is any sustained concern about the social consequences of the much-heralded 'unleashing' of market forces.

The lack of concern is particularly remarkable in the face of the American experience. After all, we in the United States constitute a sort of natural laboratory – an ongoing experi-

130

ment in the social and economic consequences of market-driven social policy. And the results of that experiment are not pretty. What is odd about the American celebration of conservative policies is that you can read it daily in the editorial pages of newspapers that simultaneously confront you with story after story, page after page describing the deterioration, desperation and danger that are the ominous underside of the advance of these policies in the United States:

- rising poverty and homelessness;
- increases in preventable illness;
- galloping inner-city drug abuse;
- and not least, sharp rises in our already staggering level of violent crime, which has long set us apart from every other advanced industrial nation.

The curious national schizophrenia that celebrates the causes of these problems while deploring the results persists in part because we fail to make visible the connections between the two – between the 'triumph' of the market and its values on the one hand, and the growing disintegration of our social institutions on the other. I therefore want to focus on those connections – specifically, between the intensification of conservative economic and social policies and the rising criminal violence that has made most US cities nearly uninhabitable. In doing so I have several overlapping aims. I want to explore some of the roots of the current American crisis in particular; but also to suggest some general propositions, based on that experience, about the relationship between crime and what I will call 'market society'. Lastly I want to offer a warning: though each country's specific experience with these policies will naturally differ according to the variety of historical, cultural and demographic patterns that predate them, what we see happening in the United States is a reminder, and I think a grim one, of what European countries may have in store if they follow this road to the extent that we have.

The United States has long been the most market-dominated of Western industrial countries, the one with the least developed alternatives to the values and institutions of the market. And in the past decade, under the Reagan and Bush administrations, that domination has been significantly accelerated. So if this is not precisely where other nations may wind up if they adopt similar strategies for economic and social development in the 1990s and into the twenty-first century, it is certainly the general direction. And that should give you considerable pause for thought.

DIMENSIONS OF THE AMERICAN CRISIS

The basic quantitative outline of the present American tragedy is easy to sketch. If you are a young male in the United States today you are part of what is virtually an endangered species; according to data from our Public Health Service you are (at age 15–24) 73 times more likely to die of deliberate homicide than your counterpart in Austria, 44 times more likely than a Japanese youth and about 20 times more likely than a young Englishman or Dane. What is worse, those risks have risen relentlessly in the past few years (the homicide death rate among young black men has risen by about two thirds in the past five years alone), and they have risen in the face of what by conventional measures was (until quite recently) a substantial economic 'recovery' – indeed a period constantly touted as one of the longest sustained periods of 'prosperity' in our history. Nineteen ninety promised to be the most violent year *ever* in that history: the rate at which Americans were killing one another had risen a stunning 20 per cent since the previous year *alone* in cities of over a million population – and 1989 was already an all-time record in many of those cities. Moreover, of course, still more ominously, that inexorably rising violence exists simultaneously with the continuing institutionalisation of a larger and larger proportion of population. The US incarceration rate – more than triple than that of Britain (and Britain is our closest competitor in this respect in Western Europe) – has been rising even faster than the criminal violence it was supposed to stop. The prison and jail population, having passed the one million mark in 1993, now constitutes a city about the size of Detroit, or of Birmingham in Britain. If we add those euphemistically described as 'under correctional supervision' – on probation or parole – we have a city of four million, making it the second largest city in the United States. It is predominantly a city of the young and the poor, especially, but not exclusively, the young minority poor – at the start of the 1990s nearly one quarter of young black men in the nation aged 20–29 were behind bars, on probation or on parole on any given day. And it is a city whose population is not only increasing by leaps and bounds but whose staggering costs have helped to bankrupt other cities: in New York State the size of the prison budget is increasing by a stunning $50 million a month.

Beyond these bare numbers there is the unquantifiable but deeply and painfully felt social and spiritual disaster that the violence in the cities reflects. Here are some examples, drawn almost at random from one month's pile of newspaper clippings:

- The annual burning of parts of the city of Detroit in honour of Halloween.
- The beating, slashing and, in one case, hacking to death of homeless men in New York that same Halloween by a gang of masked young men out for kicks.
- The rape, beating and stabbing 132 times of a young black crack addict in Boston by a gang of young men who were looking for 'a female to rob'.

The United States is a country reeling, saddened and sickened by this plague of violence. Today many Americans are haunted by the sense that under its veneer of affluence their country is in a state of rapidly advancing social disintegration. Or as my mother-in-law, a native speaker of Polish and Yiddish, put it more succinctly and less academically: 'It is falling into pieces the whole country'

Yet for my mother-in-law, as for many Americans, the sources of that disintegration – the reasons why our country is falling into pieces – remain mysterious. That is partly because of the quite successful effort by those running the country to minimise the connections between the mounting crises we face and a decade of the systematic application of their own policies.

But it is partly, too, because those of us who believe we

see those connections have failed to bring them sufficiently to light and put them on the table for serious debate. So I would like to make a small contribution towards that end. Let me suggest several ways in which the excessive pursuit of conservative, market-driven policies aggravates the problem of violent crime.

THE CONCEPT OF MARKET SOCIETY

First let me make a distinction – which I do not claim to be an original one – between 'market economy' and 'market society'. All societies make some use of market mechanisms to allocate goods and services. And most of us would acknowledge that the exact determination of what the market does better in this regard and what is best accomplished by other means is often an empirical question. But 'market society' is a different animal altogether. By market society I mean a society – or if you will a 'civilization' – in which the pursuit of private gain increasingly becomes the organising principle for all areas of social life – not simply a mechanism that can be used to accomplish certain circumscribed economic ends. In a market society all other principles of social or institutional organisation become eroded or subordinated to the overarching one of private gain. Alternative sources of livelihood, of social support and of cultural value – even of personal identity – become increasingly weakened or obliterated, so that individuals, families and communities are more and more dependent on what we somewhat misleadingly call the 'free' market to provide for their human needs – not only material needs but cultural, symbolic and psychic ones as well. I say 'somewhat misleadingly' because despite its defenders this sort of society – as it is increasingly found in the United States for example – isn't really well characterised by the notion of the 'free' market. Economic and social power and the consequent life-chances and opportunities are not 'free' in the Adam Smithian sense; they are unequally distributed among groups, some of which have increasingly been able to protect themselves against the vicissitudes of the economic market, while others are subjected to them at an ever-accelerating pace.

As I use the term, 'market society' is an abstraction and an 'ideal type', but it has approximations in the real world, both developed and developing, and once again the United States has proceeded farther down the road towards a market society than any other advanced industrial nation. How has this affected our problem of criminal violence – and what does the American experience suggest about the general links between market society and crime?

Here there are several propositions – each inextricably related – about market society's impact on several overlapping levels of social, economic and cultural life, which in turn strongly influence the shape and dimensions of the crime problem. The close overlap is in fact what makes the concept of market society, I think, helpful in understanding the nature of crime in industrial societies today. It helps, among other things, to explain why some factors taken individually – say, the unemployment rate, or levels of poverty – may not always fit so well as explanations of crime, an issue much seised upon by some of our conservative colleagues. Looking at the role of these factors through the more holistic or 'civilisational' perspective offered by the idea of market society helps us understand why poverty, for example, is much more salient for understanding crime in some kinds of societies, at some points in their development, than in others.

Here are several links between the spread of market society and the growth of crime.

LINKS BETWEEN MARKET SOCIETY AND CRIME

First Link: Market Society Promotes Crime by Increasing Inequality and Concentrated Economic Deprivation

In the United States the rise in violent crime has – not at all unexpectedly from the standpoint of several different lines of criminological theory – gone hand-in-hand with the sharpest rise of economic inequality in postwar history, the attainment, if that is the word, of the widest gap in incomes since we began gathering statistics after The Second World War. In turn, rising economic inequality in the United States can be traced to several separate but related trends. One is the deterioration of the private and public labour markets, in which a great many former 'middle-level' jobs – especially but not exclusively in blue-collar industries – have disappeared, to be replaced by a significant rise in extremely well-rewarded jobs at the top, and at the bottom a much larger increase in poor jobs, including unstable and part-time ones.

The shift in the labour market is not, of course, a matter of mysterious workings of fate or even of politically neutral changes in technology or demography. It has been driven by conservative social policy in several ways:

- Through the flight of capital and jobs to low-wage havens in parts of the United States itself and increasingly overseas, especially Asia and the Caribbean.
- Through the lowering of the real value of the minimum wage, which ensures that new job creation has been overwhelmingly concentrated in poverty-level, low-productivity jobs.
- And relatedly by the weakening of the capacity of the labour market to organise effectively in those areas of new job creation or to hold the line against cuts in real wage levels.

The resulting tendency toward an 'hourglass' income distribution is compounded by two other effects of conservative market policy: the erosion of income support benefits for low-income people and the unemployed, and a pattern of systematically regressive taxation in which, for example, the top 1 per cent of income earners have seen their pre-tax income rise by 85 per cent and their tax burden *drop* by 23 per cent, while in the 1980s the bottom 20 per cent of the population saw a real income decline of about 12 per cent and a tax burden *rise* of 3 per cent. The result of these compounded distributional policies has been to raise the top to unprecedented pinnacles of wealth and personal consumption, while dropping the poor into a far deeper and more abysmal hole than they were in before – which was already the deepest among the advanced industrial societies.

Today there are not only about seven million more poor

Americans than there were in 1979, but they are much poorer both relative to the affluent and, often, in absolute terms. And as the job structure has narrowed and income support shrivelled, it is now far more difficult, as surveys have discovered, for them to get *out*, at least through legitimate means, a fact that is not lost on the urban poor, especially the young.

Second Link: Market Society Promotes Crime by Eroding the Capacity of Local Communities to Provide 'Informal' Support, Mutual Provision and Effective Socialisation and Supervision of the Young

Obviously, this is closely related to the first link: it is in part a function of declining economic security and rising deprivation in low-income communities, as well as the rapid movement of capital and opportunities for stable work that are the hallmarks of the advance of market society. Under the sustained impact of market forces, communities suffer both from the long-term loss of stable livelihoods and from the excessive geographic mobility that results from that loss. That is compounded, in the United States, by the crisis in housing for low-income people, as market forces drive up the cost of shelter at the same time as they drive down wages. The loss of stability of shelter in turn helps destroy the basis of local social cohesion. Local communities suffering these compound stresses begin to exhibit a phenomenon some researchers call 'drain' – as the ability of families to support themselves and care for their children drops below a certain critical point, they can no longer sustain those informal networks of social support and help that can otherwise be a buffer, a cushion, against the impact of the economic grinding of the market.

For if you are having a rough time you cannot lean on your neighbours or your cousins – even if they still live in the same community – because *they* are having a tough time too; and there are therefore decreasing resources, both emotional and material, to offer anyone else. This is one phenomenon of the truly advanced market society that distinguishes the impact of economic strain today from what it was, say, in the depression of the 1930s – and which helps to explain the strength of those linkages today. It is also a link between two theoretical traditions that are often seen as competing – those that emphasise economic strain or 'opportunity' and those emphasising 'social disorganization'. This helps us to understand the next link.

Third Link: Market Society Promotes Crime by Stressing and Fragmenting the Family

Again, this is deeply enmeshed with the first and second links. The growing economic deprivation and community fragmentation in the United States today have put enormous pressure on family life, and it is partly through this pressure that the growth of market society affects crime. There is of course much talk about the sanctity of the family among American conservatives, but the reality is that market policies have brought unprecedented disaster to low- and even middle-income families across the country. These connections are many and complex: let me just mention just two of them for now.

First, the long-term economic marginalisation of entire communities that characterises market society in the United States tends to inhibit the formation of stable families in the first place, as the sociologist William J. Wilson (1987) has powerfully argued, by diminishing the 'pool' of marriageable men – men who are seen as capable of achieving a legitimate livelihood that can support a family.

Secondly, the deterioration of the labour market and the spread of poverty-level wages has meant that a great number of families – especially young families – can only stay afloat by working two or even three jobs. The real income of families with children headed by someone under 25 dropped by over 23 per cent between 1973 and 1987, and even that level of stability has only been maintained because family members are working harder and longer in the paid labour force. This has given us a generation of parents, especially young parents and single parents, who have virtually no leisure time and who are (a) constantly stressed to breaking point and (b) absent from home and the community for most of the time.

Now, I want to stress that to recognise the troubling results of these strains is not to blame the parents for them.

But one result is that the socialising and nurturing capacities of many families are weakened, and children in the United States are too often thrown back on their own resources and their own peer groups for guidance, support and supervision. Some of our conservative colleagues, of course, make much of this result in their own explanations of rising crime – but conveniently ignore its *causes.*

Again, the pressure of market forces on community stability aggravates the strain on families. At one time families facing adverse economic conditions could look to *other* families in the community for help; parents burdened by overwork could look to informal networks of relatives and friends to help care for their children. As market society advances, families are increasingly severed from these informal connections and forced to struggle against the uncertainties and deprivations of the market economy alone. The resulting 'social impoverishment' fuses with economic deprivation and insecurity to produce overwhelming stresses – stresses long associated, in particular, with violent crime behind closed doors – domestic violence and child abuse. I do not think it is by accident, for example, that the foster-care caseload in New York City tripled during the reign of the Reagan and Bush administrations, or that child-abuse reports in California rose by over 300 per cent.

These adverse impacts on families are all the more severe because of the fourth link between market society and crime.

Fourth Link: Market Society Promotes Crime by Withdrawing Public Provision of Basic Services From Those it Has Already Stripped of Livelihoods, Economic Security and 'Informal' Communal Support

Once again, this process has been most advanced in the United States, which prior to the 1980s already ranked lowest among several industrial countries in the rate at which public benefits brought families and children out of poverty. It became much more miserly during the 1980s; for example, while income benefits brought one in five families out of poverty in 1970, the figure was less than one in nine in 1990.

And beyond public income support there have been

substantial cuts in those public services that could forestall or repair some of the damages inflicted by the compound impacts of economic deprivation, family stress and community breakdown. Here the effects of market society's advance are too numerous to detail; but we can single out the effects of declining preventive health and mental health care, which might have helped to intervene with some of the children most at risk of delinquency and drug abuse; the tragic shortfall of effective intervention for families at high risk of severe child abuse; and the continuing inability to develop nurturing and accessible child care for low-income families whipsawed by low wages and overwork.

All these impacts also must be understood in the light of the next link.

Fifth Link: Market Society Promotes Crime by Magnifying a Culture of Darwinian Competition for Status and Resources and by Urging a Level of Consumption That it Cannot Provide for Everyone Through Legitimate Channels

That cultural context of course helps explain – among other things – why economic deprivation is so salient as a root of crime in market society, but not necessarily in others.

I will not dwell on this here: it has been a recurrent theme in criminological theory. My own favourite exposition of this point is that of the great Dutch criminologist Willem Bonger. He believed that, as he put it, 'To make prosperity and culture as general as possible' was the 'best preventive against crime'. But he stressed that he meant 'prosperity, not luxury': for 'There is not a weaker spot to be found in the social development of our times than the ever-growing and ever-intensifying covetousness, which, in its turn, is the result of powerful social forces'. Bonger (1936, p. 154) wrote that in the 1930s; what he would see today would surely blow his mind.

A full-blown market culture promotes crime in several ways: by holding out standards of economic status and consumption that many – in the United States in increasing numbers – cannot legitimately meet, hence creating pressure to meet them in other ways; and more subtly by weakening other values that are more supportive of the intrinsic worth of human life and well-being. One of the most chilling features of much violent street crime in the United States today is how directly it expresses the consumerist values of immediate gratification in the pursuit of material satisfaction – some American delinquents will cheerfully acknowledge that they blew someone away for their running shoes. The point is not simply to bemoan the ascendancy of those values among some of the urban young, but to recognise that they are, as Bonger (1936, p. 154) said, the 'result of powerful social forces' – a direct and unmediated reflection of the inner logic of market society, part of the total package that we must be prepared to accept, if we accept that package at all.

There are other links – but there is no time to go into them. I think we need to consider the impact on crime of the specifically *psychological* distortions of market society – its tendency to produce personalities who are less and less capable of relating to others except as consumer items or as means to the consumption of other goods. And we need to consider the long-term *political* impacts of market society that are related to crime – in particular its tendency to eclipse the alternative political means by which those dispossessed by destructive social and economic policies might express their function and their desperation in transformative rather than predatory ways.

The central point is this: it is not simply by increasing one or other discrete social ill that conservative market policies stimulate crime: it is through the growth and spread of a multifaceted civilisation that is at its core inimical to sustaining the economic, social and cultural requisites of social order and personal security. In the words of my favourite English social theorist, it is a 'false magnetic pole that sets all the compasses wrong'.

These trends are having their most concentrated impact on the young. As we move closer to a fully fledged market society they are increasingly left to grow up on their own, without much consistent support or guidance, formal or informal, from a coherent community of purposive adults; sometimes with untended physical or psychological damage; always with the lure of the exploding consumer marketplace before them; and with gradually receding opportunities to participate in that marketplace on the level that they are continually urged to desire. That is a recipe for disaster, and it helps explain why our American cities are the most dangerous and volatile in the developed world.

My central point is that these outcomes are not accidental or peripheral to the growth of market society: they are direct expressions of its central logic. As we debate the market's role in our global future, these are some of the real-world consequences we should consider.

Note

1. This chapter is based on a paper given at the Conference on Crime and Policing, London Borough of Islington, 1990.

References

Bonger, W. (1936) *An Introduction to Criminology* (London: Methuen).

Currie, E. (1985) *Confronting Crime* (New York: Pantheon).

Currie, E. (1990) 'Heavy with Human Tears: Free Market Policy, Inequality and Social Provision in the United States' in I. Taylor (ed.), *The Social Effects of Free Market Policies* (London: Harvester).

Currie, E. (1992) 'Retreatism, Minimalism, Realism: Three Styles of Reasoning on Crime and Drug in the United States' in J. Lowman and B. MacLean (eds), *Realist Criminology* (Toronto: University of Toronto Press).

Currie, E. (1996) *Is America Really Winning the War on Crime?* (London: NACRO).

Wilson, W.J. (1987) *The Truly Disadvantaged* (Chicago: Chicago University Press).

8 Crime, Criminology and Government

Russell Hogg

This chapter explores in a general way the relationship between criminological knowledge and governmental practices. The notion of government I have in mind here is not confined to the political executive or the state, but encompasses the calculated supervision or regulation of conduct in a much more general sense. This is the sense in which Michel Foucault has explored particular regions of power/knowledge and discipline, and what he calls 'governmentality' in his studies of modern medicine, psychiatry, the prison and sexuality. Foucault and the work by others that he has stimulated or influenced is the major intellectual resource upon which this chapter draws,[1] but it would be misleading to suggest that it defines some entirely new and original intellectual epoch. Many of the themes and concerns are apparent in the earlier sociology of Durkheim, Weber and Norbert Elias, amongst others.[2]

The notion of government used by Foucault began to be systematically elaborated and disseminated in the humanist rediscovery and reworking of classical philosophical and other works in the sixteenth century and thereafter.

> 'Government' did not refer only to political structure or to the management of states; rather it designated the way in which the conduct of individuals or of groups might be directed: the government of children, of souls, of communities, of families, of the sick. It did not only cover the legitimately constituted forms of political or economic subjection, but also modes of action, more or less considered and calculated, which were destined to act upon the possibilities of action of other people. To govern, in this sense, is to structure the possible field of action of others (Foucault, 1983, p. 221).

It is important to make the point that the humanism of the early modern period did not simply rediscover the classics but 'decanted the political wisdom' of classical scholars and learning into practical arts of government in such diverse areas as political ethics, warfare, medicine, jurisprudence, agriculture and husbandry. Central to the development of these arts of government, especially after the eighteenth century, is the positive knowledge of their own objects – populations, individuals, economies and so on – they necessitated. They are not emanations of modern states, but amongst their conditions of existence. Foucault approaches particular techniques and rationalities of modern government in their specificity and by reference to their irreducible effects. It is from within this perspective that I suggest we might approach the study of criminology.

THE 'FAILURE' OF CRIMINOLOGY

The characteristic preoccupation of criminologists with the 'failure' or 'crisis' of criminology may assume a new and different significance within such a project. The following is a fairly typical expression of this preoccupation, widely shared amongst criminologists of otherwise diverse theoretical and political persuasion:[3]

> The present state of criminology is one of abject failure in its own terms. We cannot say anything convincing to the community about the causes of crime; we cannot prescribe policies that will work to reduce crime; we cannot in all honesty say that societies spending more on criminological research get better criminal justice policies than those that spend little or nothing on criminology (Braithwaite, 1989, p. 129).

Considered in terms of the goal of reducing crime, or transforming the conditions that give rise to it, criminology has perhaps been an 'abject failure', although it is not obvious how you would go about showing this one way or another. After all the means of 'subjectively' apprehending what constitutes a crime and of officially knowing the incidence, trends and so on with respect to crime are themselves vitally bound up with the modern configurations of knowledge, power and government of which criminology is a part.

The content and meanings of crime – the thresholds of acceptable personal aggression, criminalisable forms of dishonest acquisition and other 'crimes' – are not stable over long time spans, nor in many cases over shorter ones. This is connected with changing moral sentiments concerning what is acceptable, 'civilised', 'normal' conduct and so on, as well as shifts in law and the organisation of control. There is little doubt, for example, that the tolerance for interpersonal violence in modern Western societies is very much less than it was in the middle ages or even in the eighteenth and nineteenth centuries, and that such violence was more commonplace in these earlier societies (Elias, 1978, 1988; Beattie, 1985). Current concern with phenomena such as spouse assault, child abuse, sexual harassment and violence in sports suggests that the boundaries of acceptable physical force and interference continue to be in a state of flux in modern societies. The wellsprings of such change in mentalities, sensibilities, perceptions and attitudes (as well as in formal legal categories) are complex and cannot be explored in any detail here.

A question that is raised, however, is whether it can plausibly be claimed that 'scientific' discourses, such as those generated by criminology, somehow manage to stand outside these socio-historical processes. Is for example the 'increase' in crime, commonly referred to by criminologists as a sign of failure, actually to be counted as such; or can it be more properly seen as an 'achievement' of modern government to which criminology has made an important contribution? Can criminology's success or failure be disentangled from the part it plays in specifying new objects of knowledge and intervention and producing new ways of thinking, knowing and acting. Thus the deviant 'types' and conditions 'discovered' by criminology – from abnormal body types to 'broken homes' to poor housing to unsupervised adolescent leisure – may be considered not only as 'pathologies' to be eliminated but perhaps more revealingly as supports for a proliferation of strategies of inquiry, administration and government. These bring a vast range of novel objects within the scope of practical governmental calculation and knowledge.

One glance at any pre-sentence (or social inquiry) report would reveal the presence of criminological (and allied) discourses. The utility of criminology is hard to deny. It authorises and validates judgements and decisions, it helps construct, allocate and sometimes efface criminal responsibility, it defines new horizons of social intervention and influences the deployment of government resources, and it provides 'vocabularies of motive' for the criminals who offend as well as the judges that send them down. It is, in an important sense, an indispensable component of the modern apparatuses of government.

Thus criminology need not only be approached as a failed or unrealised project for the elimination of crime, but may be examined as a 'positive' practice in its own right – positive in the sense of being a 'force' in the world, with certain describable conditions of existence and definite (limited) effects that are irreducible to any historical *telos* or to the (failed) designs of its practitioners.

Such a view of criminology does not labour under the rationalist illusion that these types of knowledge stand outside of government, politics and power; that the utility of criminology depends on the epistemological efficacy of the general theories and research results it produces, the idea that because they have failed to adequately explain crime 'criminologists have had little of use to say to policy makers' (Braithwaite, 1989). This latter view suggests that criminology's utility depends on the validity with which it represents (reflects, describes, explains) some pre-existing social reality (the causes of crime, the motives of criminals and so on), which in turn is 'implemented' by the institutions of government. The history of criminological thought and its relationship to the government of crime provides little warrant for such assumptions about its workings.

For one thing they seriously underestimate the complexity of the relationships between 'science', power, government and politics (cf. Garland, 1985). In this sense the production and circulation of criminological knowledge and programmes are also *governed* practices, dependent on and relative to particular institutional, technical and normative conditions and frameworks. Such claims also reflect the familiar enlightenment vision of modernity within which social life is progressively subjected to the mastery of knowledge and rational management, the notion that social and economic realities – crime, poverty, unemployment, racism and so on – can be rendered transparent to knowledge and malleable in the face of rational strategies of control, management and transformation.[4] Questions of crime and punishment might be thought to provide salutary lessons against rationalist pretensions of this kind and to demonstrate very clearly the limits and ironies of systems of social control.[5] Such an awareness is to be found amongst much criminological theory going back at least to Durkheim and including most notably the symbolic interactionist, labelling and phenomenological traditions of theorising about crime. However, all too frequently it has tended to be lost or hidden in the effort to identify the covert logics and functions served by apparently 'failed' attempts at control.[6]

The 'failure' of criminology to produce theories and programmes that 'work' (in the sense intended by their authors) has however never served to inhibit its continuing role in such debates or attempts at the governance of crime problems – the flow of research funds, the demand for expert policy advice and commentary, the development of tertiary courses of study, the establishment of institutes and so on. Even its most radical critics are not immune from these effects, as Stan Cohen has indicated:

Every attempt I have made to distance myself from the subject, to criticise it, even to question its very right to exist, has only got me more involved in its inner life. This is, of course, not just a personal experience but the shared fate of most of us who some twenty years ago embarked on a collective project of – no less – constructing an alternative to criminology. The more successful our attack on the old regime, the more we received Ph.D's, tenure, publishers' contracts, and research funds, appeared on booklists and examination questions, and even became directors of institutes of criminology and received awards from professional associations (Cohen, 1988).

If it is appropriate to talk of the 'failure' of criminology, therefore, perhaps this should be understood as *intrinsic* to the criminological project and studied as such; not as a condition to be transcended by a general theory or in some higher theoretical synthesis, let alone a moment of political emancipation.

In speaking of criminology and government, therefore, I want to emphasise two things: first, the 'productive' or constitutive role and uses of criminological ways of knowing and thinking in the modern organisation of government – the functions they fulfil, the new techniques and forms of administration they enter into and the new forms of reality they define; second, that there are very real limits to such forms of government, despite the widely fostered illusion that rational theories and solutions exist or await imminent construction. That there are limits does not therefore mean that government (and criminology) are without effects or are useless. On the contrary, the effects are manifold and issue in the expectations and demands that the promise of government creates and sustains and the perpetual attempts at government – at reform, innovation, evaluation and so on Law and order debates over recent decades in Britain, North America and Australia provide as good an example as any of this perpetual cycle.

GOVERNMENT, POWER, KNOWLEDGE

Foucault's explorations in 'governmentality' are closely connected to both the substantive concern with power/knowledge relations that runs throughout much of his work and his 'genealogical' method. As is already indicated above, Foucault's conception of government is not tied to a repressive, coercive or negative model of power; power as mere restraint or control. This is not to say that repressive modalities of power do not play an important role in the government of conduct, most obviously in an area such as criminal justice. But government encompasses much more, as do the practices of criminal justice. It would otherwise be difficult to account for the specificity and diversity of modern forms of criminal justice: for the rise of modern imprisonment since the late eighteenth century, with its close attention to the minutiae of carceral practice (the creation of purpose-built prisons with a distinctive architecture, attention to such matters as ventilation, individualised confinement, diet, time-tables, physical routines and so on); the proliferation of other forms of penalty and regulation from probation to various forms of licensing; and so on. These all have their coercive/repressive elements no doubt, but they involve much more besides. Many of these forms of regulation, let alone those that operate alongside criminal justice (social work, psychiatry and so on), are as Foucault argues directed at operating on the conduct of others, modifying and disciplining habits, desires and actions.

Foucault's genealogical method entails a focus on the irreducibility of events and practices:

> genealogy retrieves an indispensable restraint: it must record the singularity of events outside of any monotonous finality; it must seek them in the most unpromising places, in what we tend to feel is without history – in sentiments, love, conscience, instincts; it must be sensitive to their recurrence, not in order to trace the gradual curve of their evolution, but to isolate the different scenes where they engaged in different roles (Foucault, 1977a, pp. 139–40).

As regards the question of power, this leads him to privilege 'how' questions over 'why' questions. Attention is directed not primarily at institutions or the 'originating structures' of society, to grand legitimating instances (hegemony) or ideologies, or to power as a privilege that accumulates or condenses and is possessed in the hands of a class or a general apparatus such as the state; but rather to the 'little question', 'flat and empirical' of 'what happens', to an examination of power in its 'capillary form', at the point of its exercise and hence to an appreciation of power and government from the vantage point of *technique* (Foucault, 1980, 1983, 1991). In this 'ascending' rather than 'descending' conception, 'power is not homogeneous but can be defined only by the particular points through which it passes' (Deleuze, 1988, p. 25).

Modern government is made up of a complex array of

techniques and practices for managing individuals and populations, through for example the organisation of space and time (architecture, building codes, calendars, timetables and so on), a variety of measures for rendering individual lives into discourse (the foremost amongst these being confessional technologies, but there are many other related ones, including visitation, inspection, examination and so on), forms of training and bodily discipline (pedagogy, bodily exercise) and other technologies that align self-improvement with social objectives to conserve and enhance the population (sanitation, savings, insurance). The crucial point about these techniques is that they do not have any necessary belonging – to particular subjects or apparatuses of power (classes, the state) or to a particular historical *telos*. They are 'free' to migrate between different institutional, cultural and historical settings. The confession is a very good example, a technique that was deployed in medieval ecclesiastical institutions, but which can be seen to be central to modern practices and apparatuses of government in Western culture in fields as diverse as medicine, sexuality, criminal justice, psychiatry and so on (Foucault, 1980b, pp. 58–65; Hunter, Saunders and Williamson, 1993). Thus there is no grand plan or principle or historical trajectory to be discerned in the workings of history and power: 'not a timeless and essential secret; but the secret that they have no essence or that their essence was fabricated in a piecemeal fashion from alien forms'. . . . What is found at the historical beginning of things is not the inviolable identity of their origin; it is the dissension of other things. It is disparity (Foucault, 1977a, p. 142).

'Sciences' like criminology tend to conceal from themselves the ignoble and mundane foundations of their claims to scientificity and the effects they have on the limits they impose. The critical and radical variants typically aspire to abolish the great apparatuses and ruling ideologies of power, only to leave intact these formative techniques and practices.

Thirdly, if government is about the calculated supervision or management of life, it depends on knowledge of the object to be regulated. The entire history of modern criminological knowledge is unthinkable outside the institutional configurations of modern government – the production of statistics on a massive scale, the knowledge of individuals, particular social strata, urban habitats, and so on generated by a vast array of new institutions and technologies of government, from prisons and reformatories to police to schooling to the rise of the modern newspaper and journalism to the forensic uses of photography. The neologism, 'governmentality', captures this necessary interrelationship between the practical, institutional side of government (its organisation, techniques and practices) and the forms of knowledge and calculation that render these intelligible at the same time as they are incorporated within them.

Thus the prison is not simply a place of containment, but also a laboratory for documenting the characteristics, lives, habits and so on of inmates – for the elaboration of a science of crime. Of course the prison – through its architecture, its bureaucratic organisation and so on – also aims to render its own practice transparent to knowledge. The prison seeks to governmentalise not only its inmates but its staff and its own workings as well, as Bentham well understood when he designed the panopticon. Calculated management depends, as Rose puts it, on the 'inscription' of the characteristics of the object to be regulated, on reducing it to a practicable object in the form of bureaucratic dossiers, reports, statistics and so on (Rose, 1989, p. 6). In Foucault's studies of 'governmentality' he emphasises the importance of population as an object of knowledge and a target of intervention since the sixteenth century. This represents a shift of focus from the individual body and its disciplinary control, the focus of his studies in *Discipline and Punish*, to the regulation of the social body. There is no sense, however, in which one subsumes or is more important than the other. The importance of the social body and its regulation can be witnessed in the rise of sciences such as demography and epidemiology, and in the preoccupation with all those vital features of populations – birth, death and marriage rates, morbidity, habitation, urban conditions, the habits and morals of the people (divorce, crime, delinquency, suicide, and so on). The roots of criminological knowledge are to be found as much in these practical preoccupations, objects and techniques of government as in the disciplinary focus of the prison.

Of absolutely central importance here is the rise of modern

statistics (the 'science of state'), which provided the 'avalanche of printed numbers' necessitated by modern government (Hacking, 1990, p. 2, 1991). But it would be mistaken to see in this simply as a neutral information-gathering exercise. The different techniques of modern criminological thought (and of government more generally), especially statistics, do not simply measure problems as if they constituted some pre-existing reality or datum. Much more profoundly they are the means for bringing them within the domain of knowledge and government – of rendering them thinkable, calculable, a practicable object of government.

The great statistical inquiries and projects of the nineteenth century centred in particular on the enumeration of 'abnormal' phenomena, both at the level of population – crimes, suicides, disease, vagrancy, 'suspicious' persons and habitats, irregular pleasures and past-times, and so on – and at the subindividual level, for example Lombroso's anthropometry and (later) mental testing. On the basis of practical knowledge of such 'pathological' phenomena, statistical laws, theories and discourses of normality (normal human functioning) were elaborated and deployed in a range of institutional settings.

CRIME AND CRIMINOLOGY: THE 'RATIONALISATION' OF MODERN SOCIAL LIFE?

Criminology's place and role in the modern organisation of government is thus integrally bound up not simply with the greater incidence of crime and deviance in modern urban societies, but with a general tightening and refinement of disciplinary and regulatory controls over the individual and social body. Modern societies may (according to some at least) be freer societies but (and this, paradoxically, may explain the greater 'freedom' they enjoy) they are also much more thoroughly regulated societies. This is in turn related to an intensified sensitivity (which is not by any means confined to the authorities) to the disorderly, the potentially disruptive and to social risks of all kinds: to whatever interrupts or threatens the security, health and efficiency of the population.

This has spawned a preoccupation not only with crimes, but with the management of all manner of minor deviancies – of conduct, speech, habit, bodily functions and deportment; in short, of manners. The categorical proscriptions on grossly immoral acts, such as killing, trail off into more subtle and continuous forms of invigilation and tutelage that operate in the body of society and not simply through the more visible institutions and rituals associated with penal controls. As Norbert Elias in particular has shown, these attempts to impose external constraints and codes of manners on personal conduct, which he examines by reference to the long struggles of European absolutism to transform and pacify the aristocratic warrior ethos of feudal societies, have in the West come to constitute taken-for-granted forms of interior governance for large sections of the population. This amounts to a long-term shift in the psychic life, the personality structure, of the individual such that certain forms of conduct simply become unthinkable for many people (Elias, 1978, 1982; cf. Foucault, 1977b, p. 178) on what he calls the 'infra-penality' embodied in discipline in schools, workshops, the army, prisons and so on).

Writers such as Erving Goffman have also written in great and perceptive detail of the subtle, yet always fragile and incomplete, strategies of instinctive interpretation, bodily and oral presentation and negotiation of public life – of the 'body idiom', 'civil inattention' and so on that is used by individuals to secure a measure of moral order in modern urban societies (for example Goffman, 1971). As Tom Burns notes of Goffman's work in this area:

> Observing social propriety is as much a matter of general demeanour as of behaviour, and here the whole conception of comportment, or demeanour, is translated from the static (and banal) significance attached to it in ordinary discourse to become a complex of technical skills by which an individual is credited with being an acceptable, socialised person (Burns, 1992, p. 37).

Contemporary debates around the governance of conduct such as sexual harassment in the workplace demonstrate that these are dynamic and contested domains (cf. Minson, 1993).

As the work of both Elias and Goffman (amongst others) suggests, such forms of government were both cause and effect of shifts in sensibility and the instinctive life within the societies of the West. This is reflected in many areas, not the least significant of which is the transformation of the role of physical violence in domains such as the household, schooling and sports, and popular culture (such as street fighting, football, animal baiting, cockfighting and so on, involving a general lowing of the thresholds of revulsion and controls (customary and legal) directed at physical pain infliction.

It is important to recognise that these processes of governmentalisation and pacification were also directed at the practices of punishment and criminal justice, to make of punishment something other than private bodily retaliation, or a mere replication of the crime. The prolonged struggle to bring these under the supervision of public authorities (ecclesiastical, territorial and urban) was simply another dimension of the efforts to proscribe or rigorously circumscribe the private exercise of violence, to 'prevent the despotism of each individual from plunging society into its former chaos', as Cesare Beccaria put it in the second half of the eighteenth century (1963, p. 12). The public infliction of violent physical punishment (mutilation, execution, whipping, the pillory) and the public exposure of the dead bodies of offenders throughout the early modern period is testimony not only to the 'awesome' display of sovereign authority entailed in the exercise of political power, but also the widespread existence of attitudes and feelings towards violence that are quite foreign to modern sensibilities. If popular sentiments were offended by such punishments it was on account of the agents of their disposition, not the fact of such displays of public pain infliction themselves (Spierenburg, 1984). Violent physical discipline was also common in marital and household relationships and in other institutions such as schools, armies and so on.

To make of punishment something other than the expression of 'hostile feeling', a personal or exemplary retaliation in the form of pain infliction for a wrong committed, as reformers such as Beccaria and Bentham sought to do, opened the space in which we witness the birth of criminology; not as a disinterested academic discourse but as a penal rationality supplying the knowledge, forms of calculation and techniques that would align punishment with purposes other than pain infliction, that would transform the punishable element within the crime and that would disperse responses to crime across a diverse range of disciplines, agencies and forms of social intervention. The fact that punishment, punitive sentiments and the popular appeal of pain infliction on offenders have not disappeared in modern societies is indicative of the very real limits on 'modern' penal rationality, a point I will return to below.

The processes of governmentalisation of crime and punishment should not be confused or conflated with the more familiar thesis that sees in such developments the inexorable extension of social control by a centralised nation state. These historical changes involved a multiplicity of institutions, including the Christian Church, municipal authorities, the monarchy, the law, philanthropic and cooperative associations and modern apparatuses of welfare and science. Techniques of individualisation and practices and spaces of pacification were localised, especially in the institutions of the Christian Church, long before migrating to other institutional settings and eventually being more generalised across modern societies. It continues to be the case, even with respect to such a core concern of the state as law and order, that the practice of government is dispersed throughout society rather than being centralised within the state apparatus. It makes more sense therefore to speak, as Foucault does, of the 'governmentalisation of the state' rather than the 'estatisation of society' (Foucault, 1991b, p. 103).

The plurality, complexity and limits of the processes, agencies and practices I have been describing militate against the appeal of attempts to wrap them all up in general notions such as 'rationalisation' or 'statisation'. What are often seen to be inexorable and insidious extensions of social control in modern societies are much more partial, limited, flawed and ambiguous than is commonly recognised. Attempts at control, such as those associated with the creation of large bureaucratic policing and penal agencies, also engender their own range of new problems of government, from incompetence and misbehaviour to corruption and excessive violence by those intended to control and suppress it. Whilst 'state' violence, corruption and other apparent failings and ineffi- ciencies have frequently been interpreted as functional for the state or ruling groups, this is far from clear. Before at- tributing some hidden logic of control there should per- haps be an attempt to exhaust the possibilities of an account that takes limits to such forms of bureaucratic governance, that the question of regulation is one that is constantly posed with respect not only to 'criminal' and dysfunctional ele- ments within society but also with regard to the personnel and processes of bureaucratic agencies themselves (cf. Gordon, 1991, p. 27).

The effects of all this are to make a government a per- petual exercise, carried out in a diverse range of locations in ways that never enjoy complete success but always produce important and manifold consequences, including the engen- dering of new problems of government (Wickham, 1992).

I have been speaking of the limits and perpetual nature of attempts at government in the field of crime and crimi- nal justice. Recently David Garland has provided an impor- tant critique of Foucault's work in this area for what he sees as its (at least implicit) tendency to reduce penality to questions of power and instrumental control and expunge all traces of moral sentiment, emotional reaction and value as forces that shape the practice of punishment (Garland, 1990, p. 163). Garland recovers the importance of such themes – of punishment as an expression of moral outrage, an emotional outpouring of vengeful and punitive feelings – especially as they were developed in the work of Durkheim. He suggests that the modern organisation of punishment must be understood as a 'compromise formation' between 'rationalising' forces and the continuing play of these in- stinctive and affective forces that surround punishment. Rather than being seen as the more or less calculated effects of orchestrated 'moral panics' or an 'authoritarian populist' political formation, they might be more seriously understood as imposing very significant (if in no way fixed and unchang- ing) constraints on a rationalised penality, whether this as- pires to simply more efficient and humane management of existing practices, their radical transformation or their total abolition. Thus punishment may often be anything other

than functional for rational social control. As George Herbert
Mead suggested some 75 years ago, 'Hostility toward the
lawbreaker inevitably brings with it the attitudes of retribution, repression, and exclusion. These provide no principles
for the eradication of crime, for returning the delinquent
to normal social relations, nor for stating the transgressed
right sand institutions in terms of their positive social functions' (Mead, 1975).

The continuing effectivity of the 'irrational' as imposing
definite limits on the government of modern social life should
not lead us to assume that vengeful instincts relating to crime
are to be understood as fixed, 'natural' and timeless in their
content. The brief history of punishment and changing sensibilities recounted above suggests that this is far from the
case. And Durkheim, Elias and Foucault are at once, at least
insofar as they all seek to historicise and relativise phenomena commonly represented as constituting some irreducible,
presocial bedrock upon which human social organisation is
based. However this does not mean that change is easy or
that it is programmable in accordance with theories and
schemes.

This should perhaps also lead us to question the habitual
assumptions about the causes of crime and criminal motivation that are to be found in much (though by no means
all) criminology. Here the recent work of Jack Katz is of
interest. Katz eschews the whole tradition of theorising about
crime that is centred on what Albert Cohen called the 'evil-
causes-evil fallacy', the idea that 'for each "social problem"
we find much the same catalogue of sordid and ugly circumstances, which any "decent citizen" would deplore, invoked as "causes"' (Cohen, 1970, p. 125). Explanations are
sought in pathological conditions – malfunctioning individuals,
families, communities, economies, whole societies. Katz on
the other hand seeks to explore the non-material, non-rational
underpinnings of such contemporary crime and violence,
what he sees as its 'moral and sensual attractions' and the
appeals to moral right and justification that frequently ac-
company it. He suggests that much crime, and much violence in particular, can be seen as a passionate response to
deeply felt injuries to personal honour, status or authority.
Where we move beyond the formality and finality aspired

to by modern penal codes (and their common law equiva-
lents) the easy differentiation of 'crimes' and 'punishments'
may no longer be possible. Many crimes may be seen as
expressions of moral outrage and vengeful feelings against
infringements of private (although perhaps widely shared)
codes of values, much as Durkheim, Mead and Garland detect
the passionate underpinnings in organised systems of legal
punishment. Where claims to uphold the 'right' and the
'good' underpin the resort to violence, where we find not
pathology but an 'obscured similarity' between the values
and instincts of the conventional, 'civilised' culture and violent practices, some definite limits surely exist to the rationalist aspirations of much criminology (cf. Matza, 1964,
p. 62).

CONCLUSION

There are many ways of assessing the role, place and tasks
of criminology in the human sciences. Its contribution to
combatting crime or serving the needs of a transformatory
politics have attracted many adherents, but these are not
the only possibilities. The effects of criminology need not
be measured only using a barometer of progress towards a
crime-free society, whether of the socially managed or
utopian–revolutionary variety.
   There are powerful theoretical and research traditions
within (or around) criminology, stretching at least back to
Durkheim, that resist, or are healthily ambivalent towards,
such confident enlightenment projects. Within these traditions there is an awareness that criminology is not able to
escape its own 'will to power', its own entanglement within
the field of governmental rationalities. For some, an appro-
priately modest project consists of better mapping and grasp-
ing these – of telling not of criminology's success or failure
at reducing crime or ushering in the 'new' society, but of
the little (though not insignificant) role it has played in
the formation of 'the present': in producing new realities,
horizons and techniques in and for the government of social life. These neither simply reflect more or less accurately
the pre-existing reality of crime; nor do they constitute an

ideological legitimation for a system of power presided over by a ruling group or hegemony.

For those reflecting on 21 years of the 'new criminology' this may not seem like a very radical (or at all radical) agenda for criminology. In fact it quite consciously avoids the self-validating and self-authorising rhetoric of so much radical social theory. As Charles Lindblom points out, 'The radical wrongness of what exists endows neither radicals nor anyone else with the wisdom to improve it' (Lindblom, 1990, p. 13). The criminological agenda proposed in this chapter follows Pasquino in aiming

> to elicit, in the face of the present and of history, something other than either a posture of denunciation or the euphoria of world-historical expectancy. What it would rather be necessary to demonstrate would be the incessant attenuation of historical forms, to reduce . . . history to history. The political benefit . . . would be to regain contact, via this detour, with present actuality: that is to say, with the possible (Pasquino, 1991, pp. 247–8).

Notes

1. See in particular Foucault's essay 'On Governmentality', reprinted in the collection edited by Burchell, Gordon and Miller, *The Foucault Effect* (1991). This is probably the single most useful collection dealing with these aspects of Foucault's work. There is now a considerable body of literature in this field, some of which are included in the References. In generally framing the argument of this chapter I have benefited greatly from the work of Gary Wickham (Wickham, 1992) and Nicholas Rose (Rose, 1989).
2. Although out of a quite different tradition, the historical studies of Norbert Elias on the 'civilising process' and modern state formation addresses similar questions: see Elias (1978, 1982) and Mennell (1992).
3. The quote is from one of Australia's leading criminologists: John Braithwaite, 'The State of Criminology: Theoretical Decay or Renaissance' (1989), republished in W. Laufer and F. Adler (eds), *Advances in Criminological Theory*, vol. 2 (New Jersey Transaction publishers, 1990).

   The quote is one amongst many that might be selected to illustrate criminology's preoccupation with its own failure. It was also quoted in an article in *Telos* entitled 'The Crisis in Criminology' (Tennenbaum, 1992), along with quotes from Leon Radzinowicz, the founder of the Cambridge Institute of Criminology – 'Why should it be that a century of theorising and research should have made little or no apparent impact either upon the trends of crime in our society or upon our ability to modify criminal tendencies in individuals?' – and Jock Young, currently one of the leading members of the left realist movement in criminology in Britain, to similar effect. And consider other titles (of books and articles) emanating from the left realists: 'Losing the fight against crime' (Kinsey, Lea and Young, 1986), 'The failure of criminology: the need for a radical realism' (Young, 1986). See also Stan Cohen, *Against Criminology* (1988), who suggests that the 'failure of criminology' was as apparent in the late 1980s as in the early 1970s when he launched his early critiques of it.

The leftist critics of left realism in Britain – often referred to as the 'critical interventionists' – have their own conception of the fundamental shortcomings of criminology – the failure to 'locate the processes of criminalisation within a critique of the advanced capitalist state and its institutions of regulation and control' (Sim, Scraton and Gordon, 1987, p. 59). As one of the applied social sciences, criminology in its conservative, liberal and left realist guises therefore merely provides the specific forms of knowledge necessitated by the state to enhance control and stability in the long-term interests of capitalism (Ibid., pp. 1–2).

4. At the extreme (typically within radical social theory of which there are many expressions within criminology), social order as a totality is understood as a governable or transformable terrain. And there is a consistent logic at work here, for if the most 'irrational' and undesirable features of a society – violence, racism, poverty, widespread support for severe punishment and so on – are the effects of some general design (however hidden and mediated), the implication follows that it is possible to design the social order differently.

5. Many examples could be referred to, but one need only refer to the continuing profile and significance of the capital punishment debate in countries such as the United States, Britain and Australia.

6. Foucault is not immune form this tendency. In *Discipline and Punish* he suggests that the failure of the prison to eliminate crime was nevertheless recovered in a strategy in which the constitution of 'delinquency', of effectively criminalised groups, by the prison was used as a support for an extension of surveillance and control within society: see the critique of Garland (1990, pp. 164–5).

References

Beccaria, C. (1963) *On Crimes and Punishments* (Indianapolis: Bobbs Merrill).

Braithwaite, J. (1989) 'The State of Criminology: theoretical decay or renaissance?', *Australian and New Zealand Journal of Criminology*, vol. 22, pp. 129–35.

Burchell, G. Gordon, C. and Muller, P. (eds) *The Foucault Effect* (Hemel Hempstead: Harvester Wheatsheaf).

Burns, T. (1992) *Erving Goffman* (London: Routledge).

Cohen, A. (1970) 'Multiple Factor Approaches', in M. Wolfgang, L. Savitz and N. Johnson (eds), *The Sociology of Crime and Delinquency*, 2nd edn (New York: John Wiley).

Cohen, S. (1988) *Against Criminology* (New Brunswick: Transaction Books).

Deleuze, G. (1988) *Foucault* (Minneapolis: University of Minnesota Press).

Elias, N. (1978) *The History of Manners* (New York: Pantheon).

Elias, N. (1982) *State Formation and Civilisation* (Oxford: Basil Blackwell).

Foucault, M. (1977a) 'Nietzsche, Genealogy, History', in D. Bouchard (ed.), *Language, Counter-Memory, and Practice* (New York: Cornell University Press).

Foucault, M. (1977b) *Discipline and Punish* (Harmondsworth: Penguin).

Foucault, M. (1980a) *The History of Sexuality, Volume 1: An Introduction* (New York: Vintage Books).

Foucault, M. (1980b) 'Two Lectures', in C. Gordon (ed.), *Power Knowledge* (Brighton: Harvester Press).

Foucault, M. (1983) 'The Subject and Power', Afterword in H. Dreyfus and P. Rabinow, *Michel Foucault: Beyond Structuralism and Hermeneutics*, 2nd edn (Chicago: University of Chicago Press).

Foucault, M. (1991a) 'Questions of Method', in G. Burchell, C. Gordon and P. Miller (eds), *The Foucault Effect* (Hemel Hempstead: Harvester Wheatsheaf)

Foucault, M. (1991b) 'Governmentality', in Burchell *et al.* (eds), *The Foucault Effect*, op. cit.

Garland, D. (1985) *Punishment and Welfare* (Aldershot: Gower).

Garland, D. (1990) *Punishment and Modern Society* (Oxford: Clarendon Press).

Goffman, E. (1971) *Relations in Public* (Harmondsworth: Penguin).

Gordon, C. (1991) 'Governmental Rationality: an introduction' in Burchell, *et al.* (eds), *The Foucault Effect*, op. cit.

Hacking, I. (1990) *The Taming of Chance* (Cambridge: Cambridge University Press).

Hacking, I. (1991) 'How Should we do the History of Statistics?' in Burchell *et al.* (eds), *The Foucault Effect*, op. cit.

Hunter, I. D. Saunders and D. Williamson (1993) *On Pornography* (London: Macmillan).

Katz, J. (1988) *Seductions of Crime* (New York: Basic Books).

Kinsey, R., J. Lea and J. Young (1986) *Losing the Fight Against Crime* (Oxford: Basic Blackwell).

Lindblom, C. (1990) *Inquiry and Change* (New Haven: Yale University Press).

Matza, D. (1964) *Delinquency and Drift* (New York: John Wiley).

Mead, G.H. (1975) 'The Psychology of Punitive Justice', in R. Farrell and V. Swigert (eds), *Social Deviance* (Philadelphia: J.B. Lippincott, originally published 1918).

Mennell, S. (1992) *Norbert Elias, An Introduction* (Oxford: Blackwell).

Minson, J. (1993) *Questions of Conduct* (London: Macmillan).

Pasquino, P. (1991) 'Criminology: the Birth of A Special Knowledge' in Burchell *et al.* (eds), *The Foucault Effect*, op. cit.

Rose, N. (1989) *Governing the Soul* (London and New York: Routledge).

Sim, J., Scraton, P. and Gordon, P. (1987) 'Crime, the State and Critical

Analysis' in P. Scraton (ed.) *Law, Order and the Authoritarian State* (Milton Keynes: Open University Press).

Spierenburg, P. (1984) *The Spectacle of Suffering* (Cambridge: Cambridge University Press).

Tennenbaum, A. (1992) 'The Crisis in Criminology', *Telos*, vol. 51.

Wickham, G. (1992) 'Towards a Sociology of Governance' unpublished.

Young, J. (1986) 'The Failure of Criminology: the Need for A Radical Realism', in R. Mathews and J. Young (eds), *Confronting Crime* (London: Sage).

9 Criminology and Postmodernity

John Lea

INTRODUCTION

Over the last decade or more 'postmodernist' thought has had a growing influence in our intellectual culture. Developing first in architecture, cultural and media studies, literary criticism and philosophy, it has achieved a growing influence in the social sciences, sociology in particular (Bauman, 1991a; Crook *et al.*, 1992). It seems no accident that postmodern themes, stressing a generalised disenchantment with what are seen as tired and worn out ideas of scientific and human progress, coherence and truth, should achieve considerable popularity at a time of political and social uncertainty. The end of the 'post war' epoch, symbolised by the collapse of 'socialism' in the East and the welfare state in the West, provides fertile terrain for both the adulterated Hegelianism of Francis Fukuyama's 'end of history' (1989), and the wider diffusion of Jean-Francois Lyotard's expression of the 'postmodern condition' as a disenchantment with the grand narratives of the Enlightenment itself.

What has all this got to do with a humdrum backwater of the social sciences like criminology? A great deal. On the one hand the seeming impotence of society in the face of the problem of rising crime serves as a powerful metaphor for the fragmentation, uncertainty and self-satisfied indifference that, for some critics, is the prominent characteristic of 'postmodernity' (Bauman, 1991b). Criminology and penology were central pillars of the postwar 'grand narratives' of social engineering and welfare reformism (Taylor, 1982), the blueprints for the good society that are now so discredited. The crisis of modernity is a part of the crisis of criminology. For others a 'new times' of individual freedom,

diversity and difference (Hall and Jaques, 1989) has provided an arena in which new voices can be heard, previously ignored identities demand space and respect, and
hitherto ignored problems – many of them of relevance to
crime control – are given the priority they deserve.

Inevitably therefore, debate on the relevance of postmodern
themes has emerged on the radical periphery of criminology
(cf. Smart, 1995; Cohen, this volume; Young, 1992; Hunt,
1992; Schwartz and Friedrichs, 1994; Morrison, 1994; Henry
and Milovanovic, 1994). In this chapter I attempt to contribute to this debate through a discussion of particular
postmodern themes that appear, initially, to have relevance
to the problems of criminology. I conclude with a warning
against a 'loss of nerve' as regards some of the older themes
in radical criminology and an overreadiness to embrace
ephemeral and superficial accounts of the nature of postmodernity.

It is necessary to begin with some definitions, both of
criminology and postmodernism. I have always seen criminology as a 'field' rather than a particular academic discipline. That is to say, what defines criminology is the problems
that it studies, rather than the elaboration of a particular
dominant set of responses to those problems. That is why
psychologists, sociologists, lawyers, geographers and perhaps
even philosophers can all call themselves criminologists, and
why identities such as 'radical' or 'feminist' can plausibly
claim to work within criminology. It is also the reason why
criminology is such a fragmented practice and why any
postmodernist attempt to 'deconstruct' its dominant discourses
finds the job already half completed. The best definition of
criminology seems therefore to be that body of knowledges
and theories that concern themselves, one way or another,
with three questions: how and why certain categories of social
activity come to be defined as crime; why such activity occurs in different types of situations – however classified; and
how various forces in society attempt to manage and control such actions and their consequences by both formal
institutional mechanisms of criminal justice and informal
mechanisms of social control. It is in terms of these three
questions or problematics that I shall consider the relevance
of postmodern perspectives.

Postmodernism is a bit like criminology in that it too is best described as an area, a loose collection of themes, rather than as in itself a coherent philosophy. To attempt a description of postmodernism in the latter sense would be to fall precisely into the trap of attempting to articulate it as a grand narrative, or global world view, when one of its main thrusts is precisely the denial of the possibility of such standpoints. The themes that seem to me to be important, and which I shall discuss in this chapter, are fourfold.

Firstly, an important theme in postmodern and allied philosophy is that of deconstruction. Beginning with the claim that there is no necessary or logical connection between the use of language and what it purports to describe, the idea of philosophical truth outside language has then to be abandoned. Such claims have to be deconstructed and, following Jaques Derrida, it has to be recognised that every identity or definition is necessarily repressive. The act of defining is an act of excluding. Deconstruction, then, in literature 'is a matter of taking a repressed or subjugated theme . . . pursuing its various textual ramifications and showing how these subvert the very order that strives to hold them in check' (Norris, 1991, p. 39).

Secondly, the rejection of coherence and unity in the world both in the philosophical sense that there is no 'grand narrative' of truth or essence behind the appearance of chaos and contingency, and in the sociological sense that society is not, or is no longer to be encountered as, a coherent system, regulated in terms of some central steering mechanism such as capital accumulation, patriarchy or environmental adaptation by reference to the functioning – or disruption – of which social events can be reductively explained.

A third important theme concerns the nature of freedom. Postmodernism attempts a reappropriation of Nietzsche, in which freedom and self-identity are seen as emancipation from the normative constraints of the life world and social bonds, as a process of endless experimentation and expression of 'difference'. This Nietzschean philosophy finds its sociological parallel in an alleged incidental relationship between the process of personal identity formation and social values. The individual increasingly stands outside values

and orients towards them in terms of a 'tactical appropriation' (Crook *et al.*, 1992), or as a resource for the experimental creation of lifestyles that, having no generalised
coherence, consist of an endless process of bricolage. This
fragmentation and 'loss of the social' reveals a fluidity, mobility
and contingency in human relations.

It follows, and this is the final sociological theme in
postmodernism, that profound social changes are taking place.
Modern industrial societies are undergoing a process of fragmentation both at the level of social structure – class, work,
urban life, politics, and so on – and at the level of culture.
While it is possible to see this change – and the current
crisis of both socialist and liberal politics that it has, alleg-
edly, brought about – as a reflection either of the logic of
late capitalism (Jameson, 1984; Harvey, 1989) or of a functionalist process of institutional and cultural differentiation
(Crook *et al.*, 1992), the basic theme is the 'loss of the social' in the old sense that societies consisted of stable structures, classes and institutions, into which individuals were
integrated and from which they took their outlook and social roles, even if the outcome of a particular location was a
rugged individualism and an ideology of *laissez-faire*. Class is
being replaced by identity, and stable social and political
institutions by a fluid, pluralistic and contingent informalism.

In the next section I attempt to explore the implications
of these ideas for the three components of criminology
defined above. In doing so I also attempt to use criminological themes to illustrate some of the problems with postmodern ideas.

THE NATURE OF CRIME

Currently – in both critical criminology and the sociology
of law – the theme of deconstruction has become popular.
Law obviously presents itself as a 'grand narrative' *par excellence*. Such an integrated discourse with its definitions and
constructions of legal subjects and their rights and responsibilities appears ripe for the knife of deconstruction. It is,
furthermore, harder in the study of law and jurisprudence
than in criminology to ignore the relevance of fundamen-

tal philosophical issues. It is therefore understandable that a more elaborate critical appropriation of postmodernism has developed in this area than so far in criminology (see for example Santos, 1987; Douzinas and Warrington, 1991; Fitzpatrick, 1992), a debate to which the leading philosopher of deconstruction himself, Jaques Derrida, has made a direct contribution (Derrida, 1992).

Criminology, as distinct from the sociology of law, is more concerned with the processes whereby particular types of act become criminalised rather than the genesis of the categories with which they can then be described, though the two are closely related. In coming to understand what is involved in the constitution of actions as crimes, an obvious relevance is established for the first of our postmodern themes: the strategy of deconstruction. If the definition of an activity as crime is a process of repression, then the aim of deconstruction can be seen as revealing that which is hidden and suppressed by criminological discourse. Such a strategy understandably appeals to radical critics of 'mainstream' criminology. In particular some feminists have advocated a deconstructive approach as a strategy of revealing that which is hidden and repressed in an essentially 'male' discourse on criminality (Smart, 1995; Young, 1992). As far as Carol Smart is concerned,

> The thing that criminology cannot do is deconstruct 'crime'. It cannot locate rape or child sexual abuse in the domain of sexuality, nor theft in the domain of economic activity, nor drug use in the domain of health. To do so would be to abandon criminology to sociology, but more important it would involve abandoning the idea of a unified problem which requires a unified solution – at least at the theoretical level (Smart, 1995, p. 36).

Thus, taking the example of rape, deconstruction exposes how the definition of an activity such as rape involves the repression of its other characteristics – as a form of sexuality – and reveals how its explanation as a form of crime or deviance confirms this repression. Such a 'deconstructive' orientation has in fact existed for some time in radical criminology. Precisely because criminology is a relatively loose

168   *Criminology and Postmodernity*

collection of discourses, it comes as no surprise to find that
this is the case. The work of labelling theorists and social
constructionists such as Becker (1963), Spector and Kitsuse
(1977) and Pfohl (1977, 1985) in deconstructing seemingly
real social phenomena as no more than labelling or constructing activities, are in no way different from the postmodernists. Indeed Pfohl makes explicit reference to Derrida.
In some respects, therefore, postmodernism is a rediscovery
of some of the traditions within radical criminology itself
rather than the importation of new ideas from without
(Cohen, this volume). Though, as we shall see, there are
some differences.

Another tradition, well established within radical criminology and penology, is that of penal abolitionism, among
whose leading exponents are writers such as Louk Hulsman
(1986) and Nils Christie (1977). Hulsman, for example,
argued that the notion of crime at first appears to refer to
clear and fixed forms of behaviour, but on closer interrogation slides away into a plethora of different activities and
meanings that have nothing in common other than the fact
that the criminal justice system treats them as crimes.

> [The] categories of 'crime' are given by the criminal jus-
> tice system rather than by victims or society in general.
> This makes it necessary to abandon the notion of 'crime'
> as a tool in the conceptual framework of criminology. Crime
> has no ontological reality. Crime is not the object but
> the product of criminal policy. Criminalisation is one of
> the many ways of constructing social reality (Hulsman,
> 1986, pp. 34–5).

The idea of 'crime' as an essentially coercive imposition by
the state on an incommensurable diversity of problematic
situations fits well with the spirit of deconstruction. Along
with the pretensions of 'crime' to act as a yardstick for the
commensuration of harmful acts must go any totalising grand
narrative of justice or rationality, and of the criminal justice system as capable of enforcing any other than purely
local norms, of disguising under a rhetoric of universal justice and citizenship that which is tenuous, negotiated and
constantly reconstituted. Crime can no longer be given

meaning as the violation of identifiable 'natural rights', nor can it be the object of some theoretical explanation. The issue is rather the avoidance of the suppression of particularities and differences and, given the diversity of such, there can be no definite rational content to a criminal law but rather a process of constant accommodation of differences and the resolution of conflicts. If the latter could be more efficiently performed without law and criminal justice, as abolitionists argue it could, then there is no reason for not allowing it to be so. Meanwhile the subject matter of criminology itself vanishes into the shifting plurality of 'problematic situations' involving diversified and non-commensurable principles and amenable to no generalised solution. Hulsman's abolitionism firmly straddles the main themes of the postmodern perspective.

Behind the appropriation of deconstruction in contemporary radical criminology lies, of course, a politics. In the abolitionist case it is an anarchist libertarian one, that individuals should be able to sort out their own problems free of the shackles and discourses of the state and criminal law. In the case of feminist postmodernism the task is to liberate what Smart (1995) terms the 'multiplicity of resistances', those voices, in particular of women, that have been forced into silence by the theories and discourses of mainstream criminology. Both abolitionism and feminist postmodernism would reject much of the mainstream approaches to criminal justice and criminality as oppressive. They are quite right to do so. However, whether the particular approach to deconstruction that they adopt actually achieves their intended aim is another matter.

THE CRITIQUE OF DECONSTRUCTION

The immediately obvious problem with deconstruction is that of infinite regress. To abandon reference to rape in favour of sexuality leaves us with a narrative of 'sexuality' that could be further deconstructed to reveal all sorts of other discourses of power. Why should sexuality refer to anything more 'real' than rape? What about other directions in which rape could be deconstructed? The fact that we never arrive – and from a postmodern standpoint must not arrive – at any sort of rock bottom concepts that we can say 'really' describe an external reality means that methods such as deconstruction lead to infinite regress.[1] Deconstruction is like spending time with a dictionary looking up words that are defined in terms of other words, which can in turn be looked up and so on, or in Russell Berman's apt phrase, 'Deconstruction is the restaurant where one can only order the menu' (Berman, 1990).

I have previously (Lea, 1987) pointed to a similar problem with Hulsman's abolitionism. Hulsman deconstructs crime to reveal the plurality of 'problematic situations' on the assumption that there is an uncontested language in terms of which such phenomena can be located behind the discourse of criminality. However the process refuses to stop. If the concept of crime is defined by the criminal justice system and its 'power/knowledge', then certainly the concept of 'problematic' and what count as 'problematic situations' come in a very similar way to be defined by the shifting processes of power and communication within society, and neither the criminologist nor any other observer stands outside those processes. Hulsman's abolitionism fails to demonstrate the superiority of its own language and terminology: if crime has no 'ontological reality' then neither do problematic situations. Abolitionists may set deconstruction to work on the 'ontological reality' of crime only to see it devouring 'problematic situations' as well.

While in literary criticism the relativism of an infinite regression of signs may conceivably be a fruitful device, in sociology and social criticism it leads to incoherence. In practice solutions have to be found that compromise the original project of deconstruction by calling the proceedings to a halt in some arbitrary way. One variant is simply to declare some particular set of 'facts' to be 'real' or 'foundational', totally against the spirit of deconstruction itself. Such a process in traditional social constructionism was identified and criticised by Woolgar and Pawluch, in their critique of writers such as Pfohl (1977), as engaging in 'ontological gerrymandering'. That is, 'making problematic the truth status of certain states of affairs selected for analysis and explanation, while backgrounding or minimising the possibility that the same problems apply to assumptions upon which the analysis depends' (Woolgar and Pawluch, 1985, p. 216).

In order to give an explanation, for example, of increases in public concern about child battering as a product of the labelling of certain types of behaviour by child psychiatrists (Pfohl, 1977), the assumption has to be made that the labelled behaviour has been around for ages and hasn't changed. What has changed is the labelling activities. This is the only way to make labelling explanations work. In order to deconstruct current discourses of child abuse as a labelling process by professionals one has to make the assumption of a 'thing in itself', of unchanged and unlabelled 'real' behaviour, that is, a low level of actual child abuse or a diversity of behaviours towards children that have hardly changed. As Woolgar and Pawluch point out, deconstructionist sociology has been grappling with this problem for some time. On one level Becker's famous statement that 'deviance is not a quality of the act the person commits but rather a consequence of the application by others of rules and sanctions to an offender' (Becker, 1963 p. 9) was ambiguous. The radical edge to labelling theory certainly lay in its attitude to the explanation of crime and deviance as to be found not in a study of the motivations of the criminal actor but as resulting from the implicitly arbitrary nature of the labelling process. But as to whether there was a reality outside the dynamics of labelling, in the sense that one could identify the misapplication of labels, was often not clear. Radical deconstructionists such as Pfohl respond to Woolgar and Pawluch by agreeing that deconstructionist methods must also be applied to the background assumptions, with the result that what we witness in deconstructionist sociology is not a process of the discovery of what is really going on in the world but

the effect of a transformative displacement of one set of social structuring practices by some others. From within this collusion or collusion of structuring practices arises a 'true' story – the 'real facts' of the matter, the self evidency of 'things' and the like. There are no truths aside from this elusive (intellectual) formation (Pfohl, 1985, p. 230).

This shift of position by Pfohl illustrates, as Schwartz and Friedrichs (1994) note, the difference between postmodernism and the older tradition of social constructionism. While the latter attempted to attribute motives to the constructors – as with the professional bureaucratic interests of child psychiatrists identified by Pfohl in his 1977 article, postmodernism sees all knowlege as indeterminate and relative, as Pfohl's 1985 response indicates. In such a situation any stopping point to the 'narrative' is an arbitrary one.

The second variant involves transferring foundationalism from a set of 'facts' to a social subject or collection of subjects. Thus for Carol Smart the truth claims of criminology have been, or are to be, deconstructed from the standpoint of new social subjects constituting a 'multiplicity of resistances' to truth as power. It consists largely of 'lesbians and gays, black women and men, Asian women and men, feminists and so on' (Smart, 1995, p. 36). There is no disputing that much of what passes as traditional criminology is incredibly sexist and racist. However there is a problem in the method of deconstruction deployed here. Suppose we agree that the concept of 'crime' is a male discourse insofar as it marginalises phenomena that are the core of gender relations in modern society. What status does the latter statement have? One solution is to say that it is 'true' that violence is a central ingredient of gender relations – good old-fashioned foundationalism in which the truth of the statement is independent of the status of the speaker. But we now know that such truth is contaminated with (male) power. What Smart appears to be arguing is that the validity of the argument is to be found in the fact that it is being articulated by the groups she mentions. The point is surely that these social groups come predesignated as progressive forces. Smart constructs her list of resisters from the standpoint of her own 'grand narrative' concerning what is progressive in the world. If we were to extend her 'multiplicity of resistances' to embrace book-burning religious bigots, members of extreme right-wing nationalist and terrorist groups and so on – all 'resisting' what they regard as oppression – we might not find it so easy to talk about the relativisation of truth as power. That 'lesbians and gays . . . feminists and so on' (ibid.) are progressive social subjects whose counter discourses to those of 'crime' are to be listened to (even if some of them are calling for more, rather than less, activity by the criminal justice system), in fact harks back to the older notion of the radical subject as the carrier of universal concerns, of a rival, more coherent account of reality.

The third variant is to maintain the deconstructionist denial of truth claims and meanwhile resort to a simple pragmatism of 'what works'. It is exemplified in Stan Cohen's (Cohen, this volume) claim that 'Deconstructionism itself does not necessarily undermine the utility of any discourse, still less the importance of any values or the desirability of any practice'. He goes on to argue that 'This does not mean that any language game is as "good" as another. It does mean that the choice (between a radical criminology deconstructing concepts of criminality and criminal law, and a 'realist' endorsement of crime control) depends on what works, not what is true'.

So we can simultaneously understand that, on the one hand all discourses are power effects to be deconstructed, and on the other that, in order to identify social problems and take steps to deal with them, we have to use certain concepts and categories to define the problems and work out effective solutions. The only criterion for the latter is 'what works'. But if this is the only arbitrator of what discourses we adopt, then what began as a radical critique of dominant discourses of power ends up prostrating itself before them. What 'works' in any situation is precisely a product of the dominant relationships of power! It is the complete relativism as regards questions of power that lies behind the conservatism and quiescence of deconstruction. If all discourses and definitions are power effects involving repression, then power is ubiquitous. It is everywhere and therefore nowhere. All social groups are to be seen as part of the contingent plurality of differences, and any discourse of oppression or victimisation becomes just another language game with, at most, a local validity. The victim claiming she has been 'raped' is one speaker, the offender claiming that this was normal consensual sex is another. What 'works' might be to tell the victim to go home and not bother.

We are reduced to helpless spectators who can only stand and watch while victims, offenders, police officers and judges spin a yarn, bargain and compromise and produce their 'story'. Any notion that justice is being dispensed, or, more importantly, being denied, is simply part of the narrative. At the end of the day deconstruction changes nothing. It leaves us no wiser as to why certain activities, as opposed to others, are constituted as 'crime' in specific types of society and no basis for the critique of such constitutive processes. It tells us simply that power effects are always involved and that categories can be deconstructed into other categories.

Against this the older Marxist and critical theory tradition of critique is, in my opinion, immeasurably superior. The issue of the ontological reality of crime is replaced by its contradictory and historical reality. Dialectical theory is acutely aware of the repressive nature of definitions and concepts[2] but this repression is understood to lie not in the nature of the defining process as such but in the particular form of society in which it takes place. Against the assertion that crime is 'really' sexuality or economics or whatever, the aim is rather to show why certain forms of sexuality, violence or economic activity came historically to be constructed as crime, and what specific constellations of power and conflict were involved. These latter then become the basis for critique and change. The focus of critique is not from some external hypothetical standpoint of 'right' but is an immanent process based on the consequences of thinking through and acting out the contradictions of the present power relations and their discourses. Why is sexual violence by strangers a crime and by husbands not? Why is violence by workers a crime and by employers not? How are ruling and subordinate groups and classes in society actually deploying criminal law and criminalisation? These contradictions then become the basis for change and development, both reformist and, at times, revolutionary. The end product of such activity might well be the abolition of the concept of crime altogether as a way of dealing with conflicts. But if this occurs we shall be able to understand precisely the revolutionary social changes that have led to it. We shall not have deconstructed it in our heads only to reconcile ourselves again to it in reality. In the words of the Marxist legal theorist Evgeny Pashukanis,

The concepts of crime and punishment are necessary determinants of the legal form from which people will be able to liberate themselves only after the legal super-structure itself has begun to whither away. And when we begin to overcome and to do without these concepts in reality, rather than merely in declarations, that will be the surest sign that the narrow horizon of bourgeois law is finally opening up before us (Pashukanis, 1978, p. 188).

THE CAUSES OF CRIME

Assuming, then, that it is meaningful to talk about crime, we can pass to the second main problem area of criminology – the causes of crime. Here postmodern critiques may claim a relevance both as regards the possibility of explanations for social phenomena as such and at the level of the particular types of explanation that criminology has produced within its domain. The second theme in postmodernism that I identified above concerned the rejection of coherence and unity and the idea of a 'grand narrative' of truth or essence and that society is not, or is no longer, a coherent system, regulated in terms of some central mechanism that might serve as the starting point for the explanation of particular social phenomena such as crime. This obviously has a relevance at both levels of explanation.

According to Carol Smart criminology is guilty of positivism. This she defines as the doctrine that 'we can establish a verifiable knowledge or truth about events, in particular that we can establish a causal explanation, which in turn will provide us with objective methods for intervening in the events defined as problematic' (Smart, 1995, p. 34). This 'positivism' is then seen as an aspect of a modernism that involves both the adoption of 'modes of totalizing or grand theorising which impose a uniformity of perspective and ignore the immense diversity of subjectivities of women and men', and the 'assumption that once we have the theory which will explain all forms of social behaviour we will also know what to do' (ibid., p. 34).

Certainly positivist criminology – though hardly all varieties of criminology in the sense I have defined it – was a central aspect of the belief in a managed society and planned social reform that dominated the welfare state era (Taylor, 1982), and it is true that this criminology is in crisis as part of the general crisis of social policy and the welfare state. It is true that postmodernists such as Lyotard (1984) associate the failure of social planning with the grand narratives of global explanation and change that may have inspired it, and see a danger of totalitarianism lurking in such attempts at large-scale social engineering. It is less clear, however, that in advocating a modest restriction of the scientific enterprise to the domain of 'local truths', Lyotard is arguing anything fundamentally different from a previous generation of critical rationalists determined to salvage the modern scientific enterprise through the rejection of unfalsifiable holism.

Thus Karl Popper argued that we cannot study or control the whole of society for the simple reason that 'with every new control of social relations we create a host of new social relations to be controlled. . . . The attempt leads to an infinite regress; the position is similar with an attempt to study the whole of society – which would have to include this study' (Popper, 1957, pp. 79–80). Holistic experiments always go wrong because we cannot lean from our mistakes under such circumstances, 'Since so much is done at a time it is impossible to say which particular measure is responsible for any of the results' (ibid., pp. 88–9). As with social change so with scientific theory itself. For Popper science progresses through critique by falsification – but it does progress. We can never prove theories correct as we cannot observe all instances of their relevant domains, but incorrect theories can falsified as all we need is one counter-example. Hence rational theories have to be formulated in such a way that they can specify those conditions under which they would be falsified. This, for Popper, consigned to the flames Plato, Hegel, Marx, Freud and other attempts at what postmodernists would term 'grand narratives' and totalising theories. Popper first elaborated these ideas in 1936. Almost half a century later Lyotard elucidated a notion of science almost identical to that of Popper: 'Science does not expand by means of the positivism of efficiency. The opposite is true: working on a proof means searching for and "in-

venting" counter examples' (Lyotard, 1984, p. 54). He likewise shares Popper's fear about holism – grand narratives –
leading to the gulag: 'The nineteenth and twentieth centuries have given us as much terror as we can take. We have
paid a high enough price for the nostalgia of the whole
and the one' (ibid., pp. 81–2). The rejection of 'grand narratives' thus appears as a thoroughly 'modern' theme. With
a few minor adjustments the postmodern critique of metanarratives[3] can be assimilated by a sophisticated scientific
positivism.

At the level of particular explanations of crime the implications of postmodern thought are perhaps clearer. Most
sociological criminology deploys some notion of the social
collectivity, whether of the normative life world or the social structure, from which the criminal offender is marginalised and in terms of which criminality is to be explained.
The dynamics of this marginalisation varies between theories.
The stress may be on detachment and under socialisation,
on the breakdown of or contradiction between legitimate
ends and the means for attaining them within the normative structure of the life world, or on the effects of power
and domination in denying access to non-criminal methods
of grievance redress. This type of analysis is of course an
object of criticism both from within and outside criminology. Feminists have argued that the notion of sexual violence as a result of breakdown or marginalisation ignores its
alleged central role in the control of patriarchal social relations. Crimes committed by powerful individuals and corporations seem less amenable to notions of marginality than
the crimes of some sections of the poor and weak.

However it is the contrast between the very terms of this
debate and some important postmodern themes that is my
concern here. As I have noted, an important feature of the
postmodernist appropriation of Nietzschean philosophy is
a view of the individual as standing outside the normative
life world and orienting towards the latter as a resource for
the experimental creation of lifestyles in the manner of
bricolage. If freedom and the formation of personal identity are to be understood as a process of free self-creation by
means of endless experimentation and to involve the
maximisation of independence from social bonds, then the

condition of marginality becomes the general condition for freedom. Violence and 'crime' become a choice like all others – simply another experiment in 'difference'. The paradox of postmodern society becomes one in which 'crime' may be increasing but we cannot know the 'causes' of this as they are simply the general conditions of freedom itself. Very little in the way of criminological theory could survive such a fundamental reorientation. Even rational choice theory, while assimilating the decision to commit crime to a general form of calculation, usually includes as a factor in the calculation of costs and benefits of committing crime some variable such as 'willingness to commit an illegal act' (Becker, 1968), implying a cost of defying social norms and distinct from the likelihood of detection, severity of penalty and other costs. It would be necessary to remove this factor altogether in some theory of 'contingent choice', which of course would not be a distinct theory of crime at all. Any distinct criminology would disappear into a general sociology of postmodernity as the emergence of the conditions for freedom and difference through the weakening of social bonds. We might retain a notion of crime as that which impeded the development of 'difference' and plurality, but this would involve a metanarrative of justice and tolerance, which postmodernism seeks to deny.

DIFFERENCE AND RECOGNITION

There are, however, some problems with a general post-modern approach to freedom as play and experimentation. We have only to set Hegel against Nietzsche to understand freedom not as endless experimentation but as an interactive process of mutual recognition. The ability of individuals to understand their actions as free is linked to the ability to recognise those actions from the standpoint of others. Rather than dispensing with the constraints of social life, freedom requires its very existence in order to be understood as such. In this context social life is precisely the system of general norms and values that postmodernists wish to reject as 'grand narratives' (Honneth, 1992). Thus to the extent that the normative bonds of the life world are weakening, we are led to see a growing crisis of recognition rather than a diversification of opportunities for free self-creation of difference.

From this standpoint criminology is not quite so redundant. It has to be explained why particular individuals or groups find it necessary to search for and innovate new alternative structures of recognition, frequently taking a destructive form, both to themselves and their victims (Grose and Groves, 1988). Older notions such as marginality and relative deprivation still have purchase as a starting point for explaining why certain groups have been denied to sources of recognition. The element of truth in the postmodern perspective lies rather in understanding that these conditions are becoming increasingly widespread in modern capitalist societies with the decline in access to work, both as a source of recognition in itself and as a means to the achievement of mass-media-produced, consumption-oriented identities. The outcome is indeed a pluralisation of attempts to devise alternative forms of status, but the result is less the proliferation of difference than of destructive and partial forms of recognition, as with the criminal gang, or the desperate search for recognition that results in the annihilation of its potential source, as with many forms of interpersonal violence. Of course, where harmless or emancipatory activities are 'criminalised' in the interests of powerful groups such an analysis does not apply. Criminology cannot escape judgements of this type. This is why a strictly positivist criminology is necessarily reactionary. Only a radical critical criminology linked to emancipatory concerns can be consistent in its application of theory.

It remains the case of course that many forms of corporate, white-collar, organised crime and other 'crimes of the powerful' are less explicable in terms of marginalisation from sources of recognition. But here again the search for an explanation leads less obviously in the direction of any one dimensional process of fragmentation. As Harvey points out, the reorganisation of the international financial system since the 1970s 'has been a dual movement, on the one hand towards the formation of the financial conglomerates and brokers of extraordinary global power, and, on the other hand a rapid proliferation and decentralisation of financial

activities and flows through the creation of entirely new financial instruments and markets' (Harvey, 1989, pp. 160–1). This
contradictory unity of centralisation and decentralisation undoubtedly brings more opportunities for white-collar and
organised crime, while the increasing fusion of illegal and
legal finance, of organised and corporate crime, is associated with the emergence of global financial blocks (Santino,
1988). The impulse for criminality in this area lies, moreover, at the core of the capitalist form of economic organisation rather than in any new decentralising tendency. As
Box put it: 'This defining characteristic – it is a goal seeking entity – makes a corporation inherently criminogenic
for it necessarily operates in an uncertain and unpredict-
able environment such that its purely legitimate opportunities for goal attainment are sometimes limited and constrained' (Box, 1983, p. 35). Finally, the forms of status and
recognition sought by most corporate and organised criminals are entirely conventional and bourgeois and least likely
to be the result of some new postmodern proliferation
of identities. A postmodern approach, while it may grasp
certain features of the decentralised nature of 'post-Fordist'
capitalism that provide increased opportunities for crime,
has little to say about the impulse for corporate and organised
crime.

THE CONTROL OF CRIME

The final problematic of criminology is the control of crime.
Here a critical acceptance of some of the themes of
postmodern sociology may seem useful. The postmodern stress
on the fragmentation of older centralising structures of
modernity seems to accord with the increasing stress during the last decade on the role of informal preventative
processes of crime control. Of course, as every criminologist knows, the informal processes of the family, community, school and work are the most important front-line
mechanisms of crime control. But in modern society these
are always to be evaluated and regulated from the standpoint of the grand narratives of justice. During the postwar
period both the welfare state and the criminal justice sys-

tem intervened in these informal mechanisms through a variety of social rights to welfare and education, parental and children's rights and so on. Criminal justice and welfare institutions, police and social work, with their discourses of treatment, care and surveillance, seemed to many commentators in the 1970s and 1980s to be penetrating into these areas and 'blurring the boundaries' between formal institutional structures and informal community-based forms of social control, to the detriment of the latter (Cohen, 1985). The hypothesis of an incorporation of informal mechanisms as adjuncts to a repressive criminal justice system was an attractive theme to the left.

It is clear that a postmodern perspective, with its stress on fragmentation and difference as the salient characteristic of modern society, leads in a contrary direction. If postmodernisation has any meaning then it lies in the hypothesis that decentralised informal mechanisms come to dominate and partially replace formal centralised institutions and their accompanying discourses or grand narratives, and at the same time that formal criminal justice institutions operate in increasingly informal ways. The most obvious example of such processes is the growth of private, decentralised crime prevention not only at the micro level in the control of entry to particular streets, 'public' places, housing or shopping complexes, but also in the macro design of cities, the zoning of neighbourhoods the segregation of rich and poor populations and so on. Such a system has, it can be argued, begun to emerge partly as a result of the privatisation of public space or the growth of 'mass private property' (Shearing and Stenning, 1987), epitomised by the shopping mall surveyed by private security agencies, video and so on. In a postmodern world such decentralised privatised forms of crime control are decreasingly ancillary to and increasingly a replacement for the system of formal controls. The important 'postmodern' characteristics of such a system of informal controls are, firstly, that it pre-empts and avoids discourses of rights and due process through the generalised segregation of populations, and decentralised and nonfocused coercion. Control lies decreasingly in the threat of detection of and punishment for the violation of generally agreed norms, and increasingly in the general controls on entry to certain areas applied to population categories. As Mike Davis (1990), in his remarkable study of Los Angeles observes, the decline of an apartheid sanctioned by explicit, reactionary, politically centralised laws in South Africa is met by an increase in a form of apartheid – between the ghetto and the white suburb – organised through the decentralised and impartial mechanisms of private property and the regulation of space in the cities of the free world. Secondly, the decline of free public space involves a decline in the notions of the public sphere and the free citizen. The postmodern celebration of 'difference' replaces that of inclusion in the grand narratives of citizenship, though, as we have seen, such a notion fails to grasp the power implications where the blacks in the ghetto and the whites in the protected central city and the segregated and secured suburbs are all, equally, manifestations of difference. Finally, and crucially for a postmodern perspective, the accountability and control of such systems is decreasingly related to generalised discourses of democracy or generalised legal rights and increasingly to decentralised groups of 'consumers' and 'customers'. The proliferation of crime prevention serves as a metaphor for postmodern crime control.

The other side of the coin, meanwhile is that the formal agencies of social control – the police, courts and so on – act in increasingly informal ways. While remaining in theory governed by formal rules and procedures corresponding to grand narratives of justice and rights, the informal aspects of the work of such agencies come to predominate. Again, criminology has always been aware of the role of informal norms governing the work of criminal justice institutions, and indeed that such bodies would not be able to function at all without such informal procedures. But as with the role of non-criminal justice institutions in the control of crime, such informal procedures were seen as subordinated in the last analysis to generalised discourses both of justice and rights and of technical efficiency. One of the aims of radical criminologies such as left realism was to bring such informal processes, together with norms of technical efficiency, under the overall surveillance of democratic discourses of public needs (Lea and Young, 1992; Kinsey *et al.*, 1986; Taylor, 1982).

Some varieties of postmodernism attempt an annihilation not only of the grand narratives of rights, justice and needs but also of the coherent identity of social institutions themselves. Thus for Crook *et al.*, 'The very notion of "the state" as a separate and autonomous institutional entity intimately linked with the notion of "politics" and "public sphere" and clearly separated from the domains of economy, societal community and culture, is increasingly problematic' (Crook *et al.*, 1992, p. 104). In their view an important characteristic of the process of postmodernisation is that the state has become so diverse and differentiated under the impact of postwar planning and welfare policies, that it has now begun a process of 'de-differentiation' or fragmentation, in which particular state institutions effectively break away and combine with non-state institutions with which they are more adjacent in terms of practical functioning than with other state institutions. Applied to the area of crime control, such a hypothesis would imply that policing is to be seen as part of a localised subsystem of informal institutions – communities and groups defined in terms of their identities and other fragmented formal institutions – social services, magistrates courts, probation and so on, all equally disconnected in practice from centralised direction, rather than the, however imperfect and mediated, penetration into such local systems of centralised directives formulated at the level of the 'state'. Informal cautioning and plea bargaining, rather than mediations that enable the system to cope, become all there is. Anything else is empty rhetoric, the invocation of myths and rituals of justice or centralised technical rationality.

This thesis of fragmentation also has a cultural aspect in that narratives of justice and rights are themselves fragmenting. As Norberto Bobbio (1977) has noted, one of the effects of the welfare state – with its emphasis on substantive social, rather than formal legal rights – has been that the demand for rights and justice by new social movements has decreasingly involved demands for inclusion in a generalised category of citizenship and increasingly has been a matter of protection of and respect for difference.

THE RADICALISM OF MODERNITY

The idea of a process of postmodernisation as the replacement of coercive generalised notions of 'citizenship' with recognition of the plurality of difference, combined with fragmentation of the centralised state such that criminal justice institutions become increasingly responsive to such localised identities and discourses, may seem to many to be a decided improvement, an element of the progressive side of 'new times'. It may seem for example that demands on the police to develop new sensitivities to the needs of ethnic and gender identities, interpersonal and sexual relations and so on is best understood in terms of the onset of plurality and difference. However some caution is in order.

Firstly the question of power. I have already alluded to the relativistic implications of the idea of society as a plurality of difference. The panorama of decentralised crime prevention coupled with informalism on the part of criminal justice agencies, while perhaps enabling well-organised and resourced groups to secure more attention to their needs, in reality amounts to leaving the ghetto and the underclass to its own devices. Furthermore, to the extent that the social changes stressed by many postmodernists are one side of the coin of a dual process of decentralisation and globalisation (Harvey, 1989), then the question of power is posed even more acutely. The other side of the coin is the growing power of transnational capital to intervene decisively and globally to secure the conditions for its reproduction. A discourse of rights that ignores this question is a mystification (Fudge and Glasbeek, 1992). The interests of capital in meeting some needs and keeping others firmly under control should be clear. Mike Davis (1990) aptly calls his Los Angeles, where decentralised crime prevention combines with a highly militarised style of policing to keep the ghettos under control, the 'dark side of postmodernity'. The differentiation of criminal justice institutions may well involve an increasingly decentralised and fragmented informalism and 'community policing' alongside a highly effective militarised instant response to make the city safe for transnational capital. Even at the level of decentralisation and plurality, the differential power and conflicting needs of various 'identities' can lead to privatised vigilantism as the middle classes, equipped with electric fences and private police forces, keep the underclass under control not only in Third World but also in First World cities.

Postmodernism, by failing to develop a theory of power other than a diffuse and constitutive power that can note but never theorise opposition, actually comes close to autopoietic systems theory of the style of Luhman or Parsons (Calhoun, 1989; Barcellona, 1987), in which institutions function without any reference to grand narratives but simply as tension-reduction and management mechanisms.[4] By purporting to abandon grand narratives without in any sense resolving the modernistic contradiction between abstract narratives of right or justice and substantive oppression and inequality, postmodernist thought is in danger of simply reconciling itself to the power of capital.

In such a context modernist themes take on the character of a radical rebellion. For example Tamar Pitch (1995) has noted the growth in the use of the victim–offender perspective by new social movements, the women's movement in particular. An important reason for this is the attempt to recoup a notion of responsibility in which the recognition of oneself as actor is dependent on the admission of responsibility for harm on the part of the offender – a form of self-validation that, as Pitch points out, is less available in more structural notions of oppression. While such demands for self-recognition as victims may take the form of a demand for the recognition of difference, it is also surely the case that recognition by the offender of the harm inflicted involves the development of a narrative of harm and injustice that transcends the differences between the two parties to the conflict. In short the use of the victim–offender relationship, even from the stand point of 'difference' and a plurality of identities involves the emergence of 'grand narratives'. Or to put it another way, the relationship between grand narratives and localised discourses is a practical and not an ontological one. Postmodernists may abolish grand narratives or metanarratives ontologically only to see them re-emerge in the practical discourses of social movements constituting themselves as actors. This view thus sees the postmodern 'abolition' of grand narratives as largely spurious.

There is an undeniable crisis of confidence in accepted narratives of justice and truth not because they are ephemera but because of the historical obstacles to their realisation. We are back with what Habermas aptly calls the 'unfinished project of modernity'. The bourgeois universal, or grand narrative of justice and right was always a myth in the sense that it was the form taken by the particular interests of the bourgeoisie. Postmodernism simply celebrates its opposite, the cacophony of difference. Marxism located the need for the carrier of a substantive universality that transcended this opposition between the particular and the general rather than abolishing the latter in favour of the former. This carrier was of course the working class. Postmodernists may be correct that older forms of class structure have withered with the changed organisation of work. However there is no reason to suggest that the fundamental relationship of capital and labour has changed, rather that it has assumed new global forms. The rediscovery of the need for grand narratives of justice even by a diversity of new social movements raises the question of their practical achievement and hence the nature of their carrier, that class which is capable of overcoming the opposition between the plurality of demands for justice on the one hand and the interests of global capital on the other.

Notes

1. This problem of the 'infinite regress' of deconstruction has been identified in a different context by Kate Soper. Discussing the impact of deconstructionism in art and aesthetics she observes: 'But if we ask in whose interests we are deconstructing this notion of aesthetic value and cultural freedom, we shall almost certainly be referred by the critic to all those marginalized or minority identities (women, blacks, sexual and ethnic groupings, and so forth) who have been colonized or suppressed in the name of the purity of art. . . . The problem, however, is that such justifications paradoxically invoke the cultural and judgemental freedom they deny. For unless we arbitrarily call a halt to the logic of discourse theory, why should we not deny the freedom of these liberated "identities"? Why not view them in turn as the unconscious agents of someone else's cultural policing, as themselves constructed subjects blind to the propagandist purposes they are serving in the discourse which claims their liberation?' (Soper, 1991).

2. Cf. Hegels discussion of the murderer on his way to the scaffold: 'This is abstract thinking: to see nothing in the murderer except that he is a murderer, and to annul all other human essence in him with this simple quality' (Hegel, 1965, pp. 116–17).
3. The terms 'grand narrative' and 'metanarrative' have been used interchangeably in this paper
4. This theme has some elements in common with the idea of 'governmentality' extracted from the later writings of Michel Foucault (cf. Burchell *et al.*, 1991). For a discussion of developments in penology in similar terms, cf. Feeley and Simon (1992, 1994).

References

Barcellona, P. (1987) *L'Individualismo Proprietario* (Torino: Bollati Boringhieri).
Bauman, Z. (1991a) *Intimations of Postmodernity* (London: Routledge).
Bauman, Z. (1991b) *Postmodernity: Chance Or Menace?* (Lancaster University Centre for the Study of Cultural Values).
Becker, H. (1963) *Outsiders: Studies in the Sociology of Deviance* (New York: Free Press).
Becker, G. (1968) 'Crime and Punishment: An Economic Approach', *Journal of Political Economy*, vol. 76, pp. 169–217.
Berman, R. (1990) 'Troping to Pretoria: the Rise and Fall of Deconstruction' *Telos*, no. 85.
Bobbio, N. (1977) *Dalla Struttura Alla Funzione* (Milano: Communita).
Box, S. (1983) *Crime Power and Mystification* (London: Tavistock).
Burchell, G. *et al.* (eds) (1991) *The Foucault Effect: Studies in Governmentality* (Brighton: Harvester Wheatsheaf).
Calhoun, C. (1989) 'Social Theory and the Law: Systems Theory, Normative Justification and Postmodernism', *Northwestern University Law Review*, vol. 83, nos. 1 and 2.
Christie, N. (1977) 'Conflicts as Property', *British Journal of Criminology*, vol. 17, pp. 1–15.
Cohen, S. (1985) *Visions of Social Control* (Cambridge: Polity Press).
Crook, S. *et al.* (1992) *Postmodernization: Change in Advanced Society* (London: Sage).
Davis, M. (1990) *City of Quartz: Excavating the Future in Los Angeles* (London: Verso).
Derrida, J. (1992) 'Force of Law: The "Mystical Foundation of Authority",' in D. Cornell *et al.* (eds), *Deconstruction and the Possibility of Justice* (London: Routledge).
Douzinas, C. and R. Warrington (1991) 'A Well-Founded Fear of Justice, "Law and Ethics in Postmodernity"', *Law and Critique*, vol. 2, no. 2.
Feeley, M. and J. Simon (1992) 'The New Penology: Notes on the Emerging Strategy of Corrections and its Implications', *Criminology*, vol. 30, no. 4, pp. 449–74.
Feeley, M. and J. Simon (1994) 'Actuarial Justice: the Emerging New Criminal Law', in D. Nelken (ed.) *The Futures of Criminology* (London: Sage).

Fitzpatrick, P. (1992) *The Mythology of Modern Law* (London: Routledge).

Fudge, J. and H. Glasbeek (1992) 'The Politics of Rights: A Politics with Little Class', *Social and Legal Studies*, vol. 1, no. 1, pp. 45–70.

Fukuyama, F. (1989) 'The End of History', *The National Interest*, Sumner.

Grose, G. and B. Groves (1988) 'Crime and Human Nature: A Marxist Perspective', *Contemporary Crises*, vol. 12, no. 2, pp. 145–71.

Hall, S. and M. Jaques (eds) (1989) *New Times* (London: Lawrence & Wishart).

Harvey, D. (1989) *The Condition of Postmodernity* (Oxford: Blackwell).

Hegel, G.W.F. (1965) 'Who Thinks Abstractly?', in W. Kaufmann, *Hegel: Texts and Commentary* (New York: Anchor Books).

Henry, S. and D. Milovanovic (1994) 'The Constitution of Constitutive Criminology: a Postmodern Approach to Criminological Theory', in D. Nelken (ed.), *The Futures of Criminology* (London: Sage).

Honneth, A. (1992) 'Pluralization and Recognition: on the Self-misunderstanding of Postmodern Social Theorists', in P. Beilharz *et al* (eds), *Between Totalitarianism and Postmodernity* (Cambridge, Mass: MIT Press).

Hulsman, L. (1986) 'Critical Criminology and the Concept of Crime', *Contemporary Crises*, vol. 10.

Hunt, A. (1990) 'Postmodernism and Critical Criminology', *Critical Criminologist*, vol. 2, no. 1.

Jameson, F. (1984) 'Postmodernism Or the Cultural Logic of Late Capitalism', *New Left Review*, vol. 146.

Kinsey, R., J. Lea and J. Young (1986) *Losing the Fight Against Crime* (Oxford: Blackwell).

Lea, J. (1987) 'Left Realism: A Defence', *Contemporary Crises*, no. 11.

Lea, J. and J. Young (1992) *What Is To Be Done About Law and Order*, 2nd edn (London: Pluto Press).

Lyotard, J. (1984) *The Postmodern Condition* (Manchester University Press).

Morrison, W. (1994) 'Criminology, Modernity and the "Truth" of the Human Condition: a Postmodern Approach to Criminological Theory', in D. Nelken (ed.) *The Futures of Criminology* (London: Sage).

Norris, C. (1991) *Deconstruction: Theory and Practice* (London: Routledge).

Pashukanis, E. (1978) *Law and Marxism a General Theory* (London: Ink Links).

Pfohl, S. (1977) 'The "Discovery" of Child Abuse' *Social Problems*, vol. 24, pp. 310–24.

Pfohl, S. (1985) 'Toward a Sociological Deconstruction of Social Problems', *Social Problems*, vol. 32, no. 3, pp. 228–32.

Pitch, T. (1995) *Limited Responsibilites* (London: Routledge).

Popper, K. (1957) *The Poverty of Historicism* (London: Routledge and Kegan Paul).

Santino, U. (1988) 'The Financial Mafia: the Illegal Accumulation of Wealth and the Financial Industrial Complex', *Contemporary Crises*, vol. 12, pp. 203–43.

Santos, B. (1987) 'Law: A Map of Misreading Towards a Postmodern Conception of Law', *Journal of Law and Society*, vol. 14, no. 3.

Schwartz, M. and D. Friedrichs (1994) 'Postmodern Thought and Criminological Discontent: New Metaphors for Understanding Violence', *Criminology*, vol. 32, no. 2, pp. 221–46.

Shearing, C. and P. Stenning (eds) (1987) *Private Policing* (London: Sage).

Smart, C. (1995) Feminist Approaches to Criminology or Postmodern Woman Meets Atavistic Man, in *Law, Crime and Sexuality: Essays in Feminism* (London: Sage).

Soper, K. (1991) 'Postmodernism, Subjectivity and the Question of Value', *New Left Review*, vol. 186.

Spector, M. and J. Kitsuse (1977) *Constructing Social Problems* (Menlo Park: Cummings).

Taylor, I. (1982) *Law and Order: Arguments for Socialism* (London: Macmillan).

Woolgar, S. and D. Pawluch (1985) 'The Anatomy of Social Problems Explanations', *Social Problems*, vol. 32, no. 3.

Young, A. (1992) 'Feminism and the Body of Criminology', in D. Farrington and S. Walklate (eds), *Offenders and Victims: Theory and Policy* (British Criminology Conference, 1991, Selected Papers, vol. 1), BSC/ISTD).

10 Criminology and the Public Sphere: Arguments for Utopian Realism

Ian Loader

> In the struggle against the loudest voices in our societies
> – politicians, editorialists and commentators – scientific
> discourse has all the cards stacked against it: the diffi-
> culty and slowness of its construction, which means it
> generally arrives after the battle is over; its inevitable com-
> plexity, which tends to discourage simplistic or suspicious
> minds, and above all its distance from received ideas and
> spontaneous convictions (Bourdieu, 1993, p. viii).

I can still remember obtaining my battered, heavily scored
copy of *The New Criminology*, bought secondhand back in
1985 for £4. For me, then a disillusioned undergraduate
law student coming to criminology for the first time, this
was to become an important, even inspirational text. Not
only did it offer a comprehensive overview and critique of
the then strange world of criminological theory (albeit one
I later came to think of as rather too dismissive), but more
importantly it suggested the prospect of a discipline that
was intellectually ambitious, morally serious and politically
committed. I was hooked. Though it took some time to realise
it, criminology was to be my escape route from the mind-
numbing business of 'black-letter' law.

The New Criminology was a manifesto for research that was
committed, intellectually, to developing a 'fully social theory
of deviance' and, normatively, to abolishing inequalities of
wealth and power. Though today, some twenty years or so
after its publication, these ambitions remain far from realised,
the issues raised in the text's final pages remain important

ones. I therefore want to use this occasion to reflect upon one such issue: that of how criminology can and might engage with political and popular debate about crime and punishment. Few involved in the criminological enterprise can have failed at some time or other to have puzzled over this question. In a discourse so intimately connected to the business of social control, and whose subject matter is so central to the preoccupations of politicians, social commentators and public alike, the issue is raised in chronic ways for criminologists of all theoretical and political hues.

My particular purpose is to consider the relationship between criminology and what German social theorist Jurgen Habermas calls 'the public sphere'. Habermas (1974, p. 49) uses this term to describe that 'realm of our social life in which something approaching a public opinion can be formed'. It designates a set of institutional spaces – situated between civil society and the state – in which citizens can deliberate over their conflicting values, preferences and purposes. These sites, Habermas contends, should be open to all, accord participants an equal status and operate 'the unforced force of the better argument' as the sole arbiter of decision making. As such, the public sphere anticipates a future in which social integration is secured on the basis of inclusive public communication rather than through force or strategic persuasion: it is the practical embodiment of an informed, discursive democracy.

Thus conceived, the public sphere remains a normative ideal. While liberal democratic societies acknowledge the principle of public dialogue, and have partially embedded democratic rights in their institutions (Cohen and Areto, 1992, ch. 8), such societies are some distance from securing the kind of public sphere of which Habermas speaks (Habermas, 1989). The actually existing public sphere is dominated by powerful commercial interests and the unaccountable expert cultures of remote public bureaucracies, both of which share an instrumental rather than discursive orientation to the social world. The consequence is a limited opportunity for citizens to deliberate upon matters of common concern. Contemporary public life has been reduced to 'the manipulative deployment of media power to procure mass loyalty, consumer demand and "compliance" with system imperatives' (Habermas, 1992, p. 452).

How, against this backdrop, might criminologists engage with the prevailing public conversation about 'law and order'? Should they be insiders striving for relevance, or outsiders and social critics? Are certain versions of the criminological enterprise implicated in the depoliticisation of public life? Might criminology have any role to play in its democratic reconstruction? In taking up these questions I shall argue for what I term – following and adapting Giddens (1990, 1994) – a 'utopian realist' approach towards existing official and popular deliberation about crime and punishment; one that endeavours to engage with 'law and order' debates in ways that render explicit their connection with ethics and politics, while recognising – and keeping alive – the tensions that quite properly exist between the realm of social enquiry and that of politics.

The argument proceeds in the following manner. The bulk of the chapter comprises a necessarily selective account of how the criminological landscape has unfolded since the publication of *The New Criminology*. My particular concern is to conduct a critical dialogue with a range of existing traditions of enquiry (which I term – for analytical purposes – 'jobbing criminology' and 'anticriminology'), seeking to assess their understanding of the public role of criminology. I shall then be in a position to outline and defend the principal tenets of a utopian realist approach towards the relationship between criminological knowledge and politics.

INSTRUMENTAL DISCOURSES: JOBBING CRIMINOLOGY

One of the principal aims of *The New Criminology* was to challenge – and move beyond – an atheoretical, applied, correctionalist view of the discipline. Though many of its chosen targets might legitimately claim 'not guilty as charged' on this count, there is no doubt that Taylor, Walton and Young (1973) correctly identified a significant feature of the criminological project. The historically predominant ways of conceiving of criminology have evinced an instrumental orientation to the social world. They have rested on the presumption that criminology provides a set of techniques capable of generating reliable, scientific knowledge concerning crime and its causes, knowledge that can contribute to effective policy making.

This way of understanding and doing criminological research has been most evident, not so much in the sociological enquiry that provoked Taylor, Walton and Young's fire, but in those criminologies that enjoy the closest relationship to established centres of power. In Britain this kind of criminology was for a while represented by the Cambridge Institute of Criminology (Radzinowicz, 1988). It also marks the work undertaken by the internal research units of the Home Office and The Scottish Office (Clarke and Cornish, 1980a). And it manifests itself in no small measure within criminology in the United States, where criminological researchers are much more commonly housed in private corporations and research foundations (Petersilia, 1990).

These bodies of criminological research are representative of what I shall term 'jobbing criminology' (Loader and Sparks, 1993). By this I mean the practice of going from criminological job to criminological job either unburdened by intellectual agendas, or else committed only to narrowly construed and preestablished policy goals; research that proceeds with little overt reference to the political and ethical dimensions of the issues at hand. In these respects, jobbing criminology is rarely if ever a position that researchers explicitly adhere to. Rather it is an activity, and the extent to which criminologists are required to practice such jobbing will vary across time and space, depending on such matters as how and where criminology is institutionalised, the vicissitudes of research funding and the dull compulsion of the criminological labour market. It is thus no part of my purpose to isolate and criticise a distinct body of jobbing criminologists (we may all become jobbers from time to time), nor do I propose to 'rubbish' the research produced under such circumstances. My aim is merely to set out some of the salient characteristics of jobbing criminology and assess its relationship to – and effects upon – the public sphere in liberal democratic societies. For purposes of illustration I will use the work of the Home Office Research and Planning Unit (HORPU), the largest single body of criminological researchers in Europe.[1]

Jobbing criminology maintains a close and dependent

relationship to official crime control agendas. This proximity places such criminology under some obvious yet chronic constraints: it delimits the range of substantive questions that can be asked and the explanatory avenues pursued; it circumscribes the role of theory in research (to what Clarke and Cornish, 1980b, describe as theory that is 'just good enough' for policy evaluation), and gives rise to a preference for the quantification of data (though the Home Office has in recent years become slightly more amenable to qualitative methodology).

Jobbing criminology further posits the criminologist as a dispassionate researcher unearthing factual information relevant to the formulation and monitoring of criminal justice policy. Within HORPU, this has generated two genres of research. First, the systematic evaluation of penal, policing and crime prevention measures. This has remained a prominent strand of Home Office research since its inception and has ranged from studies of Borstal regimes (Mannheim and Wilkins, 1955), to a more recent focus on community policing and crime prevention programmes (Bennett, 1991; Hope and Foster, 1992). The aim of such research has however remained constant: to assess the impact of such measures (on say recidivism or crime rates) and formulate guidelines for future practice. Secondly, and more recently, HORPU has begun to produce general statistical information as an aid to the construction of more rational, informed crime control policy. This is most apparent in the British Crime Survey, launched in 1982 and repeated in 1984, 1988, 1992, 1994 and 1996. Originated as a study of the extent and pattern of criminal victimisation in England and Wales, these surveys have since mushroomed to encompass such matters as the impact and fear of crime, public participation in neighbourhood watch schemes and 'consumer satisfaction' with policing.

The contours and goals of Home Office criminology have, however, changed markedly over the last decade or so. During the 1960s and 1970s Home Office research was dominated by an ambitious, theoretically sophisticated and criminologically positivist concern with the social and psychological causes of crime. This orientation one might properly describe as 'penal modernism' (Garland, 1995). It proceeded on the assumption that criminological science could contribute to the solution of social problems by producing predictive knowledge (say of offending behaviour) useful in the control of the (external) social world. By the 1980s these ambitions had been both scaled down and recast. The search for the 'underlying' causes of crime took second place within HORPU to a neoclassicist preoccupation with the rational, calculating, opportunistic offender. Much of the resulting policy focus was concerned with managing and containing the crime problem by manipulating the immediate physical environment (Clarke, 1980). It was this that prompted Jock Young (1986) to term this body of thought 'administrative criminology'.

In the midst of these changes, a number of continuities can be identified. Home Office criminology has, first of all, continued to ascribe (however implicitly) to a set of empiricist epistemological assumptions as to what constitutes 'good' research. In the 1950s and 1960s this was by no means out of step with the orthodoxy of the wider social scientific community. Of late, however, Home Office criminology has largely failed to keep pace with broader philosophical developments and their consequences for research (cf. Outhwaite, 1987; Layder, 1993). When set against the methodological pluralism that now characterises the wider sociological and criminological field, HORPU's heavy reliance on particular forms of research practice (such as quasi-experimental design) appears increasingly outmoded. Secondly, Home Office research has generally proceeded on the basis that the ends of criminal justice policy fall beyond the reach of rational, scientific deliberation, confining itself to determining the most effective means to secure objectives established elsewhere. The ethics and politics of the issues at hand remain unarticulated, buried within what is ostensibly a neutral, technical language. As a result, Home Office research tends all too easily to fall hostage to the prevailing political fashion, whether that be the Fabian socialism of the 1960s or the managerialism of the late 1980s and early 1990s.

This is not to say that jobbing criminology is wholly without institutional autonomy or unable to obtain some critical purchase on the political and policy agendas that sustain it. Far from it. Home Office research on police effectiveness, for example, exercised an important influence over policing policy in the 1980s (Clarke and Hough, 1980, 1984). Demonstrating, among other things, that returning officers to foot patrol had at best a marginal impact on crime rates, this research did much to overcome the Thatcherite political folly of the time that suggested crime could be solved by throwing more resources at the police. It also contributed to the forging of a new consensus among senior officers about the structural limitations of policing in controlling crime – not an insignificant achievement given that the police had done much in the late 1970s and early 1980s to create unrealistic public expectations of policing, only to find themselves hoist with their own petard.

Nor is it impossible for jobbing criminology to ask acute or embarrassing questions of established political wisdom about crime. One can recall, for example, the now infamous internal Home Office (1984) research on 'short, sharp, shock' regimes at detention centres, which found strikingly high recidivism rates among those who had experienced what were then the centrepiece of the Conservative government's 'get tough' law and order policy. The research was buried and the experimental regimes expanded, only to be abandoned again a few years later. This notwithstanding, it is possible to argue that Home Office research provides an ongoing check on the more impulsive and reactionary tendencies of Conservative governments, and it is often consciously designed by its practitioners to do just that.

In many ways none of this should occasion great surprise. It is a product largely of the emotionally and politically charged character of criminology's subject matter. Crime – as well as being a blight on the quality of people's lives – is the carrier of a host of social meanings and metaphor (Sparks, 1992). It is a way of focusing, talking about and giving concrete form to, what would otherwise be disparate anxieties about the nature and direction of social change. And it grasps the popular imagination in affective rather than rational ways. As a result crime can – like perhaps no other social issue – serve as a vehicle for politicians (usually those of the right) wishing to generate political capital by promising a crackdown on the criminal Other (Hall *et al.*, 1978). Against this backdrop, any modulated, research-based voice pointing out

the effects of government policy, or unearthing information that unduly complicates simplistic political world views,
is likely to prove troublesome and unpopular. If governments use social science either as a mode of legitimation,
or merely to persuade the citizenry that 'something is being done', they can always find themselves having to confront, undermine or in some fashion sidestep the findings
of such research.[2]

A critique of jobbing criminology that views it as the poodle
of its paymasters would then – in the case of the Home
Office at least – be misconceived. However in terms of its
conception of the scope of the discipline and its understanding of how that discipline might relate to the public sphere,
jobbing criminology manifests a number of distinctive and
significant shortcomings. The most overarching of these
concerns the fact that jobbing criminology is institutionally
constrained to couch its criticisms in the language of technical evaluation, this being a precondition of its effectiveness.[3] It is required to take the ends of criminal justice policy
as given and limit its evaluative claims to the utilitarian realm
of means, something that effects some important 'closures'
around the study of crime and social regulation. Three of
these warrant discussion.

Jobbing criminology tends, first of all, to pursue a chroni-
cally limited range of explanatory avenues, structuring its
enquiries largely around the question 'what works?' This focus
– as some recent scientific realist critics of evaluation have
recently noted – tends to compartmentalise the problem at
hand and disconnect the programmes under investigation
from 'the underlying *mechanisms* that give rise to them and
the *contexts* which sustain them' (Pawson and Tilley, 1994,
p. 292, emphasis in original). As such, evaluation research
tends both to fail in its own terms (generating little that is
of use to policy makers) and leave unexamined the connections between crime control and questions of social structure.

Secondly, jobbing criminology tends to bracket off the
political dimensions of its subject matter. It remains inat-
tentive to the ways in which crime control is determined by
particular kinds of political project – one thinks, in the British
case, of the relationship between neighbourhood watch and
the official promotion of 'active citizenship' (Hurd, 1988).

And it is insufficiently alive to the ways in which crime control policy is always also embroiled in debates about the kind of society in which one wants to live. Rarely in the world of jobbing criminology does one find discussion of the relationship between crime control strategies and the good society, and on the occasions when does – as in the recent discourse on community crime prevention – one gets little sense that the values at stake are deeply contested.

Thirdly, jobbing criminology has no articulated ethical standpoint. Though it rests upon a whole set of unexplicated normative assumptions about the proper role of criminology (and in this sense is never purely technocratic), it posits ethics as beyond the reach of reasoned judgement, not really of concern to criminological research. As such it is prevented from explicitly raising and discussing questions about the ethics of criminal justice policy, and from considering the impact of that policy on different moral values. What is forgotten in the process is that crime control is not only about effectiveness but always also to do with social justice; and that 'success' in such policy can consequently be assessed in normative as well as instrumental terms.

Let us illustrate these matters with an example. The last decade or so has witnessed – in Britain as in other Western societies – a proliferation of 'situational crime prevention' initiatives. These have ranged from target-hardening and improved street lighting on the one hand, to community involvement schemes such as neighbourhood watch on the other. These schemes have been subject to a host of evaluations, and we consequently have to hand a bewildering array of information on their utility – their impact on crime rates and fear of crime, the extent of displacement and so on (Heal and Laycock, 1986; Bennett, 1990). These, of course, are important questions – but they are not the only questions. An adequate criminological understanding of these developments demands also that we address such matters as the actual and potential implications of contemporary crime prevention schemes for the character of urban life; the 'visions of order' they project and their role in cementing (sometimes literally) existent social divisions (cf. Davis, 1990, ch. 4). Rarely does any of this surface in what passes for 'evaluation' in jobbing criminology.

My complaint then is not so much with the substantive claims of research produced under jobbing conditions, many of which continue to enhance our understanding of crime and criminal justice. Nor do I deny that there is a place for the systematic evaluation of policy – even if one might wish of evaluation studies greater substantive and methodological ambition (Fischer, 1985; Pawson and Tilley, 1994). My concern is that the values of an applied, technocratic, policy-driven criminology do not come to dominate the discipline, determining what gets funded and researched and what does not. For its inability to raise questions of ethics and politics prevents jobbing criminology from mounting any sustained, principled critique of the existing order of things, no matter how undemocratic, unjust or oppressive they become. The more a jobbing conception of the discipline takes hold, the more it will be that some of the most fundamental and contested issues of social order in liberal democratic societies are reduced to questions of efficient management and administration.[4] And the more impoverished the democratic public sphere will be as a result.

OPPOSITIONAL DISCOURSES: ANTICRIMINOLOGY

Since the publication of *The New Criminology* in 1973, an applied, instrumental conception of the criminological enterprise has had to compete with a whole array of loosely connected radical standpoints. Over the last two decades a host of alternative perspectives have developed original and often challenging accounts of crime, deviance, moral censure and social regulation. These have ranged from the now established traditions of Marxism (Fine *et al.*, 1979), abolitionism (deHaan, 1990) and feminism (Morris and Gelsthorpe, 1990), to emergent ones such as peacemaking (Pepinsky and Quinney, 1988) and postmodernism (Young, 1995).

These approaches manifest a number of by no means reconcilable theoretical and political differences. The relationship between Marx and Foucault (Smart, 1983). A host of feminisms continue to ruminate over the possibility and desirability of a 'feminist criminology' (Carlen, 1992). And disputation concerning the relationship of 'criminology' to other fields of enquiry rumbles on (Nelken, 1994a). Yet for my purposes – the relationship of criminology to the public sphere – these various radical perspectives can usefully be considered together. For they share a principled refusal to be seduced by official crime control agendas, and a concerted attempt to formulate ways of seeing that transcend the received traditions of criminological enquiry.

The most significant aspect uniting these otherwise disparate positions is a problematic relationship to the discipline of 'criminology' itself (Cohen, 1988). For many radicals, criminology – with its 'endless repetitions', essentialist concepts, grim utilitarianism and intimate connections to power – is viewed as an intellectual and political straitjacket to be transcended. It is charged with resting unscientifically on a range of externally generated, commonsense notions (crime, punishment and so on); or else is deemed incompatible with some favoured political or intellectual project, such as Marxism (Hirst, 1975) or feminism (Smart, 1990). Two moves have followed: first, the reformulation of the discipline's object of enquiry around concepts such as 'ordering' (Shearing, 1990) or 'problematic situations' (Hulsman, 1986); and second, the collapsing of criminology into some other framework of enquiry – usually a variant of sociology (Pepinsky, 1986; Smart, 1990).[5]

There is further within anticriminology a marked tendency to be interested in 'crime' and 'crime control' only insofar as they can illuminate some other dimension of the social. Radical positions (the contested exception of left realism aside) have largely bypassed the question of crime causation and evinced little interest in thinking about crime in terms of its effects on people's everyday lives. Cases of this abound. *Policing the Crisis* (Hall *et al.*, 1978), for example, provides a cogent analysis of how 'mugging' was used as an ideological unifier during a time of social crisis, but has far less to say about the specificity of the issue. Michael King's (1991) analysis of crime prevention abandons entirely questions of instrumental success (which he takes to be unknowable) for an account of the visions of 'community' embedded in English and French schemes. And Pat Carlen (1994) similarly notes how much recent writing on prisons is more attentive to matters of race and gender than to the fact and experience of imprisonment itself.

A third key tenet of anticriminology is its principled refusal to 'advise, consult, recommend and make decisions' concerning crime control policy (Cohen, 1985, p. 238). Drawing a parallel with sociologists of religion, Cohen argues that it is not the role of criminologists to be 'true believers' promoting effective crime-reduction strategies. Rather the proper place of the criminologist is as an outsider and social critic, posing sceptical questions of the whole business of crime control – especially as practised in societies marked by deep structural divisions, such as those of class, gender, ethnicity, age and sexuality. This role necessitates not problem solving, but the problematisation of established, taken-for-granted and hitherto self-evident ways of doing things.

This studied reluctance to accept official interpretations of 'the crime problem' or travel along established paths of criminological enquiry has considerable virtues. It has also had a quite fundamental impact on both the scope of criminology and our understanding of crime and social regulation. It has opened up some significant new frameworks of enquiry – one thinks, for example, of the emergence of penality (Garland and Young, 1983); and transformed some existing domains of substantive investigation, such as crime and the mass media (Sparks, 1992). It has also brought criminological enquiry into often fruitful dialogue with a host of cognate disciplines. Above all the anticriminological positions that have emerged since 1973 have provided a forceful reminder that the subject matter of criminology cannot be reduced to the tinkerings of management science, and that crime and crime control are matters of political rather than just technical disputation. And they have consistently and quite properly emphasised that criminological enquiry cannot be pursued adequately without posing some fundamental questions about order, power, authority, legitimacy and social justice.

These anticriminological standpoints are not, however, without their attendant problems, many of which are germane to the question of the public sphere. I want therefore in the remainder of this section to consider briefly three such issues: (1) the neglect of normative theory, (2) the dangers of 'theoreticism', and (3) the predilection for critique over reconstruction. Let us deal with each in turn.

While radical criminological paradigms have properly

emphasised (in the face of an atheoretical policy science) the necessity for theory in criminology, the prevailing conception of theory has been circumscribed in some important and in many respects disabling ways. 'Theory' has been taken to mean either – following Merton (1968) – middle-range sociological explanations of aspects of crime and criminal justice, or else abstract reflection divorced from substantive research on the practices of social regulation (Fine *et al.*, 1979). What has been absent is any sustained attention to questions of normative (political) theory. Of course there have been exceptions (Braithwaite, 1989; deHaan, 1990; Hudson, 1993). But for the most part anticriminology has lacked an explicit ethics (something it rather curiously shares with jobbing criminology), and it has, as a consequence, been unable to articulate the normative position from which a critique of the present might proceed.

A good example of this can be found in recent Foucaultian-inspired analyses of penality (Foucault, 1977; Garland, 1985; Howe, 1994). This body of research has described in immense and valuable detail the penal techniques and strategies of power employed in the production of 'docile-bodies'. Such accounts clearly imply some kind of critical judgement. Repeated reference is made to the ways in which the production of docility involves 'subjugation' and 'normalisation', and power is frequently and approvingly described as being met by resistance. Yet little or no attention is devoted to expounding the normative basis upon which such judgement is made. We are left with implied, arbitrary critique, and accounts of modern power that are 'politically engaged and normatively neutral' (Fraser, 1989, p. 19).

There has of late been a further meaning of 'theory' at large within anticriminology; one that might be termed (borrowing from Bourdieu, 1990) 'theoretical theory', and that is most readily associated with a number of postmodern writers in the discipline (Smart, 1990). In some cases this tendency involves elaborating concepts as a necessary prelude to political engagement. Theoretical development here entails taking stock of the consequences for radical political practice of the 'crisis of representation' and the poststructuralist critique of essentialist concepts (such as 'women' or 'crime'). As Howe (1994, p. 216) puts it: 'poststructuralist feminists maintain that an interrogation of one's theoretical position and a refusal of subject-based identity politics are the preconditions of a radical practice'.

To her credit, Howe is very much alive to the political predicaments to which this position gives rise (even if her attempts to reconcile a theoretical critique of essentialism with political struggles around social justice for women seem tortuous). For others of a postmodern bent, however, these issues are simply sidestepped altogether. For example, in a recent contribution to a text on *The Futures of Criminology*, Young and Rush (1994) present us with a 'reading' of left realist constructions of the 'victim'. This is a curious piece of writing. Not only does it proffer what I believe to be a serious misreading of some small fragments of left realist text, but it makes no attempt to explicate its own standpoint – it has a kind a 'view from nowhere'. What is more, I fail to apprehend exactly what bearing this mode of theorising might have on any prevailing political problem; and I see precious few signs of the 'transcendent concern for justice' that the volume's editor detects in an emerging postmodern criminology (Nelken, 1994b, p. 17).

Interrogation of one's theoretical constructs, and reflection on the conditions of possibility of criminological discourse are, of course, both important exercises. It is also true that theory should not be written in order merely to reinforce the claims and outlook of particular political factions. But this does not mean that criminological theorising should have no bearing on political problems, especially when – as in radical and feminist work – such theory claims to be moved by a desire for social change. Here the dangers of 'theoretical theory' are readily apparent. A postmodern retreat to introspective conceptual specification runs the ever-present risk of confining radical practice to the academy, and turning 'theory' into a meaningless, disconnected and rather pretentious game stripped of practical intent. As Carlen (1992, p. 62) puts it: 'The non-stop self-conscious elaboration of theoretical "positions" unrelated to their possible analytic usefulness is a peculiarly sterile practice'.

This brings me, thirdly and more directly, to the question of the public sphere. Here anticriminology has since its inception evinced a predilection for critique over what one might call reconstruction. Analytically, this has been associated with a reluctance – for fear of buttressing an unjust criminal justice system, or suspicion of idle utopian speculation – to formulate positive social policy proposals or engage in thinking about alternative institutional designs (Mathiesen, 1974). This position undoubtedly has its merits. But it has also given rise within anticriminology to what can often appear as a rather frightened, defensive and politically disabling stance. In another context, John Dryzek has encapsulated well the limits of this position:

> Pure and indirect critique can of course be forces for change. But critique that intimates no feasible or attainable alternative fails in its practical task. For the defenders of the status quo, warts and all, can argue that really, 'there is no alternative'. And if there is no alternative, then ultimately there is no critique (Dryzek, 1990, p. 31).

Politically, a preoccupation with critique has generated among anticriminology forms of engagement confined to oppositional social movements, and something of a reluctance to engage with official and popular discourse about crime in the actually existing public sphere. These stances have a legitimate place in radical criminological politics, and in hostile political environments they are indeed tempting. But, as left realism has pointed out, and as some anticriminologists have themselves recognised (Cohen, 1990), this kind of oppositional politics has its attendant costs; not the least of which is the reinforcement it provides for the – arguably widespread – public belief that criminology (radical or otherwise) either has nothing to say about pressing social concerns, or else can only contribute to public discourse a 'rubbishing' of the ill-informed claims of others. At a moment, in Britain at least, when criminology is being almost entirely marginalised from the public conversation about crime and social order (one thinks, in particular, of its absence from the anxious debates about 'lawless Britain' that followed the murder of toddler James Bulger in 1993), such a stance risks abandoning political debate about crime and punishment to the conservative forces of 'law and order' and the technocrats of 'risk management'.

IN AND AGAINST CRIMINOLOGY: ARGUMENTS FOR UTOPIAN REALISM

I want in this final section to outline and defend a third possible mode of criminological engagement with the public sphere, one that I shall term – following and adapting Giddens (1990, 1994) – utopian realism. In so doing, it is no part of my project to contribute another 'brand-name' criminology (Carlen, this volume) to an already cluttered terrain – what follows is *not* a manifesto for 'utopian realist criminology'. Nor do I propose to leave behind entirely the traditions of jobbing and anticriminology, preferring instead to draw upon their strengths and circumvent their shortcomings. My aim is to develop an open, reflexive way of approaching questions of crime and social regulation, and of thinking about the relationship between criminological knowledge and official and popular discourse on crime.

A utopian realist criminological stance endeavours to connect issues of crime and social regulation with questions of ethics and politics, and enter the public conversation about crime equipped with an articulated, principled and future-oriented set of normative values and political objectives (the utopianism). But it also seeks to engage with the *realpolitik* of crime and criminal justice, and formulate (for example, crime reduction) proposals that have some immanent purchase on the world (the realism). This approach is one that seeks to be simultaneously 'in' and 'against' criminology; it aims to be policy-relevant, while setting out to challenge and shift the established boundaries of relevance. It recognises the tensions that exist between the practice of knowledge production and that of politics, and strives to keep such tensions alive (and fruitful) through a refusal to collapse one of its constituent poles into the other.

While this approach draws inspiration from social theory (principally Giddens, but see also Unger, 1987), elements of it can be discerned in contemporary criminological writings. Elliot Currie's (this volume, 1985, 1995) recent work and Braithwaite's (1989) advocacy of 'reintegrative shaming' share much with the kind of position I am advocating here, as does Stan Cohen's (this volume) concern to be 'pragmatic about short-term possibilities [and] genuinely utopian about constructing long-term alternatives'. Utopian realism also resonates closely with aspects of left realism. However the latter's explicit rejection of utopianism (Young and Matthews, 1992) and almost exclusive focus on policy-driven victim surveys and evaluation militates against complete identification. So too does left realism's apparent lack of theoretical ambition and its unhelpfully polarising 'for us or against us' attitude to the rest of the criminological world.

Utopian realism comprises three main tenets. It must, first of all, be *systematic*: concerned with the difficult, painstaking and tortuously slow business of constructing sociological explanation. Utopian realism insists that the development of systematic knowledge regarding, say, trends in social regulation, or the relationship between crime, poverty and marginalisation, must remain central to the criminological enterprise. This means criminologists taking what Elias (1985) calls 'the route via detachment'. They must stand aside from the immediate demands of the present so as to facilitate a knowledge of that present: knowledge that obtains its purchase on the world through 'its distance from received ideas and spontaneous convictions' (Bourdieu, 1993, p. viii).

In this respect criminology is likely – and quite properly so – to be unpopular: criminological 'good sense' is often only developed and maintained at the expense of political populism and immediate impact (Carlen, this volume). The criminological enterprise is concerned with making meaningful sense of social phenomena whose hold over the popular imagination is affective rather than rational, phenomena that often resist social explanation. Criminology must therefore expect its knowledge claims to meet with some resistance ('but how would you feel if . . .?') and be prepared to treat such antipathy as something that is itself in need of explanation.

Utopian realism demands, secondly, that criminology becomes explicitly and unashamedly *normative* in orientation. Political and popular discourse on crime revolves in the main around competing 'ought claims', and criminology cannot rest content with either cursory dismissal or even explanation of this fact. Rather it must be prepared to take normative theorising seriously, and be unafraid of trading in ethical terms (conservative politicians and pundits have no monopoly over moral discourse, whatever they may think).

This means recognising that all sociological explanation and all political projects proceed, if only implicity, from normative starting points – there is no presuppositionless 'view from nowhere' to be had. It also means developing a much closer dialogue between criminology and political theory than has existed hitherto. This is necessary both in order to develop a rigorous ethical language with which to frame matters of crime, policing and punishment; and in order to make good the idea that doing criminology always also entails reflection upon questions of order, justice, authority and legitimacy – thematics that have for too long been abandoned to jurisprudence and political philosophy, and divorced from substantive criminological research (Bottoms, 1987). A normative orientation demands further that utopian realism be prepared – in whatever field of enquiry it finds itself – to articulate ethically informed models of alternative institutional arrangements (Loader, 1994). And these alternative futures should be explicitly utopian in intent; not in the expectation that they will one day be realised, but in order that such models can become an 'activating presence' in prevailing political disputation (Bauman, 1976).

Finally, utopian realism must be *prudent*, a criminology with a practical intent. By this I mean that it applies itself to, and takes seriously, contemporary problems of crime, violence, insecurity and social order, and seeks openly to compete with official and popular discourse on such matters. In so doing, utopian realism must be sociologically sensitive to the 'institutionally immanent possibilities' (Giddens, 1990, p. 155) offered by liberal democratic societies, as well as remaining attentive to the risks and unintended consequences of all social action. And it must be ready to make sound and sober political judgements about how to act in concrete historical settings (on prudence thus conceived, see Dunn, 1990). Utopian realism might, in these respects, involve a good deal of jobbing criminology. It would, however, endeavour so far as is possible to undertake such jobs, not unreflexively and atheoretically, but in a sensitive, worldly and politically astute manner, one that never loses sight of the intimate connections between crime, politics and ethics.

Taken together, these considerations demand that we abandon once and for all an instrumental, technocratic conception of the criminological project. We must acknowledge instead that utopian realism is a 'critical theory without guarantees' (Giddens, 1990, p. 155), a 'post-foundational radicalism' (Crook, 1992); one that requires the adoption of a discursive approach to the relationship between criminology and the public sphere. This approach recognises that criminology has no choice but to set out and defend its interpretations of the world in the actually existing forums of public debate, in order to try to shift the mental and institutional boundaries of the present. In so doing, utopian realism endeavours – in whatever small way it can – to generate informed and inclusive public deliberation about questions of crime and social order, and to build the kind of democratic public sphere in which such contestation can take place. This in turn necessitates not more meta-elaboration of what utopian realism might or might not entail, but the development of criminological research and reflection guided by its tenets.

Notes

I am indebted to Willem de Haan and Richard Sparks for their comments on an earlier draft of this chapter.

1. In 1996 the Unit was reorganised and Home Office research is now undertaken under the umbrella of the Research and Statistics Directorate.
2. In any such ensuing conflict for recognition, government researchers and policy makers are distinctly disadvantaged. Not only do they lack a legitimate institutional platform from which to speak, but they can always find their research-based contentions undermined by politicians all too aware that crime and punishment grip the public imagination in affective ways. David Faulkner – until 1992 deputy secretary at the Home Office in charge of criminal justice policy – provides an interesting example of this when he bemoans the way in which the managerialist criminal justice compromise of the 1980s (represented by the Criminal Justice Act 1991 and the Woolf Report) was in 1993 swept aside by Home Secretary Michael Howard in the name of political expediency (Faulkner, 1993).
3. Though it is of course possible – as Bourdieu (1990) might say – for jobbing criminologists to become habituated to technocratic domain assumptions in ways that render then unable to frame other kinds of questions about their subject matter.

4. The discussions that sometimes take place in US criminology gatherings about *methods* of capital punishment provide a particularly sickening case in point.
5. This itself endlessly repetitious arguing over the status of criminology and the repeated attempts to dissolve it into something else, must rank as one of the more futile of intellectual conversations. Would anything of *any* substantive significance follow if one day the detractors triumphed and criminology was abolished? I suspect not, and I have never quite been able to fathom why these debates generate so much excitement. Doing criminology, as Ericson and Carriere (1994, p. 94) helpfully point out, also means doing many other things, whether they be sociology, political theory, cultural studies or whatever. We should therefore stop fretting about the criminology's scope and boundaries (and yearning for order within a more 'secure' home) and 'start celebrating its fragmentary character'. Long may criminology remain impure.

References

Bauman, Z. (1976) *Socialism: The Active Utopia* (London: Routledge & Kegan Paul).
Bennett, T. (1990) *Evaluating Neighbourhood Watch* (Aldershot: Gower).
Bennett, T. (1991) 'The Effectiveness of a Police-Initiated Fear-Reducing Strategy', *British Journal of Criminology*, vol. 31, no. 1, pp. 1–14.
Bottoms, A. (1987) 'Reflections of the Criminological Enterprise,' *Cambridge Law Journal*, vol. 46, no. 2, pp. 240–63.
Bourdieu, P. (1990) *The Logic of Practice* (Cambridge: Polity).
Bourdieu, P. (1993) *Sociology in Question* (London: Sage).
Braithwaite, J. (1989) *Crime, Shame and Reintegration* (Cambridge: Cambridge University Press).
Carlen, P. (1992) 'Criminal Women and Criminal Justice: the Limits to, and Potential of, Feminist and Left Realist Perspectives', in R. Matthews and J. Young (eds), *Issues in Realist Criminology* (London: Sage).
Carlen, P. (1994) 'Why Study Women's Imprisonment? Or Anyone Else's? An Indefinite Article', *British Journal of Criminology*, vol. 34, pp. 131–40 (special issue on 'Prisons in Context').
Clarke, R. (1980) '"Situational" Crime Prevention: Theory and Practice', *British Journal of Criminology*, vol. 20, no. 2, pp. 136–47.
Clarke, R. and D. Cornish (eds) (1980a) *Crime Control in Britain: A Review of Policy Research* (Albany: State University of New York Press).
Clarke, R. and D. Cornish (1980b) 'Editorial Introduction', in R. Clarke and D. Cornish (eds), *Crime Control in Britain: A Review of Policy Research* (Albany: State University of New York Press).
Clarke, R. and M. Hough (1980) *The Effectiveness of Policing* (London: HMSO).
Clarke, R. and M. Hough (1984) *Crime and Police Effectiveness* (London: HMSO).
Cohen, J. and A. Areto (1992) *Civil Society and Political Theory* (Cambridge, Mass: MIT Press).

Cohen, S. (1985) *Visions of Social Control* (Cambridge: Polity).
Cohen, S. (1988) *Against Criminology* (New Brunswick, NJ: Transaction).
Cohen, S. (1990) *Intellectual Scepticism and Political Commitment: The Case of Radical Criminology* (Stichting W.A. Bongerlezingen).
Crook, S. (1992) *Modernist Radicalism and its Aftermath* (London: Routledge).
Currie, E. (1985) *Confronting Crime: An American Challenge* (New York: Pantheon).
Currie, E. (1995) 'The End of Work: Public and Private Livelihood in Post-employment Capitalism', in S. Edgell, S. Walklate and G. Williams (eds), *Debating the Future of the Public Sphere* (Aldershot: Avebury).
Davis, M. (1990) *City of Quartz: Excavating the Future in Los Angeles* (London: Verso).
deHaan, W. (1990) *The Politics of Redress: Crime, Punishment and Penal Abolition* (London: Allen and Unwin).
Dryzek, J. (1990) *Discursive Democracy* (Cambridge: Cambridge University Press).
Dunn, J. (1990) *Interpreting Political Responsibility* (Cambridge: Polity).
Elias, N. (1985) *Involvement and Detachment* (Oxford: Oxford University Press).
Ericson, R. and K. Carriere (1994) 'The Fragmentation of Criminology', in D. Nelken (ed.), *The Futures of Criminology* (London: Sage).
Faulkner, D. (1993) 'All Flaws and Disorder', *The Guardian*, 11 November.
Fine, R., R. Kinsey, J. Lea, S. Picciotto and J. Young (eds) (1979) *Capitalism and the Rule of Law* (London: Hutchinson).
Fischer, F. (1985) 'Critical Evaluation and Public Policy: a Methodological Case Study', in J. Forester (ed.), *Critical Theory and Public Life* (Cambridge, Mass: MIT Press).
Foucault, M. (1979) *Discipline and Punish* (Harmondsworth: Penguin).
Fraser, N. (1989) *Unruly Practices: Power, Discourse and Gender in Contemporary Social Theory* (Cambridge: Polity).
Garland, D. (1985) *Punishment and Welfare: A History of Penal Strategies* (Aldershot: Gower).
Garland, D. (1994) 'Penal Modernism and Postmodernism', unpublished mimeo.
Garland, D. and P. Young (eds) (1983) *The Power to Punish* (London: Heinemann).
Giddens, A. (1990) *The Consequences of Modernity* (Cambridge: Polity).
Giddens, A. (1994) *Beyond Left and Right: The Future of Radical Politics* (Cambridge: Polity).
Habermas, J. (1974) 'The Public Sphere: An Encyclopedia Article', *New German Critique*, vol. 3 (Fall), pp. 49–55.
Habermas, J. (1989) *The Structural Transformation of the Public Sphere* (Cambridge: Polity).
Habermas, J. (1992) 'Further Reflections on the Public Sphere', in C. Calhoun (ed.), *Habermas and the Public Sphere* (Cambridge, Mass: MIT Press).
Hall, S., C. Critcher, T. Jefferson, J. Clarke and B. Roberts (1978) *Policing the Crisis* (London: Macmillan).
Heal, K. and G. Laycock (1986) (eds) *Situational Crime Prevention* (London: HMSO).

Hirst, P. (1975) 'Marx and Engels on Law, Crime and Morality', in I. Taylor, P. Walton and J. Young (eds), *Critical Criminology* (London: RKP).

Home Office (1984) *Tougher Regimes in Detention Centres* (London: HMSO).

Hope, T. and J. Foster (1992) 'Conflicting Forces: Changing the Dynamics of Crime and Community on a "Problem" Estate', *British Journal of Criminology*, vol. 32, no. 4, pp. 488–504.

Howe, A. (1994) *Punish and Critique: Towards a Feminist Analysis of Penality* (London: Routledge).

Hudson, B. (1993) *Penal Policy and Social Justice* (Basingstoke: Macmillan).

Hulsman, L. (1986) 'Critical Criminology and the Concept of Crime', *Contemporary Crisis*, vol. 10, pp. 63–80.

Hurd, D. (1988) 'Tamworth Manifesto', *London Review of Books*, 17 March.

King, M. (1991) 'The Political Construction of Crime Prevention', in K. Stenson and D. Cowell (eds), *The Politics of Crime Control* (London: Sage).

Layder, D. (1993) *New Strategies in Social Research* (Cambridge: Polity).

Loader, I. (1994) 'Democracy, Justice and the Limits of Policing: Rethinking Police Accountability', *Social and Legal Studies*, vol. 3, no. 4, pp. 521–44.

Loader, I. and R. Sparks (1993) 'Ask the Experts', *The Times Higher Education Supplement*, 16 April.

Mannheim, H. and L. Wilkins (1955) *Prediction Methods in Relation to Borstal Training* (London: HMSO).

Mathiesen, T. (1974) *The Politics of Abolition* (Oxford: Martin Robertson).

Merton, R. (1968) *Social Theory and Social Structure* (New York: Free Press).

Morris, A. and L. Gelsthorpe (eds) (1990) *Feminist Perspectives in Criminology* (Milton Keynes: Open University Press).

Nelken, D. (ed.) (1994a) *The Futures of Criminology* (London: Sage).

Nelken, D. (1994b) 'Reflexive Criminology?', in D. Nelken (ed.), *The Futures of Criminology* (London: Sage).

Outhwaite, W. (1987) *New Philosophies of Social Science: Realism, Hermeneutics and Critical Theory* (London: Macmillan).

Pawson, R. and N. Tilley (1994) 'What Works in Evaluation Research?', *British Journal of Criminology*, vol. 34, no. 3, pp. 291–306.

Pepinsky, H. (1986) 'A Sociology of Justice', *Annual Review of Sociology*, vol. 12, pp. 93–108.

Pepinsky, H. and R. Quinney (eds) (1988) *Criminology as Peacemaking* (Bloomington: Indiana University Press).

Petersilia, J. (1990) 'Policy Relevance and the Future of Criminology', *Criminology*, vol. 29, no. 1, pp. 1–14.

Radzinowicz, L. (1988) *The Cambridge Institute of Criminology: Its Background and Scope* (London: HMSO).

Shearing, C. (1990) 'Decriminalizing Criminology: Reflections on the Literal and Tropological Meaning of the Term', *Canadian Journal of Criminology*, April, pp. 169–78.

Smart, B. (1983) *Foucault, Marxism and Critique* (London: Routledge & Kegan Paul).

Smart, C. (1990) 'Feminist Approaches to Criminology or Postmodern

Women Meets Atavistic Man', in A. Morris and L. Gelsthorpe (eds), *Feminist Perspectives in Criminology* (Milton Keynes: Open University Press).

Sparks, R. (1992) *Television and the Drama of Crime* (Milton Keynes: Open University Press).

Taylor, I., P. Walton and J. Young (1973) *The New Criminology* (London: Routledge & Kegan Paul).

Unger, R.M. (1987) *False Necessity: Anti-Necessitarian Social Theory in the Service of Radical Democracy* (Cambridge: Cambridge University Press).

Young, A. (1996) *Imagining Crime* (London: Sage).

Young, A. and P. Rush (1994) 'The Law of Victimage in Urbane Realism', in D. Nelken (ed.) *The Futures of Criminology* (London: Sage).

Young, J. (1986) 'The Failure of Criminology', in J. Young and R Matthews (eds), *Confronting Crime* (London: Sage).

Young, J. and R. Matthews (1992) 'Questioning Left Realism', in R. Matthews and J. Young (eds), *Issues in Realist Criminology* (London: Sage).

11 Moral Panics and the New Right: Single Mothers and Feckless Fathers – Is This Really the Key to the Crime Problem?

Jayne Mooney

> We have to recognise where crime begins. I don't mean that we should listen to the woolly-headed theories that society is at fault. . . . Of course not – we can leave that message to others. We must do more to teach children the difference between right and wrong. . . . It must start at home. And it must also be taught in our schools. . . . Above all, it must be taught by example (Michael Howard, July 1993, House of Commons).

In 1991 the number of crimes known to the police in England and Wales passed the five million mark; the previous ten years saw the largest numerical increase in crime in any decade since records began. Crime has been rising steadily since 1955 but there is something special about the last ten years: for the increase is over double that of any previous decade (Lea and Young, 1993). It would not take much mental agility to note that such a qualitative leap was coincident with the recession and with a period of Conservative government intent on creating a market society. But such mental dexterity has found its exercise elsewhere. For it is not in the market place but in the family that commentators of both the right and the left have chosen to find the causes of such a phenomenal increase in crime.

The trigger for the intense debate about crime in the

213

recent period has been the moral panic over the James Bulger killing. This has taken a classic form: an event, sometimes innocuous, sometimes – as in this case – utterly horrific yet extremely rare, triggers off widespread public anxieties only tangentially related or disproportionate to the original event yet rationally based because crime really is a problem, followed by a prolonged discussion in the mass media where politicians, journalists and religious leaders create a morality play and a modern demonology with only a tenuous relationship to the real problem of growing crime (Hall *et al.*, 1978; Cohen, 1972; Young, 1971). The initial event could have occurred at any period of time, there have been four convicted child murderers since 1950, but in order to set off the moral panic the existence of growing public concern about crime had to be in place. Contrast the Mary Bell case in September 1968, when two girls aged 11 and 13 were accused of strangling two young boys for what the Court referred to as 'solely the pleasure and excitement afforded by killing'. Intense media attention occurred, of course, but there was no moral panic. No one to my knowledge talked about the decline of family values, no one talked about the problem of a mother's relationship with female children, no one talked about a crisis in femininity, no one used the atypical to generalise about society as a whole. Yet today the twin folk devils of single mother and absent father are conjured up to explain the problem of youth crime.

From the arrest to the trial of the two boys concerned the press lingered on every failing of their parents' lives, especially their mothers – 'Anne Thompson could hold her drink and no one ever saw her staggering home' as the *Guardian* put it – television crews were despatched to Liverpool to interview youngsters about their moral sensibilities and the public were regaled with the image of an underclass, staffed by single mothers, fuelled by welfare, surrounded by feckless fathers and generating delinquency that is a threat to us all.

Central to this debate was the response of the government. In the furore about youth crime that followed the arrest, Peter Lilley made it clear that the crime wave was unrelated to the recession whilst the Prime Minister John Major categorically stated that to seek the causes of crime in the wider society was futile; instead we should look at problems in the family, and rather surprisingly be blamed 'socialism'. By this he meant the welfare state.

The single mother represents a crystallisation of all the hostility to the welfare state that the Conservative Party holds. She is welfare dependent, she is a scrounger of the state, she has chosen to be pregnant in order to gain priority in council housing over the respectable married poor. It is remarkable that in order to avoid putting any blame on the economy, the ills of society have become focused on its most deprived members. As Ruth Ashton, general secretary of the Royal College of Midwives put it, 'Are we really expected to believe young women get pregnant so that they can get £38.40 a week income support and spend their time in dreary bed-and-breakfast accommodation, as so many do?'

But what are the actual links between single mothers and the crimes of their offspring? Despite all the assertions, there is not a single substantial scrap of evidence. As a leaked draft cabinet paper put it, 'It does not appear . . . that the fact of lone parenthood is itself associated with crime . . . but the children of lone parents are more likely to be brought up in poor families, and this appears to be associated with low educational attainment and delinquency'. For it is poor single parents that we are, of course, talking about and there is no doubt that poverty is related to crime. But to go too far down this path would be to admit that it was the structure of society that was at fault, and perhaps even government policies.

But let us look at the other side of the coin. To what extent are single mothers, themselves victims of the massive inequalities in wealth in our society, also victims of crime? My recent study in North London shows that they experience an extraordinarily high rate of violence from their ex-partners (Table 11.1).

Thus one in five single mothers have experienced violence in the last year, twice the rate that women as a whole experience. It goes without saying that the return of such partners would scarcely reduce the rate of crime nor provide exemplary role models for their children.

In the midst of a moral panic the rhetoric of the critics of the system often mirrors the rhetoric of its defenders.

Table 11.1   Violence against women from partners and ex-partners,

	Percentages
All women	10.0
Married women	11.1
Single mothers	18.8
Single mothers living in council housing	19.2

Source: The North London Domestic Violence Survey; $n = 571$ (Mooney, 1993a).

Just so at this conjuncture: for a whole host of radical writers have begun to describe the crime crisis as a problem of masculinity. For Angela Phillips (1993) it is the loss of male role models, for Anna Coote (1993) it is a crisis in male identity as a consequence of the loss of jobs, for Bea Campbell 'the great *unspoken* in the crime angst of the Eighties and Nineties is that it is a phenomena of masculinity' (Campbell, 1993, p. 211). Hardly unspoken, the masculine nature of crime has been commonplace in criminology and the focus of many of its major debates (Parsons, 1954; Cohen, 1955). Indeed, since the mid 1970s feminist criminologists have criticised the emphasis placed on masculinity and male offending, which certainly in the past resulted in a lack of material on female criminality (Naffine, 1987). It is, however, one thing to explore the reasons why males are universally more criminal than females, it is another to explain the *rise* in crime by a crisis in masculinity. One of the most striking facts of male–female differences is that the ratio of male to female offenders has remained almost constant throughout the general rise in offending: 85 per cent of offenders were male in 1971, 82 per cent in 1979 and 83 per cent in 1989. Surely it is the wider economic forces that propel both men and women to crime that explain the change over time rather than the gender differences that serve to maintain this remarkable constancy?

But here the challenge comes from the self-styled 'ethical socialists': Norman Dennis and George Erdos in their books *Families Without Fatherhood* (Dennis and Erdos, 1993) and *Rising Crime and the Dismembered Family* (Dennis, 1993), written under the auspices of the right-wing think tank, The Institute of Economic Affairs. Unemployment and recession cannot, they maintain, be an explanation of the rise in crime because the crime rate in the 1930s was, by present standards, comparatively low. It is the disintegrating family that has sapped the strength of the working-class community, encouraged the irresponsibility of men, engendered the increase in single mothers and generated the rise in crime whilst, incidentally, being encouraged from the wings by feminists and 'new criminologists'.

Correlation is, of course, not causation; and in this case it is coincidence. The most profound change that has occurred in the social structure since the war is the massive entry of women into the labour force – although concentrated in low-pay, low-status occupations. If this has been accompanied by a rise in the level of aspirations and possibilities for women and a greater ability to deal with marriages or partnerships that do not work out, all to the good. Our brief details of the levels of domestic violence against all women, married or single, scarcely suggests that there is no justified reason for the breakup of many families, even when it is economically disadvantageous. In this light, the clause in the Child Support Act compelling women to name the father of their children, backed by the penalty of losing 20 per cent of their benefit, would undoubtedly, as Ian Sparks, director of the Children's Society, put it, expose lone parents and their children 'to greater risk of violence, harassment and poverty'.

But this greater flexibility in family relationships scarcely explains the rise in crime. The five million crimes reported to the police every year, with another ten million or more unreported, can not conceivably be blamed on that fraction of single mothers who are on income support and have adolescent sons. What we have to look to is what has changed since the 1930s and has transformed the impact of unemployment and recession.

What is different about today? Firstly, a whole generation has grown up in the aftermath of Keynsianism and no longer view their predicament as a product of natural laws of the market but rather as a fault of government policy. Unemployment and poverty are not seen as a natural disaster but as injustice. Secondly, the very inculcation of market values sows disillusionment. The meritocratic values of John Major's 'classless society' palpably contradict the experiences of young people. The exhortation to go out and find your worth in the market scarcely works when there is no market in which to place yourself. And the values of individualism and every person for her- or himself are not a stone's throw away from the values of the teenage offender who does just that and helps himself to things in his neighbour's flat, or the joy-rider who clambers into the Porsche parked just around the corner in the gentrified street near his sink estate. Finally, an ever-present mass media parades the glittering prizes of the 'haves' daily in front of the 'have-nots'. It is the 'positive' images of consumer success not the escapist fantasies of video nasties that engender relative deprivation amongst the poor. And behind all this is a blatant procession of all the world 'on the make', the corrupt business man with a light sentence, the insider dealer making a fortune overnight, the politician lying through his or her teeth. Inequality is no longer concealed, it is flaunted; mendacity no longer whispers in secret places, it is blatant in the highest reaches of public life. And the social script that the market provides does not hold society together, it actually encourages it to fall apart.

To return to basics is to examine how market society dominates and disrupts the basis of people's lives. It is not to confuse causes with consequences: it is not to transform the poor, who deserve more, into an underclass of undeserving poor. For so many of the factors that are said to lead to delinquency are a product of the predicament of poverty, not a wilful fecklessness that generates the predicament. It is not the sins of the past that lead to underachievement in school, but children in their teens realising that the future holds little in store for them. As one of the kids on a North London Estate put it:

> Although, I'm not saying I commit crimes, if you just look at some of the flash cars that can be seen in this area, you can see why crimes are committed. People need money, clothes and food. They are bored and even if there are things to do, you still need money and the dole does not

pay that much. When we leave school we can only look forward to unemployment. . . . Sometimes, it is exciting to commit crimes, especially when you get away with it (Mooney, 1993b, p. 45).

Academic achievement is of little significance if schooling has no purchase on the future. And how do you hold the children in school once the penny has dropped that there is little to gain from staying in school? To say that under-achievement and truancy correlate with delinquency, and that all are closely associated with family poverty is correct, but to imply a line of causality from family to school performance to delinquency is a nonsense. For it is the poverty engendered by the wider society that dominates both the past and the future of the kids involved. To mistake the symptoms for the causes is to reverse causality and to draw attention away from the severe social problems we face.

The Conservative government – first elected in 1979 on a law and order programme aimed at tackling crime – has, far from ameliorating the problem, faced a rise in crime unprecedented in our history. Its response to this failure has been to attempt to distance government policy from the crime wave. This act of disengagement has given rise to an extraordinary ducking and diving, where once every few years a new theory is evoked not so much to explain crime but to explain it away. Thus religious decline, public feck-lessness in taking care of property, crime programmes on television, the overfastidiousness of the criminal justice system in protecting the accused, the leniency of sentencing and prisons, and so on have all been evoked. The Church, the police, the media and the public have all been blamed, anything but the government itself.

All of this would be of mere academic interest if such torturous evasions of responsibility did not give rise to similarly uninformed policies. Cutting back on the meagre support for single mothers, creating special units for young offenders, toughening up the already wretched conditions within prisons, all of these measures will provide solace for those looking for scapegoats. They will not make one iota of difference to the crime rate.

References

The author would like to thank Thalia Nettleton for her help with the source material for this chapter.

Campbell, B. (1993) *Goliath* (London: Methuen).

Cohen, A. (1955) *Delinquent Boys: The Culture of the Gang* (Glencoe, Ill.: Free Press).

Cohen, S. (1972) *Folk Devils and Moral Panics* (London: Paladin).

Coote, A. (1993) 'Boys who can't grow up', *Independent on Sunday*, 14 November.

Dennis, N. (1993) *Rising Crime and the Dismembered Family* (London: IEA).

Dennis, N. and G. Edros (1993) *Families without Fatherhood*, 2nd edn (London: IEA).

Hall, S., C. Critcher, T. Jefferson, J. Clarke and B. Roberts (1978) *Policing the Crisis* (London: Macmillan).

Lea, J. and J. Young (1993) *What is to be Done About Law and Order?*, 2nd edn (London: Pluto).

Mooney, J. (1993a) *The Hidden Figure: Domestic Violence in North London* (Middlesex University: Centre for Criminology).

Mooney, J. (1993b) *The Miranda Crime and Community Survey* (Middlesex University: Centre for Criminology).

Naffine, N. (1987) *Female Crime* (Sydney: Allen & Unwin).

Parsons, T. (1954) *Essays in Sociological Theory*, rev. edn (Glencoe, Ill.: Free Press).

Phillips, A. (1993) *The Trouble with Boys* (London: Pandora).

Young, J. (1971) *The Drugtakers* (London: Paladin).

12 Reassessing Competing Paradigms in Criminological Theory
John Muncie

INTRODUCTION

The publication of *The New Criminology* in 1973 remains a watershed in theoretical criminology. Not only is it widely assumed to have launched an oppositional, radical and critical paradigm onto the criminological landscape, but it also opened up questions regarding the role that criminologists could be expected to play in the broader realm of political activism. In its own words, a criminology not committed to 'the abolition of inequalities of wealth and power' was bound to be ultimately reducible to the interests of the economically and politically powerful in society (Taylor *et al.*, 1973).

The New Criminology in essence was a fierce attack on traditional positivist and correctionalist criminology, arguing that this tradition acted as little more than an academic justification for existing discriminatory practices in the penal and criminal justice systems. Rather than refocusing on the illusive search for the causes of crime, this new endeavour sought to illustrate how crime was politically and economically constructed through the capacity and ability of state institutions within the political economy of advanced capitalism, to define and confer criminality on others. The study of crime could no longer be compartmentalised in a world of pathologies, deviances and otherness, but was to be used as a means through which the exploitative machinations of the state could be exposed. In short *The New Criminology* opened the door through which valuable insights could be made, not into crime *per se*, but into how society works, how social order is maintained and how such 'order' could be subjected to political challenge.

This chapter charts the fate of *The New Criminology* from the 1970s to the mid 1990s. Firstly it focuses on its role in spawning, by design, a critical and oppositional paradigm. Secondly it explores how this paradigm was subjected to its own opposition and how, by default, it became implicated in constructing the current fragmented and diverse nature of the discipline.

POSITIVISM, MARXISM AND RADICAL CRIMINOLOGIES

The New Criminology clearly constituted a radical break with existing criminological discourse. In brief, an oppositional stance was created whereby positivism's concerns for clinical and statistical proof of crime causation, its commitment to scientific determinism and the subsequent denial of authenticity and meaning to deviance, were challenged and inverted. To be accurate, such questioning of established knowledges began with the advent of the new deviancy and labelling paradigms of the 1960s. Whereas positivism asserted that crime and deviancy were a non-rational, determinate product of undersocialisation, and thus devoid of any human choice, creativity of meaning, new deviancy theory was more concerned to grant authenticity to deviant actions by recording the motives and meanings of the deviant actors themselves. It reached this position by radically shifting the object of criminological inquiry away from trying to isolate the presumed factors propelling a pathological few to break the rules of an assumed social consensus, to an analysis that rested on a conflict or pluralist concept of society in which deviance was ubiquitous and where 'crime' was constructed through the partial and pernicious practices of social reaction and social control. The adages that 'there can be no crime without law' and that 'social control leads to deviance' effectively turned the time-honoured premises of positivism on their head.

By the early 1970s this critical paradigm had effectively placed a number of counter-propositions on the criminological agenda. Criminology was reconstituted as part of a more comprehensive sociology of deviance. Questions of social control, rather than crime causation, became the central matters of concern. A determination to 'appreciate' deviance in terms of its subjective meaning to particular actors took precedence over the spurious scientism of assertions that criminal behaviour was determined by a mix of innate, genetic or physiological incapacities (born bad) or instances of ineffective child rearing, family pathology and social disorganisation (made bad). By focusing on the process of criminalisation, rather than crime *per se*, whole new areas of interest were opened up, in which definitional, rather than behavioural issues were to become central.

It is in this context that we can account for the emergence of *The New Criminology*. Despite its title, its originality lay not so much in innovation, but in the attempt to synthesise several different traditions. The concern to respect the authenticity of the diverse and unique worlds of everyday life continued a tradition established by the Chicago school and the social interactionists of the 1930s; whilst dimensions of power and social control were appropriated from the social reaction theory of the 1960s. *The New Criminology*, however, attempted to further this antipositivist radicalisation by taking the world of personal meanings and social reaction back into a critique of the history and structure of society. This was achieved through locating definitions of crime and modes of control in the precise context of the social relationships and institutional arrangements emanating from particular modes of economic production. Clearly what this work was advocating was that the key subject of criminology was not crime and deviance as behaviours, but a critical understanding of the social order and the power to criminalise. When the task of criminology was defined as one of creating a society 'in which the facts of human diversity are not subject to the power to criminalise' (I. Taylor *et al.*, 1973, p. 282) it was clear that criminology was being transformed from a science of social control and into a struggle for social justice. Much of this, of course, relied on a reworking of the theoretical premises of Marxism. In the edited work *Critical Criminology* (Taylor *et al.*, 1975) the authors of *The New Criminology* followed Marx's supposition that laws perpetuate a particular mode of economic production by arguing that bourgeois law not only acts to preserve existing unequal forms of property ownership, but also punishes the property offences of the poor whilst maintaining stable conditions for the exploitation of their labour.

Such critical readings of the deviance–crime–law–control–state nexus were indeed influential in awakening interest in analysis of the role of the law in capitalism, in particular spawning a whole series of revisionist histories of the relationship between what counted as crime, class position and systems of punishment. The central questions that were addressed came to include the following. To what extent did the law function exclusively in the interests of a dominant class? Were the interests of a ruling class and the state always in accord? Were crime and deviance adequately conceived as antistate and thus as nascent forms of class struggle?

Such complexities could certainly not be addressed by an uncritical adoption of the economic and material determinism of Marxism. Indeed a major stumbling block in the synthesis of Marxism, interactionism and social reaction was that the concerns of criminology – radical or otherwise – and its continuing observance of the concept of 'crime' do not represent a theoretical field of study within Marxism. Rather 'crime' is an ideological category generated by state agencies officials and intellectuals. O'Malley (1987, p. 77) put it rather succinctly by arguing that 'were crime to constitute a concept within Marxism, we would face the ridiculous prospect of having the subject of Marxist analysis being determined by state administrative pragmatism'. For many Marxist scholars the entire new criminological agenda was thwarted because there could be no such thing as a Marxist criminology. Retaining the concept of 'crime' as the key referent inevitably laid open the possibility of collusion with state-sponsored and engineered definitions of undesirable behaviours and actions.

CONSERVATIVE AND REALIST CRIMINOLOGIES

Ironically these 'internal' disputes of the mid 1970s were taking place against the political backdrop of a resurgence of a popular law and order politics. *The New Criminology*'s break with traditional concepts of 'crime' and 'the criminal' was reversed by the new right's rise to power and its ready identification of hooligans, terrorists, feminists, militants, homosexuals and atheists as the criminal 'enemies within'. On both sides of the Atlantic the rhetoric of the radical right revived a neoclassical paradigm of criminality as voluntaristic – a course of action willingly chosen by pathological individuals with no self-control and with a potential for universal contamination and moral degeneracy. Seizing on the perennially growing official statistics of crime, the extension of police powers, the erosion of civil liberties and the expansion of imprisonment to unprecedented levels was a dominant feature at least up to the mid 1980s (Scraton, 1987). New 'realist' criminologists of the right similarly departed from the mores of positivism by simply claiming that crime emanates from wicked, evil people who are insufficiently deterred from their actions by a criminal justice system deemed to be chaotic and ineffective (Wilson, 1974). By capitalising on the fear of crime, the notion of endemic criminality was instilled in communities and enabled the public/political debate to be dominated by images of violent crime, lawlessness and a declining morality. In the hallowed days of law and order in the authoritarian 1970s and 1980s, retribution and vindictive punishment were continually reproduced as offering the only way out. In the 1990s such responses remain, but the discourse of the New Right has been significantly tempered by an apparent failure of its policies to prevent escalating crime rates and, within the developing ethos of cost-effectiveness in all public services, a paring down of direct state responsibility and (reluctant?) acknowledgement that all that can be done is a more efficient, effective and economic management of crime and criminal justice (McLaughlin and Muncie, 1993).

This new right capturing of almost the whole terrain of law and order politics in the late 1970s also forced sections of the left to rethink their position and to move closer to the mainstream in a pragmatic attempt to counter some of its more reactionary policies. In particular the self-styled left realists gradually disassociated themselves from the 'new' and 'critical' criminologies and attempted to impact on centrist Labour Party politics in an effort to find a new realism for new times. Left realism however initiated its programme through a virulent attack on the left, rather than the right. Labelling its former bedfellows as idealist, it argued that the left had traditionally either romanticised or underestimated the nature and impact of crime and largely 'speaks to itself' through its lack of engagement with the day-to-day issues of crime control and social policy (Young, 1986). With empirical support from a series of victim surveys carried out in the 1980s, left realism claimed that the problem of crime was indeed growing and that in particular property and street crimes were real issues that needed to be addressed, rather than deconstructed as powerful vehicles in the new right's ideology. In short it claimed that people's fear of crime was rational and a reflection of inner city social reality. As crime was considered endemic it needed to be effectively policed; its causes needed to be once more established and theorised; and a social justice programme initiated to make the police more accountable to marginal working-class communities (Lea and Young, 1984).

Clearly this agenda marked a distinct break from the critical agenda of *The New Criminology*. It invoked many themes (such as crime causation) that are grounded in positivist criminology, with, for example, street crime being portrayed as caused by relative deprivation and anomie. It initially advocated not so much an attack on the continuing structures of poverty and unemployment, but more the need for responsive policing. It appeared to accept new right and media-driven definitions of what constitutes serious crime and consequently ignored, or underplayed, the equally if not more damaging consequences of business fraud, corporate crime, white-collar crime and crimes of the powerful. Analyses of the relationship between offenders and victims were thus restricted to street crime and failed to capture the harm caused, for example, by workplace injury, occupation-related diseases and environmental pollution. In total left realism tended to work within the parameters of a social democratic reformism rather than socialist politics. Within criminological theory it owed more allegiance to Merton than to Marx.

Of course the question remains whether this more pragmatic and policy-oriented approach is a suitable vehicle to take radical criminology through the 1990s and into the twenty-first century. One of the gravest dangers is that this entry into the new right's agenda will mean that debates on crime and justice will continue to circulate around the limited sets of concerns of law and order rhetoric. Can we expect that rhetoric to be broken down unless countered by a specifically oppositional and critical discourse? Equally the dismissal of critical criminology as idealist provides a ready alliance with the right in its denigration of the critical left. In particular it ignores the influential interventionist role that critical criminologists *have* played since the 1970s in developing a politics of support for such marginalised groups as black youths, prisoners, Gypsies and women, as well as establishing independent inquiries into aspects of state authoritarianism and monitoring police practices. The critical left have thus been far from silent on interventionist or policy-making issues. We must also consider the political efficacy of left realism's alignment with Labour or democratic party politics. How far can we expect it to impact on an area of policy that traditionally is clouded in reactionary tendencies?

Equally, the left has not ignored the task of developing new theoretical frameworks in which to further our understanding of processes of criminalisation. The Marxist heritage has not so much been abandoned but refined and developed. Marxist theory is now drawn upon not to deliver a sealed doctrine, but a set of provisional hypotheses or a frame of conceptual resources/deposits. For example it is now more common to find a more complex set of analyses, following Foucault, that move away from the restricted chain of criminological references – state, law, crime, criminals – to examine other arenas of social life such as medicine, welfare and sexuality, and how these networks of power are implicated in the process of control but are governed more by the knowledge and concepts that they themselves utilise than by the definite intentions of a dominant class or an oppressive state. The state may then be implicated in the matrix of power-knowledge, but is only one part of it. This direction has in turn opened up work on a variety of semi-autonomous realms, such as communities, organisations and families, in which notions of policing and control are present but over which the state has little direct influence. It is in these areas that interest in the often neglected processes of informal networks of order *and* resistance in society has been awakened.

In this context the issue of idealism versus realism becomes something of a red herring. It is surely just as 'real' to unearth the complexities of processes of criminalisation, resistance and control, as it is to be bound to public perceptions and victim surveys. The urge to 'become real' has taken many guises. Whilst the mainstream of criminology increasingly appears to be simply involved in a technocratic exercise to evaluate the effectiveness of criminal justice procedures, the critical paradigm continues to expose the discriminatory powers and outcomes of such procedures and at least retains a space in which alternative visions of criminal justice can be created. Such visions are vital in helping us to rethink social conditions in terms of them not simply being made bearable (as in left realism or social democratic reformism) but transformed into a vehicle for emancipation.

FEMINIST PERSPECTIVES

A key failing of *The New Criminology* was the total absence of any discussion or critical analysis of gender relations and women and crime. Left realism claimed to address some of these issues by placing the previously hidden dimension of domestic violence high on its agenda. The primary concern was thus with women as victims, and this indeed has been one of its major contributions to feminist politics and criminology. However realist calls for minimal policing and a decreased power for the state do not appear to speak directly to demands for safer communities for women. Theoretically, too, realism is restricted in its analysis of women's fear of crime. Never is it made explicit that the problem is one of men, masculinity and patriarchal social relations. The goal of calling into question the more discriminatory and oppressive forms of the regulation of women is thus best pursued outside realism's limited foci. Indeed some have argued that it can only be pursued outside criminology *per se.*

The development of feminist inroads into the male bastion of criminology initially took the form of a comprehensive critique of the discipline firstly for its neglect to study women's involvement in crime and criminal justice, and secondly for its total distortion of women's experiences as essentially biologically driven. Since the mid 1970s a burgeoning literature has revealed that women's crimes are committed in different circumstances to men's and that the response to women's lawbreaking is constituted within sexist assumptions of femininity that have only further added to women's oppression. This body of knowledge has now successfully demonstrated how criminology is driven by male assumptions and interests, how criminalised women are seen as doubly deviant and how assumptions about appropriate gender roles mean that women are judged less on the nature of their offence and more on their 'deviant' lifestyle. As a result some feminists have drawn more on sociologies of gender than any pre-existing criminological knowledge, to explore their subject matter with the important message for male criminology that much can be learnt about processes of control and criminalisation by focusing on these structures and processes that create conformity, rather than sole concern with those that produce deviance and criminality (Heidensohn, 1985). Others have gone further by questioning whether the focus on female lawbreakers is a proper concern for feminism, and indeed whether a feminist criminology is theoretically possible or even politically desirable. Latterly this relationship between feminism and criminology has been further problematised by a deconstructionist or postmodern position that claims the unifiers of 'women', 'crime' and 'criminology' trap any investigation in essentialist categories that obstruct the production of new knowledge (Smart, 1990). It is perhaps no surprise that deconstructionism has gathered most strength in some feminist perspectives, for it is they that were first alerted to the need for criminology to deconstruct itself if it was to break out of its gender essentialism.

MODERNISM AND POSTMODERNISM

The tendency of the social sciences, particularly within some strands of sociology, to deconstruct and question their own internal logic is slowly permeating the discipline of criminology. As some feminist critics have warned, the discipline will remain forever self-justifying unless it is prepared to adopt a more critical stance towards the key referents of 'crime' and 'deviance' (Cain, 1990). The process of deconstruction also has its origins in the work of Foucault and his location of the discourse of criminology in the combination of knowledge and power that evolved with the modern state and the emergence of the social sciences. Foucault's acknowledgement of a multiplicity of power relations and the diverse settings in which they are activated, in particular, questioned the ability of any total theory (for example Marxism) to answer all questions. For example to talk of such totalities as 'the state', 'working class' and 'capitalism' was for Foucault misleading because 'power is everywhere'. This disenchantment with *a priori* claims to truth, as represented in stark form by the way criminology has progressed through paradigmatic construction and competition, is substantiated in the postmodern insistence that we should break with the rational and totalising (modernist) intellectual movements of the past. Whilst modernism (of which criminology is but one element) attempts to ratify knowledge so that the social can be made an ordered totality, postmodernism views the world as replete with an unlimited number of models of order, each generated by relatively autonomous and localised sets of practices. Modernism strives for universality, postmodernism accepts relativity as a lasting feature of the world. In essence postmodernism challenges the logic of 'referential finalities' as the foundation of Western society. Rather it stresses the diversity and particularity of social life and accordingly asserts that no one theoretical paradigm is capable of making sense of the social world (Hunt, 1991).

Within criminology this approach implies an abandonment of the concept of crime and its replacement by a new language to designate objects of censure and codes of conduct. As Henry and Milovanovic (1991, p. 308) argue, the discipline of criminology will continue to be a part of the 'crime problem' unless criminologists and practitioners alike 'deconstruct crime as a separate entity, cease recording it, stop dramatising it, withdraw energy from it' and construct an alternative discourse that 'allows for change, chance, being, becoming, multiplicity and irony'. Exactly what form such a project might take remains unclear, but the challenge of postmodernism is one that urges us continually to address the limitations of accepted knowledges, to avoid dogmatism and to recognise the existence of a wide variety of subjectivities.

Unsurprisingly, this rejection of totalising theory and of any criteria for establishing truth and meaning, can be viewed as intellectually liberating or as intrinsically nihilistic and conservative. For example it is far from clear how total rejection of established concepts might further our understanding of the relationship between criminalisation, poverty, inequality, racism, sexual violence and repressive state practices. The failure to replace existing concepts with alternative visions can easily leave postmodernism (and us) stranded and depoliticised.

Cohen and Taylor (1992, p. 27) attempt to tread a careful path through paradigmatic essentialism and postmodern relativism by stating: 'we may agree with the postmodernist objection to the colonisation of everyone's life world by a single all-encompassing meta-narrative, but this surely does not mean that we can dispense with the imaginative purchase upon the world provided by utopian visions'. The place of critical criminology within these new discourses and theoretical dilemmas, however, remains somewhat ambivalent. In attempting to overcome the mantle of 'determinism' it has moved to a more complex understanding of the social order, yet must now strive to avoid the open-ended vagaries of deconstructionist discourse. The task remains of constructing a framework that is capable of locating discrete and specific instances of criminalisation within a general theory of the social order.

For a criminology to remain critical and ensure that theoretical production and political practice act in tandem, it must go back and rediscover some of the basic premises of the new criminology, but then adapt these to the changing contexts of the 1980s and 1990s. In particular it must reassert the centrality of primary determining contexts: incorporating those of race and neocolonialism, gender and patriarchy, and the neototalitarian tendencies of the modern state, into the previously established context of class and the structural relations of production (Scraton and Chadwick, 1991). This theoretical grounding would then enable the formulation of a policy agenda based on a principled idealism that works to expose processes of criminalisation, conformity and control, and subsequently identifies and empowers those groups that are subject to the worst excesses of state regulation (Carlen, 1990).

In the current political climate its strength lies in providing an essential antidote to conservative and social democratic (realist) discourses. In particular an ability continually to problematise the notion of crime (as a process, not an act) allows critical criminology to move beyond the limited foci of the so-called radical realists and their apparent return to the formal terrain of traditional criminology. By questioning what actually constitutes 'crime', critical criminology is able to reveal how and why the concept is regularly drawn upon within the discourse of law and order. Situating 'crime' within debates about law and order thus enable analyses of the state and state power to be once more at centre stage, and allows visions of radical alternatives to criminal justice to come to the fore. And this would seem vital if we are not to be left with levels of analyses that stop at public perceptions, subjective experiences and ideological discourse. The role of critical criminology is to ensure that these perceptions, experiences and discourses are placed within the context of the structural relations of patriarchal capitalism. These relations may not determine our behaviour in a direct and unproblematic way, but they do set the parameters and boundaries in which social relations are experienced. And it is exactly these boundaries that continually need to be questioned and challenged.

In 1974 Currie scathingly attacked *The New Criminology* for not taking us far enough into a world 'beyond criminology' itself. Subsequently the journey into 'the beyond' has opened up uneasy dialogues with Marxism, feminism, poststructuralism and postmodernism. Some of these journeys have been abandoned for the secure haven of the pre-1973 world. Others have ended in dead ends, largely because the *raison d'être* of criminology ultimately lies in the presumption of 'crime' itself. But the concept of crime will forever remain problematic: its existence dependent on legal sanction, which in turn is grounded in particular sets of economic and political relations. Competing criminological paradigms may offer alternative readings of this reality, but the biggest obstacle to the generation of future knowledge may be the restricted discourse of criminology itself.

Note

An earlier version of this chapter was published as 'Seizing the High Ground: Reflections on Critical Criminology', *Socio-Legal Bulletin*, no. 6 (1992) (NCSLS La Trobe University, Australia).

References

Cain, M. (1990) 'Towards Transgression: New Directions In Feminist Criminology', *International Journal of the Sociology of Law*, vol. 18, no. 1.
Carlen, P. (1990) 'Women, Crime, Feminism and Realism', *Social Justice*, Winter.
Cohen, S. and L. Taylor (1992) *Escape Attempts*, 2nd edn (London: Routledge).
Currie, E. (1974) 'Beyond Criminology: Review of the New Criminology', *Issues in Criminology*, vol. 9, no. 1.
Heidensohn, F. (1985) *Women and Crime* (London: Macmillan).
Henry, S. and D. Milovanovic (1991) 'Constitutive Criminology: The maturation of Critical Theory', *Criminology*, vol. 29, no. 2.
Hulsman, L. (1986) 'Critical Criminology and the Concept of Crime', *Contemporary Crises*, vol. 10.
Hunt, A. (1991) 'Postmodernism and Critical Criminology', in B. Maclean and D. Milovanovic (eds), *New Directions in Critical Criminology* (Vancouver: Collective Press).
Lea, J. and J. Young (1984) *What is to be Done about Law and Order?* (Harmondsworth: Penguin).
Matthews, R. and J. Young (eds) (1992) *Issues in Realist Criminology* (London: Sage).
McLaughlin, E. and J. Muncie (1993) 'The Silent Revolution: Market Based Criminal Justice in England', *Socio-Legal Bulletin*, no. 9.
O'Malley, P. (1987) 'Marxist theory and Marxist Criminology', *Crime and Social Justice*, vol. 29.
Scraton, P. (ed.) (1987) *Law, Order and the Authoritarian State* (Milton Keynes: Open University Press).
Scraton, P. and K. Chadwick (1991) 'The Theoretical and Political Priorities of Critical Ciminology', in K. Stenson and D. Cowell (eds), *The Politics of Crime Control* (London: Sage).
Smart, C. (1990) 'Feminist Approaches To Criminology Or Postmodern Woman Meets Atavistic Man', in L. Gelsthorpe and A. Morris (eds), *Feminist Perspectives in Criminology* (Milton Keynes: Open University Press).
Taylor, I., P. Walton and J. Young (1973) *The New Criminology* (London: Routledge).
Taylor, I., P. Walton and J. Young (eds) (1975) *Critical Criminology* (London: Routledge).
Wilson, J.Q. (1974) *Thinking About Crime* (New York: Vintage).
Young, J. (1986) 'The Future of Criminology: The Need for a Radical Realism', in R. Matthews and J. Young (eds), *Confronting Crime* (London: Sage).

13 Free Markets and the Costs of Crime: An Audit of England and Wales

Ian Taylor

Elliott Currie, one of the foremost critics of conservative penal policies in the United States, warned a British audience of the continuing rapid acceleration of crime rates that were to be expected in this country, particularly if government attitudes and policies did not change with respect to the 'freeing of market forces' (Currie, this volume). The United States was itself a laboratory, he argued, in which there could be identified a series of unmitigated disasters that would follow, in respect of rising poverty and homelessness, increases in preventable diseases, 'galloping' inner-city drug use and rapid increases in crimes of violence and crimes against property, if the forces of the free market being unleashed in Britain were not quickly harnessed in the social interest. Whilst a 'market economy' may be the most efficient known instrument for organising the allocation of goods and services in a modern society, what *was* at issue were the consequences of allowing 'the pursuit of private gain' *per se* to become 'the organizing principle for all areas of social life' (ibid.). In the last years of the Bush administration the United States was being transformed into what Currie has termed 'a market society', where 'all other principles of social or institutional organization become eroded or subordinated to the overarching one of private gain' (ibid.).

The warnings were there for Britain to see. Let me recapitulate the five distinct ways in which the advance of 'market society' promoted crime in the United States:

1. 'Market society' was promoting crime by producing a sig-

234

nificant increase in inequality, in the process generating quite destructive concentrations of pronounced economic deprivation.

2. 'Market society' was eroding the capacity of local communities to provide support for people on an informal basis, through municipal and civic provision. The subversion of local civic provision was one key element in the inability of local communities to provide for the socialisation and supervision of their young people, now hanging around suburban parking lots or downtown street corners threatening trouble and raising local fears and anxieties.

3. In terms of effects on the labour market and on childcare provision, the advance of 'market society' was a key element in the stresses and strains being imposed on 'the family unit'. The widely reported problems of family fragmentation, including the rapid emergence of the single-parent family as a 'social problem', were clearly connected to the impact that the unleashing of market forces was having on traditional patterns of life of lower-class Americans and established ethnic communities.

4. The advance of the 'market society' in the United States (for example in the pressure to privatise social services in different American cities) was resulting in the withdrawal of any kind of public or state provision for those who had lost jobs as a result of the advance of market forces.

5. 'Market society' in the United States was in the process of institutionalising what Currie calls a 'culture of Darwinian competition' for status and resources, in particular by its constant encouragement of a level of consumption that the market economy was incapable of providing for all citizens, at least through legitimate channels.

These propositions, linking 'market society' to the pressure and strains that find expression in rapidly increasing crime, were not thought by him to be an exhaustive list of 'the social effects' of 'market society' (see this volume). Nor is he arguing that all problems in contemporary societies could simply and straightforwardly be attributed to the 'freeing of market forces' – or what is sometimes called 'the rolling back of the welfare state'. The major qualifying observation

that had to be added to Currie's argument in the early 1990s
is the understanding, now shared by economists of nearly
all persuasions, that there *has* been a fundamental and irre-
versible collapse, both in North America and Europe, of
what used to be called the 'mass manufacturing economy',
with its massive employment potential. This has now either
been shifted into low-labour-cost economies, or alternatively
has simply been superseded by high-technology or service–
industrial employment, involving far less job certainty and
requiring different skills than those on offer from the male
industrial working class.

Currie's position on the twin processes of 'marketisation'
and global economic transformation, shared by this author,
clearly distinguishes between a governmental approach to
the new economic order, which recognises the need for a
national strategy of modernisation and change, and also takes
responsibility for it in terms of retraining the workforce,
underwriting the development of research and development
and providing a basic level of public infrastructure in terms
of transport, schooling, housing and so on, and in terms of
an alternative approach that throws *all* these matters to 'the
market'. The United States – certainly under Reagan and
Bush – was engaged in the latter strategy of off-loading all
these problems onto the market, and so were the British
governments of Thatcher and Major.

THE JOB CRISIS

The most fundamental effect of the freeing of market forces
in Britain has been the unrelenting rise in real joblessness.
Representation of the 'true unemployment' picture has become a matter of political contention, after a series of 29
changes to the official definitions and continuing arguments
over the government's desire to exclude from the unemployment statistics young children on 'job training schemes'
of various descriptions. In 1989, according to these government definitions, unemployment in Britain was down by 7.1
per cent of the labour force (as against 12.4 per cent in
1983), although it rose again to 10.9 per cent (3.06 million
people) in January 1993, before falling back by October to

9.9 per cent (2.8 million) (Department of Employment, 1993). Most close observers remain convinced that these figures significantly underestimated the 'true' rate of unemployment in Britain. In 1992 the unofficial Unemployment Unit recommended that recognised OECD criteria and other survey data be combined for this purpose and calculated that the real figure for unemployment in Britain in September 1992 was in the order of *four million* people, or 13–14 per cent of the labour force.

It is worth remembering that the total unemployment figure in Britain in 1979 (1 271 000 people) amounted to only 2.4 per cent of the 'economically active' labour force (Office of Population Census and Surveys, 1982). This loss of paid employment – enormous though it was in terms of national figures – was even more catastrophic in some areas than others, most notably in areas that were dependent on heavy manufacturing industry. In industrial South Yorkshire, for example, more than half of the 80 000 people employed directly in the steel and metal trades were declared redundant in the first three years of the 1980s (Goodwin, 1993, p. 150). The official data on national and regional unemployment do not tell us, however, how many young people, and increasingly young adults, have *never* had the dignity of work within the official economy and now never expect to do so. Throughout 1993 over one million people in Britain were defined as 'long-term' unemployed under the definition of looking for work for over a year, and other surveys indicate that some 467 000 people had been unemployed for more than two years; 217 000 for three years or more, 135 000 for four years or more and 99 000 for over five years (Department of Employment, 1993). These figures do not, of course, include workers who have been finally discouraged from looking for work.

One key aspect of the job crisis in older industrial societies such as Britain arises from the unrelenting attack on public sector employment and also from the state investment in private industry that has characterised government policy since 1979. In fact the particularly high level of unemployment in Britain arises from the Conservative government's ideological disdain for public provision. It is also important to recognise the distinctive effect of the demise of mass manufacturing in all the older industrial societies, with uneven patterns now occurring from year to year (not least because of decision taken by multinational corporations to shift their investments elsewhere). Some 1.5 million jobs were lost in the European Union as a whole in 1992–3, and 19.1 million people were registered unemployed across the twelve member states (11.3 per cent of the labour force). Even in Germany, which only twenty years ago was in the midst of an 'economic miracle', unemployment was thought likely to reach 10 per cent in 1994 (*The European*, 2–5 September 1993).

Our interest here must be in the relationship between the continuing rate of joblessness, the highly patterned impact this has had on industrial working-class neighbourhoods, and the massively destructive effects that this joblessness clearly has had on the self-respect of individuals and communities.

Throughout the 1980s, at least in Britain, a key governmental refrain identified unemployment as a temporary problem, which would in principle be resolved either through individual initiative ('on yer bike'), the cumulative effects of enterprise activity in general (through a kind of 'trickle-down' effect of new jobs created through such enterprise) or the long-awaited 'end to the recession' (the 'green shoots of recovery'). As the faltering 'recovery' of 1993–4 gathered strength, however (more weakly in Britain than in North America), fears were ever more widely expressed that such recovery as there was might not be sufficient to create any serious new employment. According to the latest economic wisdom in Britain, a 3 per cent growth rate would create very few extra jobs at all; and economists and social commentators in the United States, where the recovery is stronger, are starting to speak of a new phenomenon for our times of 'jobless growth' – referring to the capacity of certain high-tech and service industries to create and satisfy demand without significant additions to their labour forces.

STATE BENEFITS AND 'SOCIAL SECURITY'

Robert Reich (1987, 1991), secretary for labour in President Clinton's administration, spent the late 1980s arguing that these fundamental changes in the character of the labour market, and in global economic activity, confronted governments with a moral as well as a strategic challenge. Either they could be 'activist' governments, attempting to lead a population through the rapid social and economic changes of the time, or – irresponsibly in his view – they could let their electors, the citizens, fend for themselves in the market, blaming them for any 'market failures' or for disruptions in social order itself.

In practice, however, the 1980s and 1990s have witnessed spokespeople for free market policies and free market governments in North America and in Europe inventing a vast range of social scapegoats (from 'lager louts' and 'welfare scroungers' to 'single mothers') and also targeting the cultural and personal failings of people outside the 'enterprise culture' ('state dependency'), as essential elements in their accounts of disorder, poverty and economic failure. All such accounts have in common, of course, their exoneration of the operation of the free market forces themselves. Robert Reich's plea that governments in the 1990s should spend some time protecting and leading their citizens through times of massive change and turmoil, rather than blaming the people for their failings, seem at present to have fallen on deaf ears.

In Britain there is a continuing attack on a wide variety of the state benefits provided to different needy segments of the population, from disability benefit and housing benefit through to legal aid entitlement, which curiously has not yet been connected up in the public mind to the sense of anxiety and fear that are so widely reported for all citizens in their use of public streets and public facilities.[1] It is intriguing, for our argument here, to note the coincidence, with very little time lag, between the government's withdrawal of income support eligibility for 16–18 year olds in 1988 to a sudden acceleration in the number of criminal offences committed by that age group.[2]

All the available evidence about the reality of life in many parts of Britain suggests that the withdrawal of state benefits across a range of areas, far from creating the conditions for a new entrepreneurialism, is instead generating considerable physical and psychological dis-ease and anxiety amongst individuals and a level of pessimism or despair across whole communities or neighbourhoods on a level unknown since before the Second World War. We have become accustomed to read in our newspapers about the return of diseases and illness that were previously associated with the squalor, overcrowding and poverty of the 'dosshouses' of the 1930s or the 'rookeries' of Victorian Britain. There are now 3800 cases of scabies every year in Britain, the rate of decline in the occurrence of TB has slowed and there is some fear amongst specialists that we may be about to witness a return of the polio strains that are beyond the immune systems of one third of the population (*Independent on Sunday*, 21 March 1993). Suicide rates are significantly up, particularly amongst young men, and the pressures on the health service branches that deal with physical or psychological problems resulting from the stresses of joblessness and deprivation are rapidly rising.

HOMELESSNESS IN MARKET SOCIETIES

Another everyday feature of life in free market societies is homelessness. The truth about homelessness in this free market society is most visible in the amount of public begging that now takes place, routinely and on a daily basis, on the streets of our major cities – though it also finds expression in the popularity amongst some young people, the new age travellers, of taking to the rural roads following recognition of the lack of accommodation for them in our cities. The fact of homelessness and the struggle for shelter is also a matter of considerable conflict, of course, in inner city lodging houses and on our public housing estates, in the demeaning and desperate struggle for space and shelter that takes place amongst runaways, deinstitutionalised mental patients, youngsters in trouble with the law, 'problem families', new immigrant groups sponsored by local authorities, and many other desperately marginalised and impoverished groups. The accepted measure of 'homelessness' in Britain, which is a crude underestimate, is the number of homeless people offered accommodation by local authorities. In 1991, 160 100 households were offered such accommodation (from the limited stock available to local authorities), in contrast with the 28 400 households who were rehoused in this way in 1979.[3] But Shelter – the national campaign for homeless people – estimates that there are now nearly two million homeless people in Britain. It is important for us to register the point that 'living rough' is not only a certain cause of ill-health, and indeed early death (the average life expectancy of the homeless in one survey is 49), but also that the homeless are disproportionately likely to be victims of street crime, including violence and even murder.[4]

POVERTY AND THE UNDERCLASS

All political and academic commentary on Britain agrees that the country is embarked on a voyage of ever increasing social inequality. The debate is supposedly about whether this renewal of inequality might have beneficial consequences (in respect of enterprise and quality of life for 'the winners') or whether it might eventually produce a social disaster. One recognised measure of inequality is the distribution of 'national income' by households:

Table 13.1   Income distribution by household
(in quintile groups of individuals)

	Bottom fifth	Next fifth	Middle fifth	Next fifth	Top fifth
1979	9.6	14.1	18.1	23.1	35.3
1988–89	6.9	12.0	17.0	22.9	41.1

Source: Social Trends, vol. 23 (1993), Table 5.17.

Figures such as these illustrate the increasing amount of national income that is now being appropriated by the top 20 per cent of the population in Britain – 41 per cent in 1988–89 compared with 35 per cent a decade earlier – and also, of course, the declining proportion of national income accruing the bottom 20 per cent (down to only 6.9 per cent in 1988–89 compared with nearly 10 per cent just ten years earlier). The figures also emphasise the fundamental reversal that has occurred *vis-à-vis* the logic of the Keynesian mixed economy and welfare state of the earlier postwar period (a steady if unremarkable shift in the direction of some equality of financial and other provision).[5]

What they do not do, however, is show the actual level of *lived poverty* that is emerging among the newly residualised underclasses, on either an absolute or relative basis, or how these new emerging underclasses are actually able to live.[6] One of the most vulnerable groups amongst the new poor, the under-25s, are currently entitled (1993) to a benefit of £44.45 per week, but in December 1993 the government announced that the new 'Jobseeker's Allowance', designed to replace unemployment benefit in 1996, would cut entitlement by 20 per cent to a maximum of £36.15. The espoused intention of this move was 'to price young people into work', but evidence of this being the actual outcome is slight indeed.

A mass of survey work and interview research with young people on existing levels of benefit suggests that a much more likely consequence will be to encourage more and more young people into crime (what free market economists might call 'the rational choice'), especially in areas where the alternative or illegitimate economies around the drug trade offer a much greater return for one's labour. There are now entire estates on the fringes of many cities where the *only* significant economic activity in the neighbourhood is the drug trade.

One important aspect about this new poverty, of course, is that it has emerged in the aftermath of political and cultural rhetoric about affluence and the 'leisure society', and in a context in which everyday consumption is everywhere assumed to be a defining feature of social existence as well as a key resource in the construction of identity. But this ascendancy of a 'society of consumption' coincides with many years of government endeavour to drive down the level of state benefit paid to the unemployed or the otherwise 'economically inactive', and some three or four years of sustained manipulation by governments of entitlement to state benefits to force a significant number of unemployed people into work on miserably low levels of pay.

It may be that adults and young children can sustain a life of considerable and unremitting material deprivation and poverty for some years, though it must surely involve a sense of resignation and a loss of self-worth: in 1993 some 1.5 million families (including 2 970 000 children) were living on income support in Britain, compared with only 923 000 children in receipt of supplementary benefit in 1979 (White, 1994). Levels of poverty like this may be morally unforgivable in an 'advanced society' but they are not necessarily socially explosive. Absolute poverty may grind a person down without necessarily causing angry resistance or recruiting the sufferers into a life of crime.[7] Where the government's drive against state benefits is really hitting home in the 1990s is among the 16–25 year olds, who are assumed in government rhetoric to be living in the parental home and to have fewer living expenses than adults over 25. But it is precisely this generation of young people who are most heavily involved with the culture of individual and group consumption – on which, ironically enough, the whole enterprise culture of the 1990s so heavily depends.

Evidence suggests that, taken together, the material poverty and the relative social deprivation involved in being youthful and on state benefit are socially explosive. Some kind of disposable income is absolutely essential to a meaningful existence as an adolescent in the society of consumption, but it is also clear that the systematic and continuing exclusion of young people from challenging and useful education, as well as from the amenities of a civilised existence that are routinely available to young people in other advanced societies (sophisticated leisure facilities, travel) may place a vital limitation on the horizons and imagination of British youth. There is no question that the limited horizons of education for youth in Britain have contributed in a major way to the shallow jingoism and sexism of young British working-class males, and there is no escaping the crime that has been engaged in by young working-class males, particularly in areas of high long-term unemployment.[8] Empirically speaking, it seems clear that the escalation of burglary, car theft and street crime coincided with the removal of state benefits from young people in the social security changes of 1988, but from a cultural point of view it is important to understand that this 'riot of crime' has been engaged in by young people whose limited aspirations in life have been unchallenged and unaided by a system of education and socialisation of working-class men that is traceable to the early years of the nineteenth century.

THE TROUBLED CONDITION OF THE BRITISH HOUSEHOLD

The twists and turns of government rhetoric around 'law and order' leading up to the infamous Blackpool conference and the 'back to basics' speeches of September 1993, resulted in the identification of the 'single mother' as the newest 'folk devil' – on whom could be laid various sins of commission that 'explained' the continuing problems of crime and delinquency in British streets (See Mooney, this volume). It was always the most tortured and misogynist of arguments, borrowed, in its most recent form, from the work of Charles Murray, sworn enemy of the welfare state and policy advisor to President Reagan.[9] The argument, at its most essential, was that young women in Britain were intentionally getting pregnant in order to 'jump the queue' for council housing. Once they had been provided with such public housing, these inadequate (and loose-moralled) young women were proving, more often than not, to be poor mothers; and, given the absence of fathers as alternative role models, the consequence was the production of cohorts of literally 'uncivilised' boys and young men, beyond the control of their mothers and the rest of civil society.[10] In Britain the political thrust for these arguments seems to have been informed in no small measure by a quite unmistakable increase in lone motherhood in this country throughout the 1980s, far in excess of other European member states, with the significant extra burden this was imposing on the Exchequer (in respect of the cost of various state benefits, other than just public housing provision alone). In 1991 there were 236 000 births outside marriage in Britain (30 per cent of all live births), compared with only 91 000 in 1981 (12.5 per cent); and the 'welfare bill' for the 1.3 million one-parent families (and the 2.1 billion children living in them) was put at £6 billion compared with £2.4 billion 10 years earlier (Braid, 1993).

The official debate about single parenthood in Britain in the early 1990s has been fantastically coded in ideological terms. The problem identified by government spokesmen, and then by Normae Dennis and George Erdos in their extraordinary little polemic about *Families without Fatherhood*, focused on families headed by lone, unmarried women as being inherently problematic and dysfunctional.[11] These families lacked the stability and guidance – the 'reality principle' – that can only be provided by a father, which Dennis and Erdos believe to have been a widespread feature of parenting by working-class fathers in northern England throughout the first half of this century. It is certainly possible to accept some of the commonsense argument that has been developed by government spokespeople and echoed by Dennis and Erdos (that is, that a child does well when both parents in a nuclear family arrangement provide consistent affection and attention), but it does not follow that all forms of nuclear family (such as the mining families that Dennis described in *Coal is Our Life* (1956)) are very good at it; and by extension that *only* nuclear families, of the kind neither government spokesmen nor Dennis and Erdos could conceivably now reinvent (working-class families existing on a single 'family wage') can provide such consistent and reliable support to children. Nor does it follow that single parenthood – meaning, for this government and Dennis and Erdos, single mothers – is the one key variable to explain crime in the 1990s – more powerfully, indeed, than unemployment itself.[12]

Current governmental rhetoric about crime and the family is the extraordinary limited vision and the perverse kind of causal accounting that is displayed with respect to the quite fundamental structural changes that are taking place in what used to be called modern, mass-manufacturing society, and the deep consequences these changes are undoubtedly having on private lives, families and households.

It is not only that there is high and long-term unemployment on a scale comparable, in some senses, with the 1930s. It is also that the context in the 1990s is absolutely dominated by ideological pressures and assumptions of 'competitive and possessive individualism'; that everyday life is highly privatised and built around the immediate and fleeting

pleasures of individual consumption; that the idea of neighbourhood life in most of our cities is extremely fragile and
there is a crushing sense of loneliness and isolation in most
people's lives. When problems of living do arise, there is an
almost total absence of publicly provided community support. Where intact nuclear families do exist, depending on
the position of these families in the housing and labour
market, they are either poor or, in two-career families, 'overaccelerated' and exhausted. *These* are the given, dominant
and influential features of 'market society', and the rise of
the single-parent family is one of many potentially disruptive *consequences* of these changes in the domestic sphere.
So also, it must be said, are a range of other human problems arising out of the pressures on private households in
'market societies': child care professionals in Britain now
routinely speak of a 'parenting crisis' that expresses itself
in rising numbers of reported cases of child abuse (44 000
on the register in 1990), in about 98 000 children running
away from home every year; in 10 000 telephone calls a day
to Childline, in rising rates of teenage suicide, depression
and anorexia and in steep rises of drug abuse, especially
among 17–20 year olds and among girls. A high proportion
of adults in Britain's prisons (some 57 per cent in one study)
have indeed spent some time 'in care' (Phillips, 1993).

It requires a particularly narrow – misogynist or specifically fiscal purpose – to single out the single mother as being
either the secret and significant cause of all these problems
or, indeed, as being the most serious issue for public
discussion.

MAKING SENSE OF CRIME IN MARKET SOCIETY

Currie's predictions as to what might happen in terms of
escalating lawlessness in this country in the absence of any
challenge to the logics of government policies *vis-à-vis* the
wholesale embrace of 'free market society' have been sub-
stantially confirmed (Table 13.2).

There can be no mistaking the continuing acceleration
of the overall number of crimes being reported to the police, and the increasing prevalence per head of population

Table 13.2   Recorded crime per 100 000 population, England and Wales, 1977–91[13]

	Total (per 1000 offences)	Rate (per 100 000)
1977	2636.5	5368
1978	2561.5	5215
1979	2536.7	5139
1980	2688.2	5459
1981	2963.8	5971
1982	3264.2	6577
1983	3247.0	6546
1984	3499.1	7047
1985	3611.9	7258
1986	3847.4	7707
1987	3892.2	7773
1988	3715.8	7396
1989	3870.7	7681
1990	4543.6	8986
1991	5276.2	10 403

Source: *Criminal Statistics, England and Wales*, Cmnd 2134 (London: HMSO, 1991), Table 2.2.

in England and Wales, especially since the late 1980s. There is little doubt, in fact, that England and Wales experienced one of the fastest rates of increase in reported crime of any late industrial society during this period; we want to suggest that the *speed of this increase in crime*, along with all the widely reported increases in popular fear and anxiety with respect to personal safety and the security of one's home, is itself a measure of the *extremely rapid subversion* of the welfare state and the whole Keynesian postwar settlement under the attack of Thatcherism and the 'free market society'. What has been affirmed – after the fact – is the importance of that welfare state – in its provision of a minimal level of personal security ('from the cradle to the grave'), on the one hand, and 'full-employment' Keynesian economic policies on the other – in providing a reasonable sense of order in the everyday lives of the majority of the population. In countries where national, governmental responses to the 'crisis of mass manufacturing' and the emergence of a new global economic order have not involved the wholesale demolition of postwar welfare provision (the Scandinavian and Benelux

248   *Free Markets and the Costs of Crime*

Table 13.3   The increase in property crime, England and Wales, 1979–91

	Burglary	Theft/handling of stolen goods	Robberies
1979 (number)	549 100	1 416 100	12 500
1991 (number)	1 219 500	2 761 100	45 300
Increase (%)	122	95	262

Source: *Criminal Statistics, England and Wales* (London: HMSO, 1991).

countries and France, Germany and Canada) there is currently no debilitating national crime problem, at least in the specific form that exists in England and Wales. By far the largest increases in reported crime in England and Wales have been in property crime – that area of activity in which young people in particular, and other unemployed people, try to supplement whatever state benefits they are accorded with goods and commodities 'their money' would never allow them to buy, or alternatively to the monies they can realise through the resale of such stolen property (Table 13.3).

Figures of this kind must surely be seen, at least in part, as evidence of the real difficulties that are now confronting people (especially the young and the unemployed) in England at the end of the twentieth century (in a 'free market society' that has increasingly been transformed into what Joseph Schumpeter called a 'workforce state') in their attempt to obtain the basic level of income or material security that was taken for granted by earlier generations. There is no escaping the massive impact of this new poverty on the young and the unemployed, and no obvious reason for denying that this poverty is one major element in the rapid increase in property crime in England, especially burglary. Nor, it must be emphasised, is there any obvious reason why this will not continue for many years to come.

As we recognised earlier, conservative critics such as Dennis, Erdos and others have always responded to declarations of this kind, especially in their unqualified form, by pointing out that the poor do not always steal. Their familiar refrain is that in the 1920s and 1930s the high rates of unemployment (of male 'breadwinners') did not result in anything like the rates of crime currently being reported for Eng-

Table 13.4 Car crime, England and Wales, 1979–92

	Thefts of motor vehicles	Thefts from motor vehicles	Total
1979	309 245	278 349	587 594
1991	572 196	931 287	1 503 483

Source: Labour Party, *Putting the Brakes on Car Crime* (December 1992).

land and Wales. But, again as we suggested earlier, in the 1920s and 1930s the United Kingdom as a whole was a well-established industrial society, with the bulk of the population earning its living from the profits of mass manufacturing and a 'grand compromise' of power between capital and labour more or less universally accepted as a fact of life. Workers as a whole derived some sense of compensation for their lack of material wealth from the sociability and neighbourliness of the 'working-class community'. In the 1990s, in contrast, if not actually a victim of a corrupt 'casino capitalism', Britain is a society in thrall to a particularly radical experiment in social reorganisation, in which very little care or concern is evident for those who lose out from such a reorganisation, and in which a culture of possessive individualism is inescapable. Television programmes and magazines (for example *Hello!* magazine, the quintessential product of our time) seem obsessed by the lifestyles of individuals who have been successful in business or the media; great interest is shown in the material goods that have been acquired by the successful (from items of clothing to cars) and in the various pleasures of personal consumption in which they indulge. In contrast to the nineteenth century, the heyday of Victorian capitalism, the successful businesspeople of the 1990s seem to feel no pressure to make any display of social concern or charitable endeavour. The image is of individual self-indulgence, as a reward for one's business success or clever market initiative. It is surely no surprise, in such a social climate, that two of the other areas of the increase in reported crime in England and Wales in the late 1980s and early 1990s are 'car crime' on the one hand and drug-related crime on the other.

Car crime (Table 13.4) and drug-related crime evince public anxiety for perfectly understandable, commensense reasons.

Car theft can involve a disabling loss of mobility for whole households and families (which may include elderly relatives or children who need access to family transport), and in this country insurance companies do not generally, provide replacement vehicles under warranty. Car theft also provokes popular anxiety with respect to the real danger presented by the 'joy-riding' activities of young car thieves, especially in heavily populated urban areas. Warranted or otherwise, drug crime evokes a fear of addicts desperately searching for money for the next 'fix' and stoping at nothing to get it.[14] The reason for most recent fear, of course, is that the escalating drug trade in the inner cities is causing a major problem with respect to armed robberies and the use of firearms generally.[15]

Car crime and drug crime have another feature in common: they involve the possession and ownership – however momentarily – of a consumer product (a car) or a sensation (individual consumer pleasure or the instantaneous high), which have become ever more valorised in English 'market society' in the mid 1990s. Car ownership is no longer, if it ever was, simply a matter of having access to a means of transport other than a train or bus: it is unambiguously an item that, through its make or model, speaks loudly of the status of its owner. Equally unambiguously it is a powerful symbol of personal style and, particularly, sexuality. Particular models of car are encoded in television advertising as providing a measure of the owner's elective identity, most usually an exiting participant of the enterprise culture what is ahead of the mass of society. The Peugeot 405, we were informed in a television advertisement in 1993, in which the car speeds through a sugar cane field and sets it ablaze as it passes, 'takes your breath away'. The attractions of the drug 'high' – either as an escape from a humdrum or despairing life of unemployment or as a radical accentuation of the seductive pleasures of a life of continual and varied consumption, are a surprising contrast. But in both instances the pleasure of drug use is a pleasure that is *understood and shared* by the successful practitioner of life in the market society and the inner-city crack cocaine user.[16] In principle there are no limitation in 'free market theory' to the exercise of consumer choice or free will ('only the market decides'),

for example with respect to the types of harm that might
be involved in such choices, either for those making the
choices or for others; and this truth has presented Conservative and Republican governments in free market societies
on both sides of the Atlantic with a series of strategic dilemmas (for example whether there is ever a justification
for market interference). Resolution of these dilemmas usually
involves a lurch in the direction of moral fundamentalism
(for example the spate of video censorship and the regulation of prime-time television and theatre enacted in Britain
in the mid 1980s). But as events in the first few months of
1994 demonstrated, such campaigns carry the danger of
exploding in on themselves, since there is no guarantee that
those who call for a 'back to basics' moral regime are themselves resistant to the temptations of 'consumption', and
'pleasure', in any of their various guises.

Calls for the restoration of a unitary or traditional set of
'basic' values – or for that matter for the restoration of the
lost power of the head of the working-class household –
really do not connect very closely to the lived realities of a
society that has been undergoing such fundamental transformation as Britain over recent years. In particular, we would
argue, they do not take into account the transformation of
Britain (England, in particular) from a rather sleepy, friendly
but essentially undynamic, unprofessional and inefficient
mixed-economy welfare state, into a harsh, energised and
overaccelerated society, belatedly trying to deliver professional
quality in terms of goods and services, but cripplingly divided
across lines of class, gender, ethnicity, 'position in the housing
market' and age. We are hectored nearly every day by government ministers blaming one fragment or other of this social
configuration for the ills of the society as a whole (by which
they really mean the possessive individualists who are this
government's preferred constituency): it is always someone
else's fault. But what may now be urgently required in Britain
is a kind of moral rhetoric that can pull these different fragments together in a shared sense of community, a shared
destiny, rather than consigning more and more fragments
to an outer wilderness inhabited by the 'other', non-citizens
about whom, by implication, we should not be concerned.
We need a sense of moral order that could work across the

whole of a society composed of quite different fragments, some of which are now struggling for survival in a competitive market society. Such a moral ethic would clearly need to take into account and tackle the rank inequalities of economic resources and social power that besmirch this society (most notably across divisions of class, gender and race), but whilst also enshrining a powerful sense of universal citizenship within this society. It should comprise not only a universalistic script with respect to rights – the traditional preoccupation of left and libertarian thinkers – but also an outline of universal obligations; and this public agenda (of citizens' obligations and rights) should not only be part of the private language of academic public lawyers, but part of the public vision of social democratic politicians, particularly when speaking of issues of law and order, and moral order, in a legally and ethically regulated market economy.[17]

We are a long way from that at the moment, and indeed the logic of contemporary development still presses in the other direction. It is vitally important that social democratic commentary in the late 1990s should be critical of the continuing privatisation of government responsibilities with respect to 'the preservation of the peace' at the local level (policing, crime prevention and provision of neighbourhood leisure and social facilities generally)[18] – nearly all of which are currently being subjected to a narrow cost–benefit evaluation in the name of free market principles. In the critique of the way that public functions are being delegated to private police forces or security firms, social democrats will find ready allies amongst many police forces.

WHAT CAN BE DONE?

It is vital for social democrats not only to have an alternative vision for society and some sense of the policy decisions and strategies that might help move society in that direction, but also to focus on practical examples of good practice, against which worthy visionary thoughts can be tested 'in reality'. Good work has been done along these lines by the left-realist school of criminology in Britain, particularly in its work on the priorities and community accountability of local policing, and especially in relation to victims of crime. But social democratic criminologists should never speak as if the problems of crime are in principle resolvable simply through the actions of police or even through 'multi-agency collaboration' in crime prevention (for all the benefits that such collaboration may have in stiffening the sinews of otherwise fragmented local communities). It should be part of a social democratic responsibility to lay bare the shallow short-termism of the Tory argument about penal discipline – summed up in Home Secretary Michael Howard's refrain that 'prison works' (with the prison population climbing to 47 423 in February 1994 up 2200 from the beginning of the year and rising by 350 per week).[19]

It is not only that the increase in the prison population serves mainly to increase the overall proportion of state investment being diverted from more useful areas into the newly privatised areas of the penal industry. It is also that historical evidence, to which our free market government seems so oblivious, shows that crime rates only decline in periods of job creation (the 1860s, the early 1920s). Social democrats in the late twentieth century *must* also deal with 'the big issues' – the realities of market society with all its social and cultural effects (joblessness; the homelessness, poverty and deprivation at the heart of civil society; the massive subversion of institutions, especially local authorities but also the whole apparatus of welfare state provision with respect to health, income support and so on that until the late 1970s were working, however imperfectly, in the public interest.

It is not necessarily a matter of wanting to reinvent any of these institutions in their earlier, postwar form, but it is almost certainly a matter of wanting to reinvent the lost sense of community, public civility and/or sense of a shared citizenship that characterised English life before the free market experiment.

In this abstract but essential endeavour – of constructing a critique of free market society whilst suggesting practical alternatives by pointing to good alternative examples elsewhere – we English may have to turn, however unwillingly, to France. One of the major debates in the serious press in France at the end of 1993 focused on the detailed, strategic analyses of the European labour market that have been undertaken by the labour economist Pierre Larroutrou, taking into account all available knowledge about the continuing impact of technological change on job losses. Larroutrou argued that the only way in which there could be a significant increase in jobs in the European Union in the near future is via an EU-wide move towards a four-day working week. Adoption of this policy would create two million new jobs across Europe, with a 5 per cent loss of earnings across the existing labour force and a massive increase in leisure time. Present indications are that the Larroutrou plan stands no chance of adoption, not least because of the British government's unrelenting opposition, through its representatives in Brussels and Strasbourg, to any form of labour market regulation.

The importance of this struggle over 'labour market futures' for our thinking course, is that there appears to be no way that this debate is about to break open in such a way as to give hope to hundreds of thousands of young people and unemployed people across Europe that they will find employment in a legitimate trade. Social democrats must be involved in this debate, out of recognition of the role paid work has in constructing a full sense of citizenship in 'advanced' industrial and even post-industrial societies.

But social democrats must also be attentive to projects that improve public life and the daily lives of citizens in a more immediate fashion, short of a revolution in labour market policy or other transnational economic policies. A good example of this kind of good practice is the campaign conducted by the management of the Paris public transport authority (the RATP) to 'reclaim the territory' of the Paris underground, the Metro, which in the early 1980s had become prey to all the problems of neglect and inefficiency that bedevilled public transport systems at that time. An extensive policy of ridding the network of graffiti, regularly removing litter and repairing vandalised property was initiated in 1986, and entire stations were redecorated, repaired and redesigned with a view to passenger safety and well-being. The Metro is now regularly patrolled by a single security service, which is responsible for the policing of ticket fraud as well as handling more serious incidents.

The results have been remarkable, and are the subject of

widespread commendation in the French press. The initial investment in the reclamation strategy (the 'seed money') has now been recouped through a significant increase in use of the system, and as a result there has also been a significant increase in employment on the Metro. Assaults on passengers declined by 27 per cent between July 1989 and December 1991, and on staff by 9 per cent. Pickpocketing fell by 35 per cent over the same period (Kozar, 1992). It is hard to point to similar success stories of crime reduction in public places in Britain because the political culture, we would argue, is resistant to expenditure on any kind of public welfare provision.

The purpose of this chapter has not been to provide all the details of a social democratic programme of job creation and public investment, but rather to argue that these two areas of activity are an essential element in any social democratic programme for crime prevention at the end of the twentieth century. It is not just a question of returning a social democratic government; it is not just a question of investing more effectively in crime prevention rather than penal discipline; and it is certainly not a question of returning to moral fundamentalism. It *is* a matter of thinking about the good old questions – the big issues – of what makes for a good society, and indeed the greatest sense of security, well-being and happiness of the greatest number of people. On these issues, as on crime, the 'free market society' has clearly failed.

Notes

1. The consequences of the budget of November 1993 were that 90 000 unemployed people would lose all benefits (except those relating to their National Insurance contributions) after six months rather than one year; that 'invalidity benefit' would be withdrawn from another 70 000 people who currently qualified as physically or mentally disabled) and that the pension age for women would be raised to 65 in the year 2010.
2. I am grateful to Tim Hope of the University of Manchester for pointing out this connection. Dr Hope is currently researching the detailed relationship between the attack on state benefits and the crime rate.
3. *Social Trends*, vol. 11 (1981), vol. 23 (London: HMSO, 1993).

4. Cf. Tony Craig, 'Right for the Right to a Home', *Guardian Supplement*, 23 November 1993.

5. The move towards greater inequality in Britain is also informed by the government's interest in a deregulated labour market, resistant to the legislative intentions of the European Union, in which people will be forced to work for lower rates of pay in the interest of competitive efficiency. The government's objectives here may not be to create a South-East Asian type of sweatshop economy, as some Labour politicians have argued, but they are certainly to reduce the average rates of hourly pay in Britain (which at £6.61 per hour in 1990 were the sixth highest in the European Union, behind Denmark, Germany, Belgium, Holland, Luxembourg and Italy) (*Eurostat*, 1991). (Brussels: Eurostat)

6. I am trying to be sensitive here to the troubled and contentious issue as to whether there can be any objective, material definition of poverty or whether the definition of poverty must always be relative to standards of living that have come to be expected and taken for granted.

7. Such miserable levels of poverty can, however, contribute enormously to the break-up of marriages and families, and also to abuse of children. American social scientists visiting this country, noting the miserly level of wages and state benefits and the high cost of living in this country, often wonder out loud how the poor of Britain can live at all.

8. It is vital for social democratic observers to take on board the overrepresentation of young men in crime problems in free market England, without being blind to the number of young women who are being recruited into other trades (for example prostitution) as a result of economic pressures. It is not only that young men account for some 80–90 per cent of offences reported to the police, but also that their lawless activities in many areas of our cities are so threatening to other people wanting to make use of public space. Beatrix Campbell's extraordinary study, *Goliath*, provides a detailed analysis of the way in which lawless young men have colonised council estates (London: Methuen, 1993).

9. The 'vilification of the single mother' is nothing new in Britain – there were some particularly unpleasant instances of scapegoating at the end of the last century and in the twenty years after the Second World War. Cf. Mary Braid, 'Return of the Bogywoman', *Independent on Sunday*, 10 October 1993.

10. There are, of course, many other possible explanations of the number of lone mothers taking up the head-of-household position in Britain, not least of which is the profound lack of opportunities for women in the labour market in Britain, given the extreme underdevelopment of equal opportunities legislation in this country. It is also important to ask the question originally posed in the United States by Barbara Ehrenreich as to why it is nearly always mothers, rather than fathers, who finish up taking responsibility for children in the case of early pregnancies. In this view, not often heard in

government circles, the 'irresponsibility' is quite unambiguously the irresponsibility of men (Barbara Ehrenreich, *The Hearts of Men: American Dreams and the Flight from Commitment*, New York: Anchor Books, 1984).

11. Dennis and Erdos' argue that the 'decline of fatherhood' is the main reason for the explosion of crime in the 1980s and 1990s in Britain, which they repeatedly insist cannot be explained by the unemployment rate alone. (Norman Dennis and George Erdos, *Families Without Fatherhood*, London: IEA Health and Welfare Unit 1992).

12. Cf. for example the study by David Dickenson on Unemployment and Crime, funded by the Nuffield Foundation and reported in 'Study Links Crime to Jobless Rise', *Guardian*, 7 January 1994.

13. The statistics presented here are for England and Wales alone. Scotland displayed a very different pattern of crime throughout the 1980s and early 1990s, with significantly lower levels of increase, particularly in youth crime. Observers in Scotland have tended to attribute these differences, in particular, to the different patterns of housing tenure in Scotland (where a large proportion of the population has the security of some kind of public housing) and also to the long-established practices of Scottish juvenile tribunals, which deal with the problems of young people outside a narrowly legalistic or punitive paradigm. Careful observers of these figures will note the slight decline in overall crime in 1977 and 1978, the last two years of the last Labour government.

14. Raw statistics are extremely problematic as a measure of the size of the drug trade, since such a large proportion of the activity is conducted underground.

15. The number of armed robberies in England and Wales is still very small in comparison with the United States, but the rate is increasing. There were 5140 such robberies in 1991 compared with only 1791 in 1981. Illegal possession of firearms is also on the increase. It is important to qualify all generalisations in this are a, however, with the reminder that the number of deaths from violent crime in England and Wales (55 in 1990) is minuscule in comparison with the United States (16 000 in 1990).

16. For an analysis of the 'seductions' of crime of all kinds and the individualist pleasures that are so heavily valorised in contemporary American culture, see Jack Katz, *Seductions of Crime: Moral and Sensual Attractions of Doing Evil* (New York: Basic Books, 1988).

17. In Australia, criminologists working within the 'republican' tradition have begun to explore the potential of Aboriginal customary law (with its heavy emphasis on individual obligations to the community, as well as rights) as a vehicle for the reform of the deliberations of local magistrate courts. In this 'communitarian' tradition the greatest emphasis is on a powerful notion of 'community interest', which is frequently expressed in the 'shaming' of persistent individual offenders, but there is also a strong sense of community interest in helping offenders, particularly the young, with the problems they encounter in life. See John Braithwaite and Kathleen Daly, 'Masculinities, Violence and Communitarian Control', in Tim Newburn

and Betsy Stanko (eds), *Just Boys Doing the Business: Men, Masculinity and Crime* (London: Routledge, 1995).
18. Neighbourhood leisure and social facilities in this context refers the vital but (in England) now almost totally neglected role of parks, swimming pools, sports and community centres, and other local institutions in contributing to a challenging and worthwhile life for young people and others.
19. *Guardian*, 8 February 1994.

References

Braid, M. (1993) 'Return of the Bogeywoman', *Independent on Sunday*, 10 October.
Department of Employment (1993) *Labour Force Quarterly Report* (London: HMSO) August.
Dennis, N. (1956) *Coals is Our Life* (London: Eyre & Spottiswoode).
Goodwin, M. (1993) 'The City as Community: The Contested Spaces of Urban Development', in Gerry Kearns and C. Philo (eds), *Selling Places* (Oxford: Pergamon Press).
Kozar, C. (1992) 'Three Years Reclaiming Lost Ground', in *Public Transport Security and Environment*, proceedings of the International Conference of The Unions Internationale des Transport Public, Paris, May.
Office of Population, Census and Surveys (1982) *Labour Force Survey* (London: HMSO).
Phillips, M. (1993) 'Children in the Age of Bewilderment', *Guardian*, 16 September.
Reich, R. (ed.) (1987) *The Power of Public Ideas* (New York: Harper).
Reich, R. (1991) *The Work of Nations: Preparing Ourselves for Twenty-First Century Capitalism*(New York: Knopf).
White, M. (1994) 'Row Over "Real" Tally on Jobless and Poor', *Guardian*, 3 January.

14 Writing on the Cusp of Change: A New Criminology for an Age of Late Modernity

Jock Young

It is my belief that the last twenty years has witnessed the most profound transformation in our discipline. Heralded by the new deviancy 'explosion' of theory in the late 1960s and early 1970s and with *The New Criminology* in 1973 as a convenient marker, we have experienced the shattering of the seemingly monolithic world of modernity associated with the postwar period and the emergence of a late modernity, where the ground rules of certainty undergirding our subject have become blurred, contested, ambiguous and perpetually debateable. The changes have occurred at the level of crime, crime control and criminology itself. They are certainly not merely an intellectual product – perhaps the reverse; real changes have occurred in the world both in the quantity and quality of crime, and the public discourse on crime, whether in the mass media, in fiction or at the doorstep has radically altered. Nor, of course, is such a transformation limited to crime and criminology but is part of a wider movement into late modernity that has resonances in every sphere of life, whether cultural, architectural, sexual, biographical or economic (see Harvey, 1989). Indeed making a connection between the wide-ranging changes that have occurred within the labour market, in leisure, within the family, in changing usage of public and private space and in relationships of gender on the one hand, and the newly emerging patterns of crime and victimisation on the other, must be top of our agenda (see Young, 1998).

But let us, for the moment, note that the vast majority of advanced industrial countries have experienced a dramatic rise in crime and disorder. Victimisation has become more common in the public sphere and also, at least on the level of revelation, widespread within the private sphere. Crime has moved from the rare, the abnormal, the offence of the marginal and the stranger to a commonplace part of the texture of everyday life. It occupies the family, the heartland of liberal democratic society as well as extending its anxiety into all areas of the city. It is revealed in the highest echelons of our economy and politics as well as in the urban impasses of the underclass. At times, it seems as frequent in the agencies set up to control crime as it does within the criminal fraternity itself.

All of this has created the most profound difficulties for traditional criminology. Two crises have stretched across the last twenty years: the crisis of aetiology and that of penalty. The metanarrative of progress had as its almost unspoken assumption a decline in crime and incivilities. Yet the highest living standards achieved in the history of our species has been accompanied by a steady rise in the crime rate, whilst crime itself occurs in all the places it should not as well as being more frequent in all its traditional haunts. The failure of the 'great society' programmes of the Johnson administration, the most wide-reaching, costly and intensive social democratic attempt to engineer an end to poverty, discrimination and crime, was the prelude to an era where tackling the causes of crime became shorthand not for social engineering but for the necessity of greater discipline in the family or its transmutation into the actuarial calculation of risk minimisation. The second crisis, that of penalty, stretches from the prison revolts of Parkhurst to Strangeways today. It is a history of increase, of overcrowding, of a widespread public recognition of futility. It is paralleled by a reevaluation of the role of policing from the thin blue line to one component in the multi-agency control of crime. All of this repositions the criminal justice system from the agency that is there to control crime to that of a bit player in the social agenda playing second bill to the family and employment, and dependent on public cooperation and support.

And behind these two crises lies an underlying suspicion: for what sort of liberal democratic state is it that is unable to protect is population from crime yet brings a wider and wider swathe of its population under penal supervision? What sort of freely entered into social contract exists between state and citizen and between one citizen and another if inner cities have become areas of curfew at night for women and the elderly and where state coercion is a necessary adjunct to everyday life?

The metanarratives of progress through planning and the rule of law become tarnished and suspect whilst, more profoundly, the basic categories of crime cease to be fixed entities and become subjects of ambivalence and debate. Categories blur, categories stretch and extend, categories lose their rigidity. Various victim movements are intensely involved in this process of redefinition. Child abuse, for example, is not merely proven to be more extensive than ever thought before, but is also defined in much less tolerant terms. Indeed one can see a long-term move from what one might call the 'positive' child abuse of Victorian times ('spare the rod and spoil the child') to the notion that any physical hitting whatsoever is gross and a symptom of parental inadequacy. The green movement sensitises us to the frequently invisible crimes of pollution, environmental damage and radiation, while lobbying for new statutes and the extension of existing legislation. Most importantly, second-wave feminism is having a constant influence on both academic criminology and public debate on crime. Rape, domestic violence, sexual harassment, child sexual abuse, justified homicide all become areas of struggle where categories are reconceptualised, stretched and placed on a continuum that 'blurs' with normality, and where there is constant disagreement about demarcation. Just as libertarian socialism informed the radical criminology of the 1970s, radical feminism has been a constant source of inspiration, and sometimes irritation. The key role radical feminism gives to male violence and criminality in the oppression of women and the extraordinary influence it has had on public awareness underscores the leverage that such discourse has had on academic criminology. Meanwhile a vigorous and heated debate has occurred on all the so-called 'consensual' crimes: pornography, drugs, abortion, illicit sexual relations and even sadomasochism. Every modern political tendency has entered the arena: socialist feminism and radical feminism, right-wing libertarianism and the moral 'majority', neoliberals and social democrats. What is obvious is that academic criminology, the interior world of scholarship and research, is greatly affected not only by the empirical problem of crime (as well it should) but by the great hubbub of debate in the exterior world outside it: by politicians, journalists and activists. Whatever, one tendency is clear: the level of debate within criminology has far from abated (cf. Rock, 1994; Sumner, 1994). Indeed, standing as it does at the crossroads of law and order, at the intersection of morality and immorality, it is a discipline upon which every major intellectual and political current makes its mark.

THE CRISIS OF MODERNITY

The crisis in criminology is a crisis of modernity. The twin pillars of the modernist project of reason and progress, the use of law in the control and adjudication of human affairs and the intervention of government to engineer a just social order totter under the weight of their own inconsistencies and ineffectiveness. The legacy of the Enlightenment of the eighteenth century and the scientific revolution of the nineteenth century bequeathed us the two staple paradigms of criminology – classicism and positivism – and it is the challenge to these doctrines that has generated the intense debate that characterises the late twentieth century. The old certainties of the obvious nature of crime, the central role of the criminal justice system in its control, and the possibility of realising by government intervention a social contract that embraced all citizens have come, one by one, to be cast in doubt. The forces that brought about this transformation are, quite naturally, largely exterior to the discipline itself, although research findings and intellectual currents within the academy have developed and augmented these tendencies. This process has of course involved all areas of social policy, although it has been felt most acutely within criminology, for it is crime and the anxieties surrounding it that are, as always, the key weathervane of change in our society.

The two intellectual currents that signalled the supposed 'end of history' are neoliberalism – the market philosophy of the new right – and postmodernism, one reviving a *laissez-faire* past as the key to effective government policy, the other basing its claims on a post-industrial future where all Enlightenment certainties are rendered inapplicable. The collapse of state 'socialism' in the East and the growing doubts about the programmes envisaged by social democracies underscored the fragility of the metanarratives of progress through sustained government planning. The political response was the attempted substitution of the market for metanarrative by the emerging new right administrations. The intellectual response was the growth of postmodernism, which similarly rejected the validity of metanarratives as a guide to social, political and cultural development. Both the new right philosophy of the marketplace and post-modernism have had profound effects upon criminology. The former is obviously evident in the proliferation of texts written from a new right perspective. In these the actor is rational and self-seeking, and crime is committed where the balance sheet of profit and deficit is in the black and where opportunities are present. No metanarrative of injustice as a motivation for crime nor a sense of justice and fairness as incorporating us within the bounds of sociability are deemed necessary. Rather the human calculator exists in a universe of structured temptations and 'opportunities,' there is no cause of crime other than 'basic human frailty' (see Felson, 1994; Gottfredson and Hirschi, 1990; Clarke, 1980). The influence of postmodernism is less obvious, and on the face of it might be seen to have only a marginal impact. And it is true that explicitly postmodern work in criminology only arrived very late in the day, long after the tumult in literature and cultural studies. Yet as Stan Cohen has perceptively indicated in this volume, postmodernist themes were present in criminology from the early days of labelling theory in the 1960s, and continued through abolitionism and social constructionism before coming out as full blown postmodernism in the late 1980s (for example Pfohl, 1985).

Indeed if one reexamines labelling theory and its critique of traditional criminology one can find the majority of postmodernist themes. The concept of the social construction of the label was a precursor to 'deconstructionism', the notion of a plurality of voices defining reality was present in their unruly conception of social order, as was the idea of 'a hierarchy of credibility', where male, white, older, upper-class definers of reality exerted their dominance. The language of the label and its idealistic power in social construction was widely explored, and indeed was the intellectual progenitor of today's 'politically correct' terminology. A conflict theory unwilling to tie itself to the dynamics of class or a wider, overreaching narrative of control was content to locate power within the everyday micropolitics of human intervention. And even the loss of unitary subject into a locus dissected by competing social texts can be vividly found in the work of Erving Goffman. But above all the perspective drew its orientation from a critique of the intrusion of the state, in the form of both welfare and criminal justice, into the lives of individuals. That is, it accused the state of imposing a metanarrative, either of determinacy or of evil, that was not only incorrect in its essentialism but actually self-fulfilling in its effect. The irony, then, is that postmodernism arrived comparatively early in the postwar development of criminology and that many of the recent converts to its cause do not seem to have realised that there exists a rich and developed tradition that predates them (for example Smart, 1990).

Yet whilst both postmodernism and neoliberalism were busily writing off metanarratives, the proliferation of new social movements centring around feminism, the environment and ethnicity were creating new narratives, with their own conceptions of progress and social contract. All of these impacted upon criminology, although the role of feminism – particularly centred around victim movements – has been the most crucial. It is in this mêlée of new ideas, responding to cultural and social change occurring both through the affluent period of the 1960s and 1970s and the recession that followed it, that criminology has been set adrift.

BACK TO BASICS

It is the core contention of this chapter that to understand the development of criminology one must situate it in the context of the exterior problems of crime, in particular its extent and perceived distribution, and the wider political and social currents of the time. In the latter instance the major metanarrative concerns the emergence and transformation of liberal democracy and the key notion of the social contract. The changing notion of the social contract has, of course, been the staple of political philosophy within the academy, and the pivot of social and political discourse in the wider society. This has centred around two problematics: individualism and meritocracy. Namely, how can a society based on self-seeking individuals cohere and hang together, and how can a society legitimating itself in terms of rewards allocated by merit in the market place reconcile gross inequalities of property and opportunity? These problems of social order have obvious repercussions for criminology, the study of legality and disorder, and it is within this discursive flux that criminology has evolved. To point to this seemingly obvious external context does not, of course, suggest that the interior history of criminology is without its own momentum, nor that it cannot, at times, purposively attempt to cut itself off from outside influences. Indeed the history of academic positivism within criminology has been precisely to do this: to rewrite the history of the subject as if political philosophy was not its concern (see Matza, 1969) and to consign discussions of social contract and classicism to the prehistory of the discipline (see Beirne, 1993). Of course, it is because such an attempt at blinkered authority has been so successful that it is necessary to state the obvious.

THE MODERNIST PARADIGM: A WORLD AT ONE WITH ITSELF

The modernist project has, over the century, involved the greater and greater incorporation of the population into full citizenship. Such a social contract is based on the notion of a citizenship, not merely of formal rights, but of substantive incorporation into society. In the terms of T.H. Marshall's famous essay (1950), citizenship should involve not only legal and political rights, but social rights: a minimum of employment, income, education, health and housing. In these terms the full-employment, high-income economies

of the Western world in the postwar period up to the recession were well on the way to achieving full citizenship for
the mass of the population. I am well aware that, in reality,
there were considerable pockets of extreme poverty, of the
continuing existence of massive social inequalities and of
the contradictions that such a welfare society engendered
(see Offe, 1984), and of the fact that it was *male* full employment that was actually being referred to, but this does
not concern us here. What is of importance is that the consensual politics of the period quite clearly, and on a bipar-
tisan level, saw society in terms of a social contract enveloping
the vast majority of adults. Let us examine the major premises of the modernist paradigm as a discourse relating crime
and deviancy to the normal citizenry.

1. *Citizenship resolved:* the long march of citizenship is either
   resolved or is on the brink of resolution. The incorporation of blacks and women into full citizenship in a formal sense of legal and political equality is accompanied
   by the achievement of social equality for the vast majority of citizens.
2. *The interventionist state:* the role of the state is to intervene in order to achieve in a piecemeal fashion social
   justice as part of a metanarrative of progress. It is Keynesian
   in economics and Fabian in its social policy. The twin
   pillars of modernity are the rule of law and the welfare
   state as represented by neoclassicist legal theory and social
   positivist notions of planning. The state protects and the
   state delivers.
3. *Absolutist social order:* the vast number of citizens accept
   the given social order as the best of all possible worlds.
   Unemployment is low, the level of wealth is the highest
   in the history of humanity and the average income has
   annually increased since the war. The social order is viewed
   not only as just but as obviously in the interests of all,
   the major institutions of work, the family, democratic politics, the legal system and the mixed economy are accepted
   without much question. The rules are seen in absolute
   terms: they are obvious, clear-cut and uncontested. The
   end of ideology is at hand and Western values represent
   the end point of human progress.

4. *The rational conforming citizen and the determined deviant:* the vast majority of people are rational and freely embrace the consensus of values. The exceptions are a tiny minority of professional criminals and a larger, but still small, number of criminals and deviants who are determined by psychological and social circumstances. The large-scale rational criminality and dissent that were possible prior to the modern advances in citizenship cease to exist. No longer is the rational criminal, the spectre that haunts the work of Beccaria, a large-scale threat or possibility. People by and large do not choose deviance – they are propelled into it.

   We thus have the classicist citizen and the positivist deviant: both discourses coexist. The role of positivism is to explain any deviation from the rational, absolute, obvious norm of conformity.

5. *The narrow conduit of causality:* causality is reserved for those who deviate; explanation for or conformity to absolute rules is, of course, unproblematic – aetiology is after all only necessary when things go wrong. Deviance occurs because of problems located not so much in the present as in the past: the conduit of causality is individualised and sited frequently in the family. The notion of sizeable, socially distinguishable groups occupying identifiable space is replaced by the atomistic individual, a random product of some unusual family background. The dangerous classes of premodernity become the individual deviant in modernity; it is not till late modernity that the spatial and the social pariah reoccurs with a vengeance in the concept of the underclass.

6. *The assimilative state:* the role of the welfare state is to assimilate the deviant at the margins into the main body of society. To this end a corpus of experts builds up skills in the use of the therapeutic language of social work, of counselling, of clinical psychology and allied positivistic disciplines.

THE CHALLENGE TO MODERNISM

Let us look first at the major forces that have both disoriented and regalvanised the discipline. The four factors are *the rise*

in the crime rate, the revelation of hitherto *invisible victims,*
the *problematisation of definition*, and the growing awareness
of the *universality of crime and the selectivity of justice.* Each of
these factors generated a diverse theoretical response, sometimes exaggerating their relevance and sometimes evoking
an outright denial. All of them, however, sensitised criminology
to the breadth of analysis necessary for the explanation of
crime. All of them subverted and undermined the compla-
cency of the modernist paradigm.

The Rising Crime Rate

The majority of industrial countries have seen a considerable rise in the rate of recorded crime in the post-1960s
period. This has had an impact on theories of causation,
has given rise to a crisis within the criminal justice system
because of the experiential rise in demand upon it and has
qualitatively upgraded the public's prioritisation of crime
as a problem. Indeed of all the factors that have given rise
to changes in our conception of crime and to a reappraisal
of the criminal justice system, the rise in crime is the central motor of change. But let us first look at its effect on
theories of causation. The rise in crime from 1960–75 occurred during a period of full employment, of living standards rising to levels greater than had been known in human
history, and in the context of a vast expansion in welfare
provision. The widely held belief in social positivism – that
crime was caused by bad social conditions – was clearly contradicted, for as the West became wealthier the crime rate
rose. It is true, of course, that in the recession of the 1980s
social positivism was to an extent rehabilitated, but the impact on criminological theory of rising crime in a period of
prosperity was profound. Indeed most of the major theoretical developments since 1960 have been a response to this
anomaly. Thus on the right, neopositivism and control theory,
especially in the work of Travis Hirschi, James Q. Wilson,
Charles Murray and Hans Eysenck, picked explicitly on the
failings of social positivism and in response greatly developed theories of individual positivism. In particular, changes
in the family became high on their aetiological agenda (see
Mooney, this volume). Indeed criminologists of all persua-

sions have shifted their attention to the informal systems of the control of crime, whether it is the family, the community or the process of public shaming. A fundamental shift has occurred from viewing the criminal justice system as the thin blue line in the war against crime to viewing the institutions of civil society as being of crime importance.

Such an increase in crime threatened not only social positivism, but the neoclassicist pillar of modernism. For governments all over the Western world have committed more and more money to the criminal justice system in order to combat crime, yet the crime rate continues to increase. In the United States such a penal crisis has reached epidemic proportions: the state is able neither to protect its citizens from crime nor to maintain a society where imprisonment is a comparative rarity.

Lastly, the effect of the increase in crime has been to increase public anxiety. The social contract of modernity has placed the state in the role of monitoring public safety. Within a lifetime, particularly for urban dwellers, crime has grown from marginal concern, an exceptional incident in their lives, to one that is an ever-present possibility. Nor is it simply that government expenditure on crime control has increased and hence public expenditure through taxation, but so has the direct public cost in terms of locks and bolts and insurance on homes. Crime has moved from being a side issue of public concern to a central political issue.

The Revelation of Invisible Victims

The existence of a dark figure of crime unreported to official agencies has been known since the work of Adolphe Quetelet, the Belgian founder of social statistics in the 1830s. Its true extent was a matter of speculation until the first large-scale victimisation surveys in the United States commencing in the 1960s (The National Crime Survey). The extent of the dark figure varies between surveys, but commonly only about one third of offences are known to the police. Thus the British Crime Survey estimate in 1991 was fifteen million crimes compared with the some five million officially recorded. Comparing the two data sets is fraught with problems, but this does not concern us here. What is of importance is that the crime rate is at least three times that shown in the official figures, and must of course be considerably higher given that victimisation surveys themselves have a substantial dark figure of crimes unreported to interviewers (see Young, 1988).

Thus on top of a rising crime rate we have clear indications that the 'true' extent of crime is extremely widespread. The fifteen million crimes in England and Wales would represent one serious crime occurring each year for every four people in the population. Of course crime is more focused than this, and in urban areas one finds about one half of respondents being victimised at least once in the last twelve months (see Kinsey *et al.*, 1986). Such findings underline the fact that experience of crime is a normal rather than an exceptional event in people's lives. This immediately creates problems for the modernist view of crime. For, far from being the product of exceptional circumstances, such a 'normal' occurrence must have its genesis in widespread conditions within our society. This normalisation of crime points to its endemic origins.

Furthermore it is also apparent that the hidden figure varies considerably with the type of crime committed. Property crime in general has high reporting rates, often because of reasons of insurance, whereas crimes of violence and sexual assault have much lower reporting rates, not only to the police but to conventional victimisation surveys. Nor is it merely that certain types of crime have higher hidden figures, crimes against certain victims are much less revealed in the criminal statistics than others. In general, the more socially vulnerable the victim and the more private or intimate the setting of its commission, the least visible the crime.

Such a distinction between visible and invisible crimes almost turns the modernist paradigm on its head. For it suggests that the image of crime presented in official figures is fundamentally flawed. That is, not only are the figures quantitatively inadequate – and crime much more common than we previously believed – but what we see as the most serious crimes – violence and sexual assault – are grossly underestimated and frequently occur in intimate and private settings.

Up until now I have talked about the findings from conventional criminological research within the discipline, but the full force of this change in orientation has come from movements exterior to criminology. In particular, feminist research and scholarship has profoundly changed our images of crime. Their task has been to conduct a series of studies and undertake a systematic analysis to reveal the hidden victimisation of women. In particular this has been influenced by the radical feminism of the post-1960s period. For radical feminism pinpointed violence against women as a central means of excerting control over women in a patriarchal society. It revealed the extent of such violence and it situated it in terms of the relationship between men and women.

The revelation of widespread violence and sexual attacks occurring throughout the class structure creates problems for the conventional location of the causes of crime within the lower class and on the margins of society. It does not preclude class analysis. Certain types of invisible crime may well be more prevalent amongst the lower classes, but other types of crime, particularly crimes of violence, may be much more widespread and less class-linked than has been traditionally assumed. The social positivist pillar of modernism is thus suspect, or at least must be considerably more specified. But it is not only the positivist pillar that is disturbed by such findings, the intimate, family or private-centred nature of much violence and sexual crime also creates problems for neoclassicism. For the fundamental building block of classicism based in social contract theory is the coming together of self-interested individuals who rationally recognise that in order to avoid a war of all against all it is necessary to regulate their conduct and empower the state to intervene against activities that violate the general interest. 'Individuals' in neoclassicism refers not so much to atomistic individuals as individuals within their families. That is, the family unit is seen as a unitary interest and such private interests come together publicly in social contact (Pateman, 1988). Threats and dangers to one's self-interest come from *outside* the family. Because of this, modernism conceives of the criminal as the stranger. The exposure of the intimate nature of much violence – whether domestic violence, rape, homicide or child abuse – breaches this modernist certainty.

The Problematisation of Crime

Up to this point I have discussed the impact on conventional
notions of crime generated by its increase in quantity and
the discovery of a wide range of hitherto unacknowledged
offenders and victims. This has been concerned with the
exploration of the dark figure of crime, implicitly assuming,
for the moment, that there is indeed a 'real' figure of crime
that can be more and more accurately ascertained. The
problematisation of crime takes us a stage further. For a
whole series of questions have arisen, both from social movements outside the discipline and within criminology itself,
with regard to what actually is criminal and how our conception of crime is constructed. Note that for modernism,
crime was obvious: a house broken into, a person assaulted,
a car stolen. It was an objective fact that could be described
more or less accurately and its size ascertained with increasing precision with each advance in measurement. The breach
in this orthodoxy occurred from the 1960s onwards with
the sustained critique of positivism developed by labelling
theorists. In 1967 Edwin Lemert summarised a revolution
in thinking about crime and deviance when he wrote: 'This
is a large turn away from older sociology which tended to
rest heavily upon the idea that deviance leads to social control.
I have come to believe the reverse idea, i.e. social control
leads to deviance, is equally tenable and the potentially richer
premise for studying deviance in modern society' (Lemert,
1967, p. v).

For the labelling theorists the quantity of crime, the type
of person and offence selected to be criminalised and the
categories used to describe and explain the deviant are social constructors. Crime, or deviance, is not an objective
'thing', but a product of socially created definitions: deviance is not *inherent* in a particular behaviour, it is a quality
bestowed on it by human evaluation. For example to kill someone can be an act of heroism if committed by a police officer
confronting armed robbers, but it can be an act of extreme
immorality if committed by the robbers. Likewise to inject
morphine can be a necessary and legal act if administered
to the terminally ill, but it can evoke all the prohibitive
powers of the state if committed by a street junkie. But these

are extreme contrasts, and reality consists of a series of defined graduations. Thus the social definition of what is criminally violent will consist of a gradient between seriously violent and non-violent, and it will change over time as public sensitivity to violence changes. Therefore determining the 'real' rate of violence involves two questions: what changes in behaviour might be deemed violent, and what changes are there in the public tolerance of violence? It is this recognition of the *dyadic* nature of crime that is the major accomplishment of the labelling tradition. For crime rates are no longer obvious summarisations of forms of behaviour, but are processes where both human action and definition are subject to change. The dark figure of crime therefore not only expands as more crime is revealed by more sensitive measuring techniques, but also expands if social definitions became less tolerant of crime. Such a position makes extremely precarious the positivist desire for objective and precise measurement in order to emulate the physical sciences. Crime becomes problematised, indeed instead of the clear-cut distinction between crime and non-crime, it is easier to view behaviour as a continuum between tolerated and criminalised behaviour where the cut-off point varies over time and between different social groups. How hard, for example, does a slap have to be to evoke criminal sanctions, and at what point does appropriating other people's property become theft?

It is scarcely surprising that such a perspective should arise within the academy, given the extraordinary level in which the nature, size, limits and, indeed, existence of social problems are debated within contemporary society. Over the last twenty years we have seen a burgeoning of pressure groups seeking both to extend the boundaries of criminalisation and to introduce decriminalisation, to redefine the limits of traditional social problems and to introduce new problems, to recategorise crimes and to redefine problems. Let me cite just a few: the feminist movement, animal rights campaigners, environmentalist groups, anti-racist activists, child protection agencies, and movements both to legalise drugs and to legally restrict other drugs (particularly tobacco). What constitutes crime, therefore, becomes contested and subject to public debate. To take rape as an example, feminist

researchers not only argue that the level of rape is much
higher than conventionally recorded, they also trenchantly
challenge conventional definitions of rape. Thus rape in
marriage becomes in many legislatures a criminal offence
and the existence of widespread 'date rape' is claimed. The
argument thus shifts from determining the 'true' figure of
obviously coercive sexual encounters – stranger rape accompanied by violence – to determining the exact nature of
rape and defining the limits of coercion and consensus in
sexual relationships. The debate thus begins to centre around
what constitutes consenting sexual intercourse, that is, the
lines are redraw between coercive and consensual relationships. It further highlights the existence of a continuum:
for in an unequal society a large number of heterosexual
encounters can be deemed coercive, particularly when a
woman is totally dependent on her husband economically,
or when her employment prospects are dependent on her
male superiors. Indeed some radical feminists would argue
that all heterosexual relationships are coercive and that rape
is simply a matter of degree, whereas others would make
much more rigid distinctions. And precisely such a continuum
problem occurs with a whole series of other serious crimes,
including child abuse and domestic violence.

There is also a point where the revelation of more and
more hidden crime becomes extremely problematic. The
exposure of past sexual abuse, for example, can become a
seemingly bottomless pit that embraces a greater and greater
proportion of the population. What are we to make of, for
instance, claims that over 50 per cent of women have been
sexually abused in their childhood? It is not the aim of this
chapter to deliberate on such assertions, merely to point to
the heated public debate that such revelations generate.
Indeed organisations have been set up to protect families
against what has been called 'false memory syndrome', whilst
on the other hand some therapists now specialise in 'un-
blocking' memories of supposed child abuse.

The Universality of Crime and the Selectivity of Justice

Traditionally, criminology has seen crime as being concentrated in the lower part of the class structure and being

greatest amongst adolescent boys, that is, its focus has been on lower-class, male youths. The first serious force to unbalance this orthodoxy was the work of Edwin Sutherland, particularly his article, 'White Collar Criminality', written in 1940. He wrote:

> The theory that criminal behaviour in general is either due to poverty or to the psychopathic and sociopathic conditions associated with poverty can now be shown to be invalid . . . the generalisation is based on a biased sample which omits almost entirely the behaviour of white-collar criminals. The criminologists have restricted their data, for reasons of convenience and ignorance rather than a principle, largely to cases dealt with in criminal courts and juvenile courts, and these agencies are used principally for criminals from the lower economic strata. Consequently, their data are grossly biased from the point of view of these economic status of criminals and their generalisation that criminality is closely associated with poverty is not justified (Sutherland, 1940, p. 10).

Here well before his time, Sutherland captured the problem of universality and selectivity that was to fixate the criminology of the late 1960s onwards. Crime is much more widespread than the stereotypes of the criminal suggest, and furthermore the criminal justice chooses a particular 'sample' based not on random selection but on the stereotype itself. This time bomb of Sutherland's ticked away until the 1970s, when its full implications began to be widely acknowledged. This was due to two types of influence: the multitude of self-report studies, particularly of delinquency, which flourished during the period, and the increased number of revelations of crimes of the powerful. A whole series of texts pointed to the widespread occurrence of white-collar crime: Frank Pearce's *Crimes of the Powerful* (1976), Dennis Chapman's *Society and the Stereotype of the Criminal* (1968), for example, and in high places, The President's Commission on Law Enforcement and the Administration of Justice (1967).

The revisionism of the early 1970s pointed to the endemic nature of crime (*universality*) and emphasised the systematic class bias in the focus of the criminal justice system (*selectivity*). And if universality made conventional positivist notions of causation unlikely, selectivity pointed to fundamental problems in the neoclassicist idea of equality before the law. Furthermore criminology itself became a suspect discipline, for how could the scholar possibly generalise from a sample already chosen by the criminal justice system (see Hulsman, 1986; Sumner, 1990). Indeed crime, as Hulsman put it, seemed to have no 'ontological reality'.

However, just as the first wave of class-orientated revisionism pointed to the endemic nature of crime, the new revisionism, with its feminist orientation, pointed to a drastic caveat. For feminist criminology not only widened the notion of victimisation, it also pointed to the implications of the extremely low offending rate of women. This in itself was commonplace: criminological texts have always indicated that women have a remarkably lower offending rate than men. What is of key importance is that feminist criminology brought the matter to centre stage: it hammered home the centrality of the male–female differential. Pivotal work such as Eileen Leonard's *Women, Crime and Society* (1984) systematically exposed the androcentric bias in criminology. Theory after theory, whether it is differential association, anomie, subcultural theory or social deprivation, breaks down when women are put into the explanatory equation. Furthermore, not only is the importance of informal control rather than the deterrent impact of the criminal justice system highlighted in the low offending rate of women, the fact that such control is exerted within a patriarchy, rather than as a bland social pressure, situates it within the social structure of society.

Thus the old certainty of social positivism – that poverty and unemployment lead to crime – becomes problematic once the criminality of those high in the social structure and women are taken into account. The first should have an extremely low crime rate, which they do not, whilst women, because of their comparative impoverishment and high rate of unemployment, should have a high rate, which they palpably fail to exhibit. Crime thus occurs in places where it should not, and does not occur it places where it should.

As we approach the end of the century, events have taken this process further. The endemic nature of crime – at least

for males – has become more evident as the crime rates
have risen, indeed in the United States penal supervision
(that is, of course, of just those who have been caught) has
become commonplace. And for sections of the US population commonplace means normal. One in four black males
in their twenties are either in prison, on parole or on probation in any twelve-month period. This proportion must
surely be higher in the great cities of the United States,
and no shame can presumably accrue from such an occurrence. As for selectivity, a whole series of spectacular acts of
discrimination and prejudice have generated widespread
public distrust of the impartiality of the criminal justice system. The Rodney King incident in Los Angeles and the various
examples of dramatic injustice in the UK – including the
cases of the Birmingham Six and the Guildford Four, as
well as many of the activities of the Midlands Serious Crime
Squad – revealed just the tip of the iceberg of malpractices
that growing sections of the public view as commonplace in
the more mundane work of policing (see Kinsey *et al.*, 1986).

Table 14.1 US population controlled by penal law, 1993

	In prison	Controlled by penal law*
Total population	1 in 135	1 in 40
Black males	1 in 24	1 in 13
Black males in twenties	1 in 15	1 in 4

* In prison, on parole or on probation.
Source: Bureau of Justice Statistics, 1995 (see commentary by Currie,
this volume).

Before I turn to an explanation of these events, let us
examine in tabular form the fundamental changes that have
occurred.

SHIFT INTO LATE MODERNITY

It is my contention that during the last third of the twentieth century a dramatic shift has occurred both in our perceptions and in the reality of crime and its control. This

Table 14.2   The shift into late modernity: changing conceptions of crime and its control

1. Definition of crime	Obvious	Problematic
2. Prevalence of offenders	Minority	Extensive
3. Incidence of victimisation	Exceptional	Normal
4. Causes of crime	Distant, determined, exceptional	Present, rationally chosen, widespread
5. Relationship to 'normality'	Separate	Normal/continuum
6. Relationship to wider society.	Leakage	Integral
7. Locus of offence	Public	Public/private
8. Relationship of offender to victim.	Stranger, outsider	Stranger/intimate, outsider/in group
9. Locus of social control	Criminal justice system	Informal/multi-agency
10. Effectiveness of social intervention	Taken for granted	Problematic: 'nothing works'
11. Public reaction	Obvious and rational	Problematic: irrational 'fear of crime' and moral panics
12. Spatial dimension	Segregated	Contested space

has involved both change and revelation, that is, the world has changed but in changing has made it more easy to perceive the underlying reality of crime. There is a remarkable agreement on the timing of this change. 'It all began', James Q. Wilson wrote, 'in about 1963. That was the year to overdramatize a bit, that a decade began to fall apart' (Wilson, 1985, p. 15). And indeed diverse commentators, be it Wilson, or Herrnstein and Murray in their controversial *The Bell Curve* (1994) or Eric Hobsbawm in his magisterial *Age of Extremes* (1994), all pinpoint the change that occurred in all areas of life in this period. The theoretical signal for this change within criminology and the sociology of deviance was undoubtedly the emergence of the new deviancy theory. This early burgeoning of postmodernism vividly grasped the transformation that was under way. It oversaw the shattering of modernity, in particular in its elaboration of the collapse of absolute rules, its insistence on the precarious nature of causality and its stress on the irony of the self-fulfilling and oppressive nature of social intervention as part of a meta-narrative of progress.

The changes that occurred inevitably involved instabilities in the two spheres of order: that of reward and that of community, namely what citizens saw as the adequacy of their reward in the market place and how they viewed the balance between their desires as individuals and their responsibilities to the community. The motor behind such a change was the rising demand upon citizenship both in terms of formal equality and, substantively, the increase in what was demanded of citizenship. Behind such a surge in aspiration lay the incessant development of a markct socicty in the postwar period. The market brings together wide swathes of the population into the labour market. It creates the practical basis of comparison: it renders visible inequalities of race, class, age and gender. It elevates a universal citizenship of consumption yet excludes a significant minority from membership. It encourages an ideal of diversity, a market place of self-discovery, yet provides for the vast majority a narrow, slatted individualism. It creates 'uninterrupted disturbance of all social conditions, everlasting uncertainty and agitation', yet depends on a relatively uncritical acceptance of the given order. The market flourishes, expands and beckons, yet it undercuts itself. It does all this but it is not a mere transmission belt: the mores of the market may be the dominant ethos of the age but this ether of aspiration is shaped, developed and given force by the human actors involved. It is in this light that the problems in the two spheres of order – relative deprivation and individuation – must be viewed. For these are the key to the crime wave in the postwar period.

RELATIVE DEPRIVATION AND INDIVIDUALISM

Relative deprivation, it must be remembered, is a creature of comparison. It can occur both when things get better and when they get worse, *providing* comparison is easy or is made easier. It is often absent when the gulf between people is large and has existed for a long time; it is frequently slight when differentials gradually and imperceptibly get worse. To grasp this principle is to move towards an understanding of the last third of the twentieth century. As Eric Hobsbawm charts in *The Age of Extremes* (1994) the postwar years involved a massive movement towards full citizenship of each of the subordinate categories of society: the working class, women, blacks and youth. Opportunities increased, greater equality was often realised and much more frequently talked about; expectations rose and by the 1960s the rhetoric of liberty and revolution was in the air. This was not an era of satisfaction, despite full employment and exceptional living standards. The *paradox of equality* is that as differentials narrow differences become all the more noticeable. Relative deprivation did not disappear with rising wealth, it was not ameliorated by widespread gains of citizenship – on the contrary it grew worse. Then after the golden years came the recession of the 1980s and 1990s – the era of mass unemployment and marginalisation. The gains of economic citizenship have been dramatically removed, and in a Keynesian era are seen not as the result of some natural catastrophe but as a failure of government. The mood of the unemployed is not self-blame but system-blaming (see Mooney, this volume). Relative deprivation persists but it has been transformed. It no longer involves comparison across the serried ranks of the incorporated, it has become a comparison across the divided labour market and between those in the market and those excluded.

But relative deprivation alone does not explain the rise in crime and disorder from the 1960s onwards. Relative deprivation breeds discontent. Discontent can manifest itself in many ways, and crime is only one of them. The lethal combination is relative deprivation and individualism. For Hobsbawm it is the rise of individualism that is pivotal: 'The cultural revolution of the late twentieth century can thus be understood as the triumph of the individual over society, or rather, the breaking of the threads which in the past had woven human beings into social textures' (Hobsbawm, 1994, p. 334). It is individualism that leads discontent to generate the 'Hobbesian jungles' of the urban poor, a 'universe where human beings live side by side but not as social beings' (ibid., p. 341).

NOSTALGIA AND DECLINE

There is a predominant train of thought, shared by those on both the left and the right of the political spectrum, that the last third of the twentieth century has been a period of decline, a decline that takes many forms: increased unemployment, breakdown of community, disintegration of the traditional nuclear family, lack of respect, lowering of standards, prevalence of disorder and, notably, a rise in the crime rate. The features stressed vary with the politics of the commentator, although all of them cite many of these items as indices of a world turned sour. Crucially, whatever the politics, the role of the market society is seen as pivotal for this change. Let me take what at first sight might be almighty strange bedfellows: James Q. Wilson and Eric Hobsbawm. For Wilson, a policy advisor to Nixon and Reagan and guru of the right, the cause is a culture that emphasises immediate gratification, self-expression and low impulse control. 'A liberal commercial society committed to personal self-expression', creates inevitably problems of discipline: 'a devotion to self-actualisation is at best artistic or inspiring and at worst banal or trivial. In the hands of person of weak character, with a taste for risk and an impatience for gratification, that ethos is a license to steal and mug' (Wilson, 1985, pp. 247–9). In the end, however, 'we have made our society and we must live with it' (ibid.). Indeed Wilson's work is in many ways an attempt to come to the terms with how such a liberal 'free' society can work, extending from his initial 'realist' beliefs in the power of law, punishment and policing to his later, much greater, emphasis on family, the first five years of life, character and social training (Wilson and Herrnstein, 1985; Wilson, 1991, 1993).

Eric Hobsbawm, the Marxist historian, reaches the same conclusion – but this time with considerable irony – when he notes how capitalism needs the presence of precapitalist values: trust, honour, discipline, commitment to community and to family. Thus he writes:

As we take for granted the air we breathe, and what makes possible all our activities, so capitalism took for granted the atmosphere in which it operated, and which it had inherited from the past. It only discovered how essential it had been when the air became thin. In other words, capitalism has succeeded because it was not just capitalist. Profit maximisation and accumulation were necessary conditions for its success but not sufficient ones. It was the cultural revolution of the last third of the century which began to erode the inherited historical assets of capitalism and to demonstrate the difficulties of operating without them. It was the historic way of the neo-liberalism that became fashionable in the 1970s and 1980s, and looked down on the ruins of the communist regimes, that it triumphed at the very moment when it ceased to be as plausible as it once seemed. The market claimed to triumph as its nakedness and inadequacy could no longer be concealed (Hobsbawm, 1994, p. 343).

So the cause of such a decline is a *deficit*, and this shortfall is a result of the triumph of market values themselves. A market society cannot exist without the oxygen of non-market values and relationships: the market undercuts its own existence. Of course such a deficit is underwritten by the recession of the latter part of the century: commentators of all political persuasions recognise this, but even social democrats acknowledge that the impact of the recession has been severely worsened by the culture of individualism. The solidarity of the working-class community and family, which saw the people through the 1930s, has given way to fragmentation. In the place of collective values there is every person for themselves, in place of working together there is internecine strife and criminality (Dennis, 1993; Seabrook, 1978).

The diagnosis of decline and deficit is followed, perhaps inevitably, with the prescription of *nostalgia*. Politicians of all persuasions share a preoccupation with the notion of returning to the past, of rekindling the half-warm memories of family, work and community. After all, the essence of the widespread appeal of Etzioni's communitarianism is the attempt to bolt on to a shattered society all the steadfast certainties of the past: a world where everyone pulled together.

Thus a novel bipartisanship of nostalgia is presented before us. It is a world of full employment where the market is extended to embrace the marginalised and absorb all individuals – depending on one's political persuasion. It is a society where we must support the family or curb the feckless single mother – depending on one's party preference. It is a time to rebuild community, to return to basics, to encourage the collective values of yesteryear.

There are mistakes both in the prescription and the diagnosis. Much of this centres on the misunderstanding of individualism and of the deficit that is seen as its inevitable result. Let us put the argument in logical order: market society engenders a culture of individualism, which undermines the relationships and values necessary for a stable social order and hence gives rise to crime and disorder. Upon this both Wilson and Hobsbawm would agree, but Hobsbawm adds an ironic twist: market society is, in fact, dependent on the values and relationships that predate it and that the culture of individualism dissolves and disintegrates. I want to examine two key aspects of this argument. Firstly, to what extent is contemporary capitalism undermined by rising crime and disorder? Secondly, to what degree is the culture of individualism an unmitigated deficit?

In Merton's famous theory of anomie the cultural ideals of meritocracy are subverted by the existing structure of society. In Hobsbawm's critique the reverse is true: the values of society undermine the structure. For both, one consequence of such a contradiction between culture and structure is crime and disorder. I am certain that both of these ironies in the constitution of market societies – the first in what I have demarcated as the sphere of justice, the second in the sphere of community, both clearly alluded to by Durkheim – are crucial in the generation of crime in advanced industrial societies. Indeed they are at the core of the claim by radical criminologists that crime is an endemic rather than a peripheral feature of social order. Yet it would be as wrong to suggest – as Hobsbawm does – that such endemic disorder is in fact a systemic problem *for capitalism* as it would – as an earlier generation of radicals maintained – that crime is not much of a problem *for anyone*. Rather we must pinpoint who actually suffers from crime in this present period, as well as the social consequences of endemic criminality. Certainly the growth of individualism has been the great shaper of the latter part of the twentieth century. Certainly this is a product of market forces; but the impact of the market is contradictory, as is individualism itself. Let us immediately clear up the notion that capitalism always needs a great degree of social order. This is true only of specific periods: the universally orderly population of the

modernist period was necessary only with Fordist production and full employment. It is in the newly emerging industrial nations that a massive orderly population is necessary,
if anywhere. Neoliberalism triumphed in the First World and
in the recent period, when order amongst the marginalised
part of the population – and also the most disorderly – is
of declining necessity to capital.

The underclass of today are not needed, their labour
unnecessary, the inculcation of punctuality and discipline
irrelevant, their consumption demands useful but easily
controllable. The disorder of their communities may be at
times an embarrassment to politicians – as in the case of
the Los Angeles riots – but their impact is negligible. It is
media circus without relevance for capital. The underclass
destroy their own areas, they turn in upon each other; they
at times threaten the police, who are specifically employed
to be both threatened and threatening. Indeed leading theorists of the right such as James Q. Wilson speculate as to
how far an area has 'to tip' before it is unrescuable and
'realistically' not worth state intervention. New York City,
the leading financial centre of world capitalism, can exist
with crime rates at a Third World level, yet its economic
performance is unabated by the crime that surrounds it.
Order must occur, of course, in financial transactions and
precontractual norms exist in order to sustain contracts, as
Durkheim pointed out, but this is different matter than that
of the crimes of the excluded. It is anyway a matter of speculation as to exactly what level of honesty and trust is necessary for capital accumulation, a large proportion of which
occurs because of precisely opposite pecuniary virtues. The
right and the privileged – by means of gates and bars, barriers and surveillance, private guards and public policing –
can keep themselves and their property safe. The suburban
shopping mall and the new developments downtown must
be regularly swept clean of beggars, small-time thieves and
drunks; windows must be mended and vandalism erased if
customers are to consume effortlessly and without distraction. But none of this poses much of a threat, although it
does provide a ready rhetoric for politicians and the basis
for influential criminological texts (Wilson and Kelling, 1982).

Neoliberal policies around the world attempt not only to

roll back the state, but also to draw back the parameters of civil society. They put the social contract back on the table and attempt to exclude the lower orders from its orbit. The poor are denied decent education, health care, legal rights and they are, as Galbraith (1992) has pointed out, easily outvoted – their political rights are not so much denied as rendered inconsequential. And lastly in the field of law and order, areas that have poor schools and patchy social services also have desultory policing. Here the police react only to gross disturbance, they are not the servants of the local citizenry, they are its warders. Law and order, like so many aspects of the welfare state, are least provided where they are most needed. Yet law and order, like health care and education, are needed by the mass of citizens. Crime control in particular is a political unifier, for it is a shared problem for the mass of the population. The capitalist system in the First World requires political order and economic stability, but crime – with its fitful intransigence and inconsequential rebellion – is of no great threat, indeed it is, as Wilson suggests, an inevitable consequence of a 'successful' free market system. But what is inconsequential to the system is profoundly deleterious to the citizen, and particularly so with the rising demand for a better and safer environment coupled with a general intolerance of violence. Indeed we have something of a paradox here: a rising popular demand for law and order at a time when there is a declining systemic need for them. It is for this reason that law and order are of great ideological importance to neoliberal politicians of the right whereas they are – or at least *should* be – of more direct material consequence to social democrats.

CRIME AND DEFICIT

Let us now turn to the problem of individualism and deficit. The language of criminology is rife with the notion of deficit: the causes of crime are lack of material goods, falling standards of social training or a general decline in values. Take your pick: the preferred deficit varies with the politics of the commentator, yet each involves a loss and an individualistic response to it. I would like to reverse this nostrum:

the cause of crime is not so much that a world has been lost as a that new world has not yet been gained. Let us briefly look at each of these deficits in turn, but first of all let me stress that I am not arguing that considerable and often heartless losses have not been experienced during the last part of the twentieth century. The recession has caused widespread misery, whole communities have been destroyed and families torn apart, whilst the values of the market have profoundly transformed social life. All of this suffering and divisiveness has certainly occurred, but its cause has not been simple deficit: it has involved rising demands as well as falling returns, a questioning of conformity rather than a passive deviance, a conflict in standards as well as a lack of values.

To take the lack of material goods first, here surely simple deficit theory works? The recession coupled with the rise in individualism, and the material harshness of the market in combination with market values, are frequently seen by social democrats as the obvious causes of crime in the present period. Herein lies a pitfall for radical analyses of crime. The danger is, quite simply, that for many social democrats working within criminology the aetiological crisis is over. We are back in the old formula: bad conditions lead to bad behaviour. The rhetoric is simple and seductive: for have not the cuts in the welfare state been swingeing and irresponsible and is not the gap between rich and poor widening? Furthermore, to the conceptual armoury of declining material conditions have been added market values. Conditions have worsened and individualism is rampant in a market society. What else but rising crime could result?

However, it is not as simple as this. Lack of material rewards clearly does not mean absolute poverty, and crime rose throughout the late 1960s with rising living standards: it is relative deprivation that is a potent cause of crime. So perhaps even here we should refer to a relative deficit. That is, the relative material standards of individuals compared one to another, a sense of inequality, of unjust reward commensurate with merit. So as groups begin progressively to demand greater equality of reward and fuller citizenship, their relative deprivation increases and, if no collective solution is forthcoming, crime will occur. Thus the prognosis for South Africa, for example, is that it will become more and more crime ridden unless progress is seen to be substantial, tangible and possible in the future. Half-hearted progress or mere proclamations of equality will not remove feelings of relative deprivation; on the contrary they will exacerbate them. Such a situation, wherever it happens, of fuller citizenship demanded but thwarted is scarcely a simple deficit. For it involves not only a static comparison with those who are more successful and have rising aspirations, it also includes those who perceive themselves as being below the line of equality and those who are actively stretching the limits. Both Durkheim and Merton realised this: they in no way embraced a fixed, positivistic concept of deprivation (cf. Katz, 1988).

Yet social democratic interpretations of crime frequently convey the notion that crime is about simple deficit, that it will disappear as we approach greater equality (it may well not, for the paradox of equality is that relative deprivation can increase with greater equality of reward) and that crime is somehow something that 'tops up' the income of the poor. This is simply not true: crime, whether street robbery or embezzlement, is rarely committed in order to reach the median wage. The poor do not steal Beetles but Porches, looters do not carry home a booty of baked beans but camcorders, no one – apart from a tiny few – takes illicit drugs to feel normal (see Mugford and O'Malley, 1991). And the rich do not commit crimes in order to ensure comfort in future retirement – they have already secured that – they do so in order to excel in their affluence and to exult in their edge over all comers. Furthermore the rich, as Ruggiero has nicely pointed out, do not pursue crime because of a deficit of opportunities; far from it, they have a surfeit of criminal possibilities just as they do legitimate opportunities (Ruggiero, 1996, 1993). It is a question of being below limits and going beyond limits: it is relative deficit and transgression; a fact recognised by Durkheim and Merton with their invocation of both a sense of unfairness and of infinity of reward.

Let us turn now to the second deficit, that of social cohesion: the decline in the strength of the family and the community. Here a notable political polarisation is evident: for

if those on the left talk of deficit of reward, on the right
the preferred deficit is lack of control. And if social positivism reemerges in the first deficit, then neopositivism has
even more dramatically reemerged with the second. The
traditional role of biological or psychological positivism has
been to explain crime and deviance as a pathology of the
individual and to avoid ascribing causes to endemic problems within the structure of society. Thus the positivism of
the modernist period has ascribed deviance to the failure
of a few isolated, dysfunctional families. The emergence of
mass crime and deviance necessitates a latching on to causes
that are at once widespread but do not imply there is something drastically amiss with the structure of society. Neopositivism, particularly the work of Charles Murray (1990,
1994) and Travis Hirschi (Gottfredson and Hirschi, 1995)
have focused on the re-decline of the family and the central competence of socialisation in the first five years of life.
Such a *market positivism* does not question human rationality and choice (albeit it is remarkably restricted to conformist
outcomes), but sees criminal choices as the result of low
impulse control and antisocial individualism engendered in
childhood. For on the fulcrum of human decision making
the long arm of freedom needs the heavy counterweight of
early discipline. The widespread nature of such a problem
is seen as a result of women choosing to have children outside wedlock or cohabitation This problem is often seen as
localised in an underclass and is a product of welfare dependency. A culture of individualism encourages young
women to have children who are inadequately socialised and
whose activities are subsidised by the taxpayer.

   This is not the point to enter into a debate with this thoroughly disagreeable and factually incorrect argument, but
what is of immediate relevance is its notion of how crime is
caused by social deficit. Crime is seen to occur because of a
failing of the system of socialisation, whether it is family or
community, single parent or underclass. Crime is thus seen
as a leakage, the result of a faulty container. The mistake
here is twofold. Firstly, to explain crime as the result of a
lack of control ignores why people wish to commit crimes.
It removes motivation from the equation, and thus ultimately
rules out any generation of motives to criminality from within

the social structure itself. Secondly, it assumes that the container is a physical object that has, so to speak, sprung a leak. The attitude of individuals to the control asserted by their family or community is completely ignored. They are not social actors reflecting their surroundings, rather they are objects more or less controlled by their environment. In fact the habit of obedience, deference and willingness to defer to family, neighbours and the local community have all declined, partly because of the system's inability to provide acceptable opportunities and partly because of an unwillingness to accept authority just because it is authority. The decline in unthinking obedience is perhaps one of the most significant changes in the twentieth century. This loosening of social ties is not a mechanistic process but a result of greater demand for individual autonomy: its roots lie not in deficit but in aspiration.

Finally, let us look at the third supposed area of deficit: decline in values. I have already indicated that one of the characteristics of late modernity is an intense debate about values. Crime and deviance are no longer measured by the absolute standards that modernity offered: their definitions are contested and publicly debated. If this is a deficit then it is a decline in certainty not a failure of concern. Yet we can go further than this, for in the areas of violence and quality of life one can detect a clear rise in standards. The increased sensitivity towards child abuse, domestic violence and animal rights are examples I have already used. But the demand to be freed from the fear of crime and to be freely able to walk the streets of our great cities at night is part of a general concern for the lived environment and green issues. This rising demand for law and order is, as I have noted previously (Young, 1995), paradoxical in that it is frequently accompanied by a deterioration of behaviour. Yet the perpetrators and the protestors are not, I suspect, the same people, and the frequent finding that reported rates of serious violence rise much faster than homicide rates suggests that an overall long-term change in tolerance is occurring. This does not suggest a deficit, indeed as Norbert Elias has famously portrayed we are witnessing a civilising process rather than an unmitigated tide of barbarism. In particular the entry of women into the labour market, and

hence more fully into the public arena, has led to a growing intolerance of male violence and incivilities. It is not
merely the provision of more opportunities and of raising
living standards, it is about justice and merit. It is not about
more social control, of mending the leaks in the system, it
is about incorporation: of families and communities whose
norms are not simply obeyed, but accepted and embraced.
It is not a question of creating a monolithic consensus in
value, but of continuous diversity and change. And in essence all of this revolves around the notion of citizenship.
That is, a citizenship that is concerned with equality, a citizenship that is not fixed in limits but subject to rising aspirations, a citizenship whose substance and content is subject
to redefinition, disagreement and debate.

Let us return now to individualism. A creature both of
Janus and Pandora, the individualism of the latter part of
the twentieth century is both contradictory and unpredict-
able. It is a product of market society, surely, but the way in
which individualism develops can have both antisocial and
profoundly social consequences. The individualism that begs
us treat others like commodities can also be the individualism that refuses treatment like a commodity. The desire for
self-actualisation can mean, of course, the cold-blooded pursuit
of growing selfish interests, but it can also mean resistance
to being put upon. The increasing demand for self-expression can be at the expense of others, but it can also be the
demand for a world where self-expression is possible. The
cult of the individual is at worst a motive for violence to
achieve one's aim, but it may well involve a growing abhorrence of violence against the individual. In short, if the dark
side of the dialectic of individualism is crime and villainy,
the bright side is a whole host of new social movements, a
new sensibility about the environment and a lowered tolerance to violence. And there can be little doubt of the central role that second-wave feminism and the green movement
have played in the genesis of a new individualism.

THE SOCIAL CONTRACT OF LATE MODERNITY

The social contract of modernity has broken down in part
because it was ill conceived, in part because the world has

changed. Let us look at the transition to late modernity in terms of three areas: goals, modus operandi and terrain. If the goal of modernity was the elimination of absolute deprivation and the creation of opportunities within a society of consensus, that of late modernity must be the distinctly different tasks of tackling relative deprivation and the move towards a more meritocratic and diverse society. We live in a society that is grotesquely unmeritocratic. By this I do not mean the inequalities of inherited wealth, *which surely is the problem at core*, but the way that from the top to the bottom desiderata are distributed, with the logic of merit entering as only one of a series of entirely contingent factors in the calculation of reward. At times one confronts blatant unfairness, at other times a *chaos of reward*, where there seems no rhyme nor reason to distributive justice. Indeed such a process is widely recognised by the population as the key principle of distributive justice: 'the luck of the draw' – an extremely unmeritocratic concept. Unfairness is blatant and unapologetic, for example and most obviously the allocation of individuals in the labour market, whether to the primary or secondary sectors or to the ranks of those excluded from long-term employment, has only a partial relationship to merit. Too often the barriers of class, race, gender and age are self-evidently more influential than those of merit and talent. The destructive effect on society of such widely perceived unfairness, uncertainty and even arbitrary good fortune readily fuels relative deprivation and discontent.

In terms of methods of operation we must construct a new contract of citizenship that emphasises diversity rather than absolute values, that does not allow the state and its experts to bestow problems but involves and encourages intense democratic debate and evaluation, that is not a citizenship of rights but one of reciprocity between each citizen and fully recognises the necessity of reciprocity between citizen and state in the enactment of social goals and institutional change.

Finally, the terrain in which modernism flourished has fundamentally changed. It is not possible to return to the world of the 1950s. We must work on the terrain we are now given. We cannot return to full employment in the sense of puberty to grave, nine to five, men only. We cannot return to the Kelloggs cornflakes image of the nuclear family, with its patriarchal structures and lifetime permanence. We cannot return, except in soap operas, to the community of perpetual interference, observation and meddling. We cannot return to the thin blue line that protects us against crime and a welfare state that decides our priorities and bestows our problems. We cannot return to monoculture, moral certainty and absolute values. We cannot return to the uncontested, the unambiguous, the unequivocal and the undebated.

The switchback of modernity takes us ever forward, closing down accustomed paths and offering us new panoramas and possibilities. 'All that is solid melts into air', but it must be remembered that all that was solid was often oppressive, unthinking and unexamined. Reason takes apart the old basis of trust but enjoins us to form new and more rational bases of order. Crime occurs when citizenship is thwarted, its causes lie in injustice, yet its effect is, inevitably, further injustice and violation of citizenship. The solution lies not in the resurrection of past stabilities, based on nostalgia and a world that will never return, but on a new citizenship, a reflexive modernity that will tackle the problems of justice and community, of reward and individualism, which lie at the heart of liberal democracy.

CONCLUSION

We live in a time when there has been massive structural change: when there have been fundamental changes in the primary and secondary labour markets; when the employment patterns of women have radically changed; when structural unemployment has been created on a vast scale; when communities have disintegrated; when new communities have emerged in a multicultural context; when patterns of leisure both in the cities and the countryside have been manifestly restructured; when patterns of social space have been redefined; when the agencies of the state, particularly the police, have undergone a systematic transformation and reappraisal by the public. And these structural changes have been accompanied by cultural changes that are no less dramatic: patterns of desire have been transformed; the global village, engendered by the mass media, has become an ever-present reality; the old patterns of reward and effort have been redefined; institutionalised individualism has permeated areas of social life that were hitherto sacrosanct; and the naturalistic language of the market place has challenged and threatened the metanarrative of social democracy and modernity. In any fully social theory all of this must be related to the quantum leap in crime and incivilities that we are now experiencing. If ever there was a need for a new criminology it is now: it is our task to create such a criminology and to break with the atavistic discourse of positivism and neoclassicism that masquerades as contemporary theory.

I have talked about the failure of the twin pillars of modernity: I do not want to suggest that the way out of this impasse is a postmodernism of relativism, defeatism and acquiescence; the times call for a realism that will take the project of modernity forward, a criminology for the period of late modernity, a social democracy for the twenty-first century.

References

Beck, U. (1992) *Risk Society* (London: Sage).

Beirne, P. (1993) *Inventing Criminology* (New York: State University of New York).

Bureau of Justice Statistics (1995) *Correctional Populations In The United States* (Washington: US Department of Justice).

Chapman, D. (1968) *Society and the Stereotype of the Criminal* (London: Tavistock).

Clarke, R. (1980) 'Situational Crime Prevention', *British Journal of Criminology*, vol. 20, no. 2, pp. 136–47.

Dennis, N. (1993) *Rising Crime and the Dismembered Family* (London: IEA).

Felson, M. (1994) *Crime and Everyday Life* (Thousand Oaks, CA: Pine Forge Press).

Galbraith, J.K. (1992) *The Culture Of Contentment* (London: Sinclair-Stevens).

Garland, D. (1985) *Punishment and Welfare* (Aldershot: Gower.

Gottfredson, M. and T. Hirschi (1990) *A General Theory of Crime* (Stanford, CA: Stanford University Press).

Gottfredson, M. and T. Hirschi (1995) 'Natural Crime Control Policies', *Society*, Jan/Feb, pp. 30–6.

Harvey, D. (1989) he Conditions of Postmodernity (Oxford: Blackwells).

Herrnstein, R. and C. Murray (1994) *The Bell Curve* (New York: The Free Press).

Hobsbawm, E. (1994) *The Age of Extremes* (London: Michael Joseph).

Hulsman, L. (1986) 'Critical Criminology and the Concept of Crime', *Contemporary Crises*, vol. 10.

Katz, J. (1988) *The Seductions of Crime* (New York: Basic Books).

Kinsey, R., J. Lea and J. Young (1986) *Losing the Fight Against Crime* (Oxford: Blackwell).

Lemert, E. (1967) *Human Deviance, Social Problems and Social Control* (New Jersey: Prentice-Hall).

Leonard, E. (1984) *Women Crime and Society* (New York: Longman).

Marshall, T.H. (1950) *Citizenship and Social Class* (Cambridge: Cambridge University Press).

Matza, D. (1969) *Becoming Deviant* (New Jersey: Prentice-Hall).

Messerschmidt, J. (1986) *Capitalism, Patriarchy And Crime* (Lanham, MD: Rowman & Littlefield).

Messerschmidt, J. (1993) *Masculinities and Crime* (Lanham, MD: Rowman & Littlefield).

Mugford, M. and P. O'Malley (1991) 'Heroin Policy and Deficit Models', *Crime, Law and Social Change*, vol. 15, pp. 19–37.

Murray, C. (1990) *The Emerging British Underclass* (London: IEA).

Murray, C. (1994) *Underclass: The Crisis Deepens* (London: IEA).

Offe, C. (1984) *Contradictions of the Welfare State* (London: Hutchinson).

Parsons, T. (1947) 'Patterns of Aggression in the Social Structure of the Western World', *Psychiatry*, vol. 10, pp. 167–81.

Pateman, C. (1988) *The Sexual Contract* (Cambridge: Polity Press).

Pawson, R. and N. Tilley (1994) 'Evaluation Research And Crime: A Scientific Realist Approach', mimeo.

Pearce, F. (1976) *Crimes of the Powerful* (London: Pluto).

Pfohl, S. (1985) 'Towards a Sociological Deconstruction of Social Problems', *Social Problems*, vol. 32, no. 3, pp. 228–32.

President's Commission on Law Enforcement and the Administration and Justice, 1967 *The Challenge of Crime in a Free Society* (Washington: Government Printing Office).

Rock, P. (ed.) (1994) *The History of Criminology* (Aldershot: Gower).

Roshier, B. (1989) *Controlling Crime* (Milton Keynes: Open University Press).

Ruggiero, V. (1993) 'Organised Crime In Italy', *Social and Legal Studies*, vol. 2, pp. 131–48.

Ruggiero, V. (1996) *Organized and Corporate Crime in Europe* (Aldershot: Dartmouth).

Rustin, M. (1994) 'Incomplete Modernity: Ulrich Beck's Risk Society', *Radical Philosophy*, vol. 67, pp. 3–12.

Seabrook, J. (1978) *What Went Wrong?* (London: Gollancz).

Smart, C. (1990) 'Feminist Approaches to Criminology', in Gelsthorpe L. and A. Morris (eds), *Feminist Perspectives in Criminology* (Milton Keynes: Open University Press).

Sumner, C. (ed.) (1990) *Censure, Politics and Criminal Justice* (Milton Keynes: Open University Press).

Sumner, C. (1994) *The Sociology of Deviance* (Milton Keynes: Open University Press).

Sutherland, E.H. (1940) 'White Collar Criminality', *American Sociological Review*, vol. 5, no. 1, pp. 2–10.

Sutherland, E. and D. Cressey (1966) *Principles of Criminology*, 7th edn (Philadelphia: J.P. Lippincott).

Wilson, J.Q. (1985) *Thinking About Crime*, 2nd edn (New York: Vintage Books).

Wilson, J.Q. (1991) *On Character* (Washington: AEI Press).

Wilson, J.Q. (1993) *The Moral Sense* (New York: The Free Press).

Wilson, J.Q. and Herrnstein R. (1985) *Crime and Human Nature* (New York: Simon & Schuster).

Wilson, J.Q. and G. Kelling (1982) 'Broken Windows', *The Atlantic Monthly*, March, pp. 29–38.

Young, J. (1988) 'Risk of Crime and Fear of Crime', in M. Maguire and J. Pointing, *Victims of Crime: A New Deal* (Milton Keynes: Open University Press).

Young, J. (1995) 'Incessant Chatter: Recent Paradigms in Criminology', in M. Maguire, R. Morgan and R. Reiner (eds), *The Oxford Handbook of Criminology* (Oxford: Clarendon Press).

Young, J. (1998) 'From Inclusive to Exclusive Society: Nightmares in the European Dream' in V. Ruggiero, N. South, I. Taylor (eds) *European Criminology* (London: Routledge).

Index